Field Manual
No. 3-4
Fleet Marine Force Manual
No. 11-9

*FM 3-4/11-9
Headquarters
Department of the Army
US Marine Corps
Washington, DC, 29 May 1992

FM 3-4

NBC PROTECTION

Editor's Note: Requirements of Change 1, 28 Oct 92, and Change 2, 21 Feb 96, have been incorporated within the document. Changed or new material is indicated by an asterisk (*) for Change 1 material and by two asterisks (**) for Change 2 material.

MEMORANDUM, SUBJECT: Request to Change Chemical Proponent Field Manual Distribution Restriction Statements, 6 October 2000, with 12 October 2000 e-mail endorsement.

Table of Contents

Chapter 4 - Nuclear Protection

Chapter 5 - Biological Protection

Chapter 6 - Collective Protection

Appendix A - Operations in Special Environments

Appendix B - Guidelines for the NBC Portion of a Collective-Protection System SOP

Glossary

References

Authorization Letter

DISTRIBUTION RESTRICTION: Approved for public release; distribution is unlimited.

*This publication supersedes FM 3-4, 21 October 1985.

HEADQUARTERS
DEPARTMENT OF THE ARMY
COMMANDER US MARINE CORPS
Washington, DC, 28 October 1992

CHANGE
NO. 1

NBC PROTECTION

1. Change FM 3-4, 29 May 1992, as follows:

Remove old pages	Insert new pages
3-9 through 3-10	3-9 through 3-10

Page 1-14. Fourth paragraph, line 7, change "TM 3-6665-260-10" to "TM 3-6665-2608-10."

2. Post these changes according to DA Pamphlet 310-13.

3. File this transmittal sheet in front of the publication.

By Order of the Secretary of the Army:

GORDON R. SULLIVAN
General, United States Army
Chief of Staff

Official:

MILTON H. HAMILTON
Administrative Assistant to the
Secretary of the Army
02091

By Order of the Marine Corps:

RONALD D. ELLIOTT
Executive Director
Systems Command
U.S. Marine Corps

DISTRIBUTION:

Active Army, USAR, and ARNG: To be distributed in accordance with DA Form 12-11E requirements for FM 3-4, NBC Protection (Qty rqr block no. 0736).

Introduction

NBC weapons are among the most hazardous on the battlefield. The doctrine of many potential enemies calls for their wartime employment of NBC weapons. In order to deter an enemy from exercising this option, US forces must be continuously prepared to fight and win under NBC conditions.

To fight and win under NBC conditions requires an application of the three fundamentals of NBC defense-contamination avoidance, protection, and decontamination, at all levels of command, coupled with an effective retaliatory response.

Avoidance

The first fundamental of NBC defense is avoidance. Avoidance addresses individual and/or unit measures taken to avoid or minimize NBC attacks and reduce the effects of NBC hazards. By taking measures to avoid the effects of NBC attacks, units can reduce their protective postures and decrease the likelihood and extent of decontamination required. FM 3-100 provides a general discussion of avoidance measures. See FM 3-3 for a detailed discussion.

Protection

The second fundamental of NBC defense is NBC protection. Protection is one of the four dynamics of combat power and consists of two primary components: actions to counter the enemies firepower and actions to maintain the health and morale of soldiers. NBC protection encompasses both of these components. Its goal is the conservation of the fighting potential of the force so that it can be applied at the decisive time and place. We divide NBC protection into three broad areas-force, collective, and individual protection.

Force Protection

Force protection involves actions taken by a commander to reduce the vulnerability of his force to an NBC attack. At the lower levels of command, battalion and below, this will require that the unit conduct a procedure called MOPP analysis. The final result of this analysis will be a determination of protective equipment to be worn by unit soldiers. However, several other decisions concerning alarm placement and automatic masking criteria will be required as a part of the analysis. Forces above battalion level will conduct a process called vulnerability assessment and risk reduction. The vulnerability assessment is an estimate of the probable impact on the force of an enemy NBC attack. It occurs both prior to and after initiation of NBC warfare. This assessment will be used in conjunction with mission, enemy, terrain, troops, and time available (METT-T) information to determine acceptable means of reducing force vulnerability to enemy attack.

Collective Protection

Collective protection addresses the use of shelters to provide a contamination-free environment for selected portions of the force. It is protection provided to a group of individuals that permits relaxation of individual NBC protection.

Individual Protection

Individual protection involves those actions taken by individual soldiers to survive and continue the mission under NBC conditions. It also addresses protection provided to an individual in an NBC environment by protective clothing and/or personal equipment.

Decontamination

The third fundamental of NBC defense is decontamination. It is the reduction of the contamination hazard by removal or neutralization of hazardous levels of NBC contamination on personnel and material. FM 3-100 provides a general discussion of decontamination. See FM 3-5 for a detailed discussion.

Retaliation

** Defensive measures alone are not an effective response to enemy NBC attacks. The US retains the right to retaliate in response to enemy NBC attack. Depending upon the situation, this retaliation may take the form of nuclear, conventional, or political options. There is no requirement that the US response be strictly proportional to an enemy attack in kind; US offensive biological and chemical operations are prohibited. See FM 3-100/FMFM 11-2, Chemical Operations for a general discussion of NBC retaliation.

Chapter 1

Individual Protective Equipment

A soldier's mission-oriented protection posture (MOPP) gear protects against NBC contamination. It consists of the overgarment, mask, hood, overboots, protective gloves, individual decon kits, detection equipment, and antidotes. Before soldiers can protect themselves against NBC hazards, they must first know what individual protective equipment is available and its capabilities.

Protective Ensemble

Various armies of the world use different types of chemical protective clothing for individual protection. Several types are available in the US Army. The type depends on the protection required, but all fall within two major divisions: permeable and impermeable. Permeable clothing allows air and moisture to pass through the fabric. Impermeable clothing does not. An example of impermeable clothing is the special butyl rubber suits worn by some explosive ordnance disposal (EOD) soldiers and decon soldiers. Most troops use permeable suits. These are known as battledress overgarments (BDOs).

Battledress Overgarment (BDO)

Note: The information on the BDO represents a more flexible approach than was addressed in the 1985 version of this manual More recent assessments of the BDO indicated that a more flexible approach was needed to optimize use of the BDOs excellent NBC protection capabilities.

Description

** The BDO is a camouflage colored, woodland or desert, expendable two-piece overgarment consisting of one coat and one pair of trousers (figure 1-1). The jacket has a zipped front, and the trousers have a fly front and zipped legs. The overgarment material consists of an outer layer of nylon cotton and an inner layer of charcoal impregnated polyurethane foam. Due to heavy impregnation of charcoal, some charcoal may be deposited on skin and clothing under the BDO; however, this will not detract from the BDOs chemical protective characteristics nor harm the wearer. The BDO presently comes sealed in a vapor-barrier bag that protects against rain, moisture, and sunlight. The BDO is water resistant, but not water proof and is normally worn as an outer garment. The BDO is normally worn over the duty uniform; however, in high temperatures it may be worn over underwear. In extreme cold weather environments, the BDO should be worn between layer 2 (bib overall, cold weather shirt, and trouser liner) and layer 3 (coat liner and field trousers) of the Extended Cold Weather Clothing System (ECWCS). In extreme cold weather environments, the BDO is sized to wear over artic/extreme cold weedier environmental clothing; however, mission requirements may dictate that the BDO be worn under artic clothing. For example, soldiers may need to wear a white artic outergarment to help ensure needed cover and concealment.

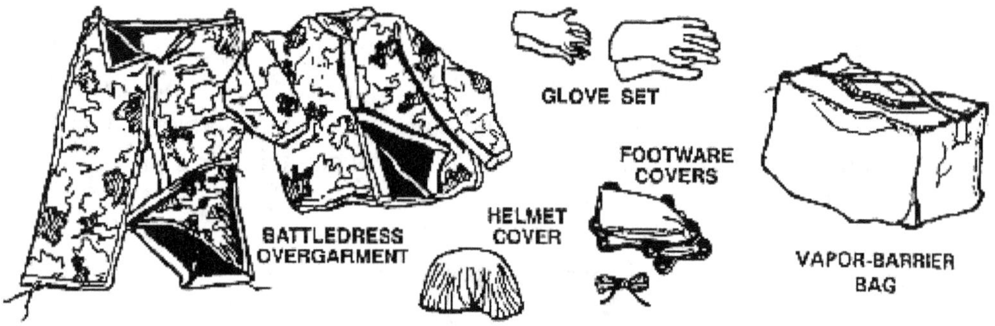

Figure 1-1. Protective ensemble.

Protection Capabilities.

** The BDO provides protection against chemical agent vapors, liquid droplets; biological agents; toxins; and radioactive alpha and beta particles. When the BDO is removed from its vapor-barrier bag and worn, its protective qualities last for a minimum of 30 days. It is recommended that the BDO be replaced after 30 clays; however, the weartime may be extended by the commander when operationally necessary. BDOs worn longer than 30 days presents a slightly increased risk to the wearer; however, the key to BDO effectiveness at anytime during wear, is its serviceability. The slightly increased risk that is incurred by wearing the BDO past 30 days is discussed in chapter 3, Chemical Overgarment Risk Assessment.

Weartime for the BDO begins when it is removed from its sealed vapor-barrier bag, and stops when the BDO is sealed back in its vapor-barrier bag. If the original vapor-barrier bag is not available, return the BDO to a similar material bag and seal with common duct tape, Donning of the BDO regardless of the time, equates to a day of wear. Extending the weartime for the BDO affords additional flexibility operational and logistical support planning. The BDO provides a minimum of 24 hours of protection against exposure to liquid or vapor chemical agent. Exchange the BDO within 24 hours of exposure to a liquid chemical agent. The BDO is not designed to be decontaminated or reimpregnated for reuse.

Serviceability.

The BDO becomes unserviceable if it is ripped, torn, fastener broken or missing, or petroleum, oils, or lubricants are spilled or splashed on the garment. For example, if a

POL spill on a BDO sleeve or trouser leg soaks through the BDO material, replace the BDO. Further, the BDO remains serviceable if the vapor-barrier bag suffers damage (i.e., pinholes, rips, tears), provided the overgarment has not been physically damaged or exposed to water, POL spills, or chemical agents. When any packaging leaks are discovered, seal/repair them as soon as possible. Common duct tape provides an appropriate and expedient way to repair the vapor-barrier bag. Sealing the bag, protects the BDO from direct exposure to moisture, smoke, and fuel solvent vapors which can jeopardize the BDO protective qualities; however, if the original vapor-barrier bag is no longer available to the soldier for overgarment storage, use a replacement storage bag that, as a minimum, is water resistant or water repellent.

Nuclear, Biological, and Chemical Equipment Bag

The NBC equipment bag is designed to consolidate and transport the CPOG, chemical protective gloves, and chemical protective boots. The bag is constructed of an abrasion-resistant nylon and incorporates a unique closure system, using velcro, two compression straps, and quick release buckles for protection from the outside cargo tie-down straps for attachment to the current developmental load-carrying equipment (LCE).

Chemical Protective Overgarment (CPOG)

NOTE: The information on the CPOG represents a more flexible approach than was addressed in the 1985 version of this manual. More recent assessments of the CPOG indicated that a more flexible approach was needed to better use the CPOGs protection capabilities.

Description.

The CPOG is a plain OD green expendable two-piece overgarment consisting of one coat and a pair of trousers (figure 1-2). The jacket has a full length zipper opening covered by a protective flap. The trousers have a fly front, and zipper closure on the lower outside section of each leg. The CPOG is made of material having an outer layer of nylon cotton and an inner layer of charcoal impregnated polyurethane foam. Due to the heavy impregnation of charcoal, some charcoal will be deposited on the skin and clothing under the overgarment; however, this will not detract from the chemical protective characteristics of the suit nor harm the wearer. The CPOG comes sealed in a vapor-barrier bag that protects against rain, moisture, and sunlight. To protect the protective qualities of the CPOG against rain, wet weather gear should be worn over the overgarment. The CPOG is normally worn over the duty uniform; however, in high temperature it may be worn over underwear. In extreme cold weather, the CPOG is sized to wear over arctic extreme cold weather environmental clothing; however, mission requirements may dictate that the CPOG can be worn under arctic clothing. For example, soldiers may need to wear a white arctic outergarment to help ensure needed cover and concealment.

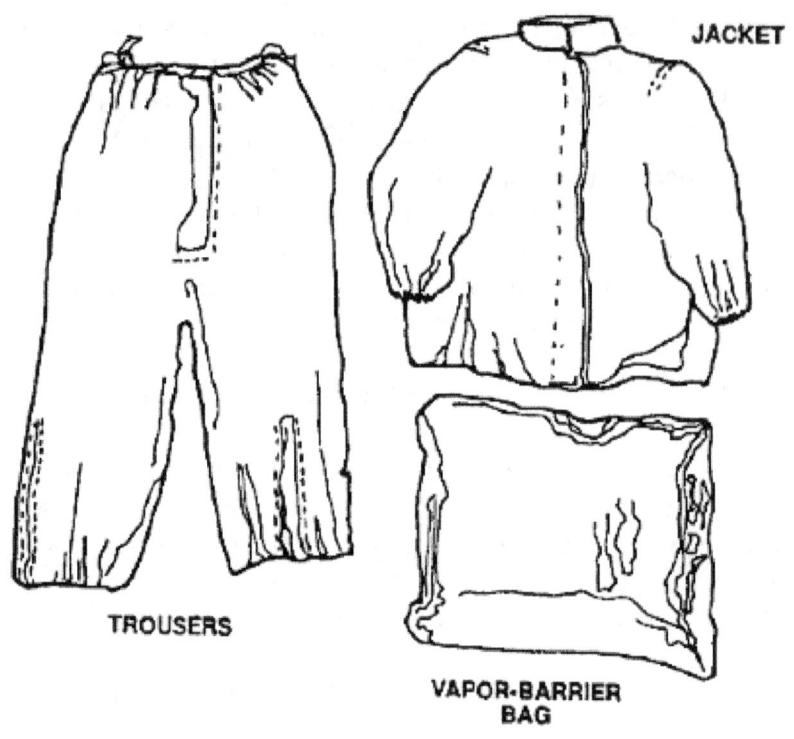

JACKET

TROUSERS

VAPOR-BARRIER
BAG

Figure 1-2. Chemical protective overgarment.

Protection Capabilities.

The CPOG provides protection against chemical agent vapors, liquid droplets; biological agents; toxins; and radioactive alpha and beta particles. When the CPOG is removed from its vapor-barrier bag, its protective qualities last for a minimum of 14 days. It is recommended that the CPOG be replaced after 14 days; however, the weartimes may be extended by the commander when operationally necessary. CPOG worn longer than 14 days present a slightly increased risk to the wearer; however, the key to CPOG effectiveness at anytime during its wear, is its serviceability. The slightly increased risk that is incurred by wearing the CPOG past 14 days is discussed in chapter 3, Chemical Overgarment Risk Assessment.

Weartime for the CPOG begins when it is removed from its sealed vapor-barrier bag, and stops when the CPOG is sealed back in its vapor-barrier bag. If the original vapor-barrier bag is not available, return the CPOG to a similar material (i.e. water proof) bag and seal with common duct tape (for example, double plastic trash bags are a possibility). Donning of the CPOG, regardless of time, equates to a day of wear. Extending the weartime for the CPOG affords additional flexibility in operational and logistical support planning. The CPOG provides a minimum of 6 hours of protection against exposure to liquid or vapor chemical agents. Exchange the CPOG within 6 hours of exposure to a liquid chemical agent. The CPOG is not designed to be decontaminated or reimpregnated for reuse.

10

Serviceability.

The CPOG becomes unserviceable if it is ripped, tom, fasteners broken or missing, or petroleum, oils, or lubricants are spilled or splashed on the garment. For example, if a POL spill on a CPOG sleeve or trouser leg soaks through the CPOG material, replace the CPOG. Further, the overgarment remains serviceable if the CPOG vapor-barrier bag suffers damage (i.e., pinholes, rips, tears), provided the overgarment has not been physically damaged or exposed to water, POL spills, or chemical agents. When any packaging leaks are discovered, seal/repair them as soon as possible. Common duct tape provides an appropriate and expedient way to repair the vapor-barrier bag. Sealing the bag protects the CPOG from direct exposure to moisture, smoke, and fuel solvent vapor which can jeopardize the CPOGs protective qualities; however, if the original vapor-barrier bag is no longer available to the soldier for overgarment storage, use a replacement bag that, as a minimum, is water resistant or water repellent. For example, the water proof bag can be used for storage.

Contamination Avoidance and Liquid Protective Suit

** The suit, contamination avoidance and liquid protective (SCALP)(Figure 1-3) is a four-piece suit consisting of jacket, trousers, and two footwear covers. The base cloth material is of high density polyethylene fibers, and the footwear covers have embossed polyethylene soles for durability and slip resistance. The jacket is a pullover design with an integral hood and covers the head, chest, and arms. An opening is provided for the facepiece of the individual protective mask. Two drawstrings, each with a barrelock, secure the hood to the facepiece, and latex bands secure sleeves around the wrists. The trousers contain a drawstring with a barrelock at the waist and latex bands on the legs to secure them around the ankles. The footwear covers consist of polyethylene soles and latex bands in the upper portion to secure them to the legs. The SCALP jacket/trousers are issued separately from the SCALP footwear covers since the sizing systems are independent of one another. The SCALP, being a disposable, lightweight, impermeable suit, is worn over the BDO, CPOG or CPU/duty uniform to provide additional protection from gross liquid contamination for periods up to one hour. The primary users are armor and EOD personnel and personnel in collective protection who may, by necessity, be forced to leave that collective protection to perform some vital maintenance or reconnaissance function. In such situations, the SCALP will also reduce reentry time. A secondary use of the SCALP is to protect decontamination personnel from being soaked during decontamination operations. Commanders must be aware that wearing the SCALP over the BDO will place additional burden on the soldier, increasing heat stress problems already associated with wearing the BDO. The SCALP weighs approximately 1.5 pounds.

Figure 1-3. Contamination avoidance and liquid protective suit.

Integrated Battlefield Aircrew Uniform

The aircrew uniform integrated battlefield (AUIB) is a standard combat uniform for aircrews designed to replace both the CPOG, BDO, and Nomex flight suit. The AUIB

12

provides NBC protection and protection against flames. It is a two-piece chemical protective uniform with a protective curtain and stand-up collar. The collar closes with a hook-and-pile tape. The suit has a slide fastener front closure with protective flap and a gusseted fastener leg closure for quick and easy donning and doffing. The wrists and ankles have hook-and-pile adjustments to ensure a tighter fit. Chest pockets are side openings for easy access when the safety harness is in use. Side thigh and calf pockets have bellows on one side for easy access. Insulated pockets for atropine injectors are provided on the upper sleeve. All pockets are lined with butyl rubber.

Toxicological Agent Protective Apron

The toxicological agent protective (TAP) apron is intended for personnel whose duties may bring them into contact with liquid chemical agents: for example, those who work with toxic munitions, perform decontamination in a field environment, handle contaminated clothing and equipment at a decontamination site, and handle and treat chemical agent casualties. On the battlefield, the TAP apron provides chemical decontamination units added protection when conducting extended decontamination operations. See FM 3-5 for further information on the use of the TAP apron during decontamination operations.

Chemical Protective Glove Set

Description.

A glove set (figure 1-1) consists of an outer glove for protection and an inner glove for perspiration absorption. The outer gloves are made of an impermeable, black, butyl rubber. The inner gloves are made of thin, white cotton. These inner gloves can be worn on either hand. If either outer glove is punctured or torn, replace the pair of gloves. When engaged in heavy work or during cold weather, soldiers should wear standard work gloves or black shells over the butyl rubber gloves to protect them from damage. The gloves comes in three thickness; 7, 14, and 25 mil. The 7 mil glove set is used by soldiers such as medical, teletypist, and electronic repair personnel whose tasks require extreme tactility and/or sensitivity and will not expose the gloves to harsh treatment. The 14 mil glove set is used by soldiers such as aviators, vehicle mechanics and weapon crews whose task require tactility and sensitivity and will not expose the gloves to harsh treatment. Use of more durable 25 mil glove set is for soldiers who perform close combat tasks and other types of heavy labor.

Protection Capabilities.

The glove protects against liquid chemical agents and vapor hazards as long as they remain serviceable. If the 14 and 25 mil glove set becomes contaminated with liquid chemical agent, decontaminate or replace them, within 24 hours after exposure. If the 7 mil glove set becomes contaminated, replace or decontaminate within 6 hours after exposure. The contaminated gloves may be decontaminated with a 5 % bleach and water solution or a 5 % HTH and water solution and reused indefinitely as long as they remain serviceable. The gloves also keep biting insect vectors and radioactive fallout away from the hands. See FM 3-5 for procedures on decontamination of gloves during the deliberate decontamination process.

Serviceability.

Exposure of the rubber to DS2, break-free, antiseize compound or any other petroleum-based products attacks the gloves rubber polymers and makes them very sticky. Avoid contact with these material if possible. However, replace the glove if the rubber is sticky. Use bleach and water to remove these compounds from the rubber gloves as soon as possible. See below for a means to determine glove serviceability.

Serviceability Test

To determine if a glove set is damaged or serviceable, either fill the gloves with air and submerge in water or fill the glove with water and look for water leaks. The preferred method for determining serviceability is to fill the glove with air and submerge it in water. Prior to submerging the glove in water, hold the base of the glove with both hands (using thumb and index fingers). With the glove fingers hanging downward, rotate the glove several times ensuring an air pocket is formed below the palm. Holding the inflated glove in one hand, squeeze the glove and examine for escaping air and then submerge in water. If bubbles escape, the glove is unserviceable.

Green/Black Vinyl Overboot (GVO)/(BVO)

Description.

The GVO is a plain Olive Drab (OD) Vinyl green overshoe with elastic fasteners. The GVO can be used to protect the wearer against NBC agents or rain, mud, or snow (environmental effects). The black vinyl overshoe (BVO) has been recently typed classified, and can also be used for NBC protection. The BVO is very similar to the GVO, except for the change in color and black enlarged tabs on each elastic fastener.

Protection Capability.

Soldiers wear the green or black vinyl overshoe (GVO/BVO) over their combat boots (figure 1-4) to protect feet from contamination by all known agents, vectors, and radiological particles for a minimum of 14 days. Protection continues past 14 days provided the GVO/BVO remains serviceable. Wearing the GVO/BVO with combat boots provides 24 hours of protection against all known agents, following contamination. Decontaminate the GVO/BVO with a 5 % bleach and water solution or a 5 % HTH and water solution. If the GVO/BVO shows signs of deterioration following decontamination (e.g., cracks, tears, punctures, rubber becomes sticky), replace the boots. See FM 3-5 for information on decontamination of the GVO during the deliberate decontamination process.

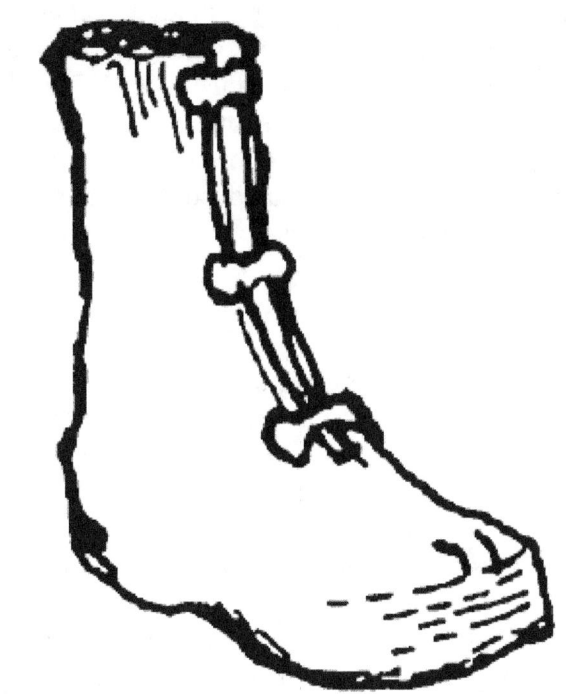

Figure 14. Green vinyl overboot.

Serviceability.

Inspect GVOs regularly to ensure their integrity is maintained, and replace if cracks, tears, or punctures are found. Continuous contact with DS2 will, over time, degrade the GVO/BVO. If DS2 gets on the GVO/BVO, rinse it with bleach and water at the earliest possible time.

Chemical Protective Footwear Cover (CPFC)

Description.

The CPFCs are impermeable and have unsupported butyl rubber soles and butyl uppers. Two variations are in the field. One has a single heal flap, and the other has the newer fishtail double heel flap. Donning instructions vary for each type. Check instructions before donning.

Soldiers wear the chemical protective footwear cover (overboots) (figure 1-1) over their combat boots. The CPFC are being replaced by the GVO/BVOs as stocks become available.

Protection Capabilities.

The overboots protect feet from contamination by all known chemical agents, vectors, and radiological dust particles for a minimum of 24 hours as long as they remain serviceable. The overboot can be decontaminated using a 5% bleach and water solution or a 5% HTH and water solution. If the CPFC shows signs of deterioration following decontamination (e. g., rips, tears, torn laces, rubber becomes sticky), replace the footwear covers. See FM 3-5 for information on decontamination of the footwear cover during the deliberate decontamination process.

Serviceability.

When wearing the overboot, avoid tearing or puncturing them. Tears and punctures can happen when soldiers traverse rough terrain. The laces may catch on protrusions, such as are found on tanks, causing the boots to rip. Replace the overboot if it is punctured or torn.

Chemical Protective Helmet Cover

This cover (Figure 1-1) protects the personnel armor-system ground troop (PASGT) helmet from chemical and biological contamination. The cover is a piece of butyl-coated nylon cloth gathered at the edge by an elastic web enclosed in the hem. It is an olive green, one size fits all cover. It is designed to keep chemical and biological agents from penetrating the kevlar helmet and the helmet cover.

NBC Protective Covers

The NBC protective cover (NBC-PC) is designed to be a lightweight, low-cost, versatile cover to be used in the field to prevent liquid contamination of supplies and equipment. The cover will be used to provide a barrier between covered supplies and equipment and liquid agents, biological agents, and radioactive dust. Protection time against liquid-agents is 48 hours. The cover can provide protection for up to six weeks without agent exposure before it begins to break down due to environmental conditions.

Protective Masks

Protective masks keep wearers from breathing air contaminated with chemical and/or biological agents. Masks are available in these categories: the field protective masks, M17-series currently issued to every soldier, and the M40-series, its replacement; the tank and aircraft protective masks, M24/M25-series, and their eventual replacement; the M42 for combat vehicle crewmen; the M43 for aviators and crewmen; and finally the special purpose mask.

M17A1/M 17A2 Field Protective Mask

An M17-series chemical-biological mask (Figure 1-5), when properly fitted and worn with the hood, protects against field concentrations of all known chemical and biological agents in vapor or aerosol form. Filter elements, in the cheeks of the facepiece, remove the agents from air entering the mask. When the air has a low-oxygen content, such as in tunnels or caves, or when the air has a high level of smoke mixtures, the mask will not protect the wearer. Do not use it for firefighting. It does not protect against ammonia vapors or carbon monoxide. It also is not designed for radiological protection. However, worn properly, it provides added alpha and beta dust inhalation protection, and soldiers should wear it in all known situations until the contamination is identified.

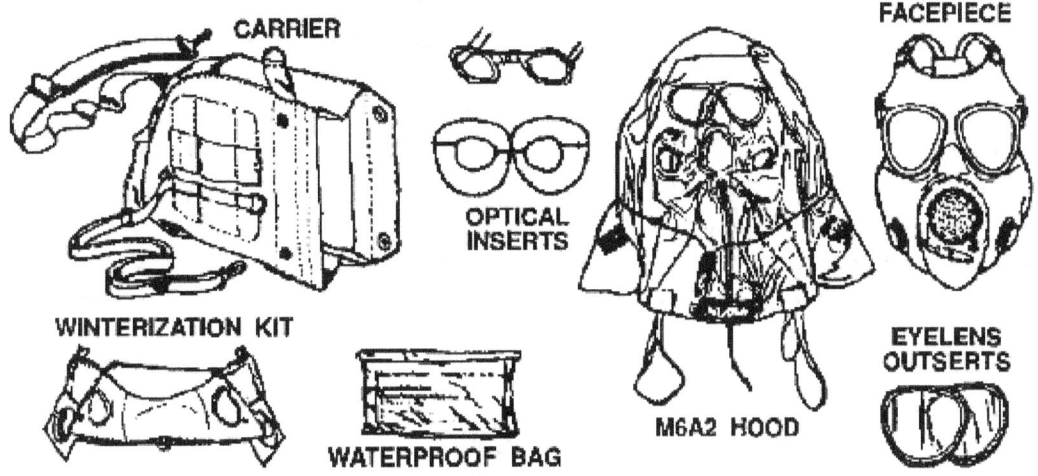

Figure 1-5. M17A2 mask and additional authorized items.

The M17A2 is the standard-A field mask. It is a modification of the M17A1 mask and has no resuscitation tube. Both masks have the following items:

- A voicemitter to facilitate communication.
- A tube for drinking water from the canteen while masked.
- Two outserts to protect the eye lenses and to prevent fogging in low temperatures.
- A carrier for storing and carrying the mask and additional authorized items. Pockets inside the carrier store such items as the nerve agent antidote kit (NAAK), Mark I, and the convulsant antidote for nerve agents (CANA). The exterior pocket of the carrier stores such items as the M1/M1A1 waterproof bag and M8 paper. The M1/M1A1 waterproof bag is used to enclose the mask to protect the filter elements from water damage. An example of use is during river-crossing operations.

Additional authorized items for use with the M17-series mask include the following:

- The ABC-M6A2 field protective mask hood. The hood attaches to the M17-series mask. It protects the head and neck from chemical agent vapors or liquid droplets, biting insects, and radioactive dust particles.
- The M4 mask winterization kit. Use it during cold weather conditions--lower than -20°F (-29°C)--to prevent frost accumulation on the inlet-valve caps. (See cold weather operations in Appendix B).

17

- Optical inserts. These are provided for soldiers who require vision correction according to AR 40-63. TMs 3-4240-279-10 and 3-4240-279-20&P give instructions on the care and maintenance of these masks.

M40 Field Protective Mask

The M40-series chemical-biological mask (Figure 1-6) as it becomes available replaces the M17-series protective mask as the standard Army field mask. The mask consists of a silicone rubber facepiece with in-turned periphery, binocular eye lens system and elastic head harness. Other features include front and side voicemitters, allowing better communication particularly when operating FM communications, drink tube, clear and tinted inserts, and a filter canister with NATO standard threads. The M40 mask provides respiratory, eye, and face protection against CB agents, toxins, radioactive fallout particles, and battlefield contaminants. The canister filter cannot be changed in a contaminated environment. The mask was-not designed for that contingency. TMs 3-4240-300-10-1 and 3-4240-300-20&P give instructions on the care and maintenance of the mask.

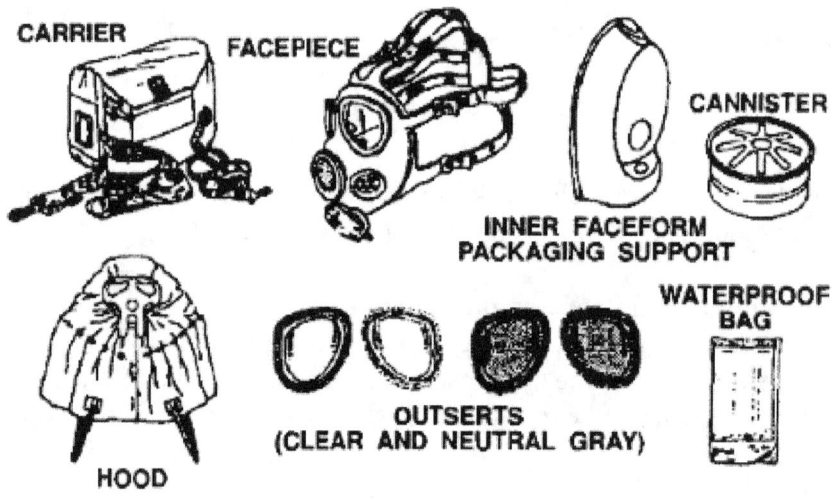

Figure 1-6. M40 mask and additional authorized items.

M25/M25A1 Tank Protective Masks

The M25/M25A1 chemical-biological masks are special masks for crews of armored vehicles. These masks, like the M17-series masks, protect against chemical and biological agent in the vapor or aerosol form.

The M25 and M25A1 masks (Figure 1-7) are essentially the same. The only difference is the higher forehead tab on the M25A1. When used in a tank or other armored vehicle, the masks couple to a filter unit, such as the M13A1 gas-particulate filter unit (GPFU). The GPFU forces filtered temperature-controlled air to the facepiece. This increases protection. It also reduces heat stress in hot weather. When wearing the mask outside the tank or armored vehicle, the wearer inhales air through the M10A1 canister.

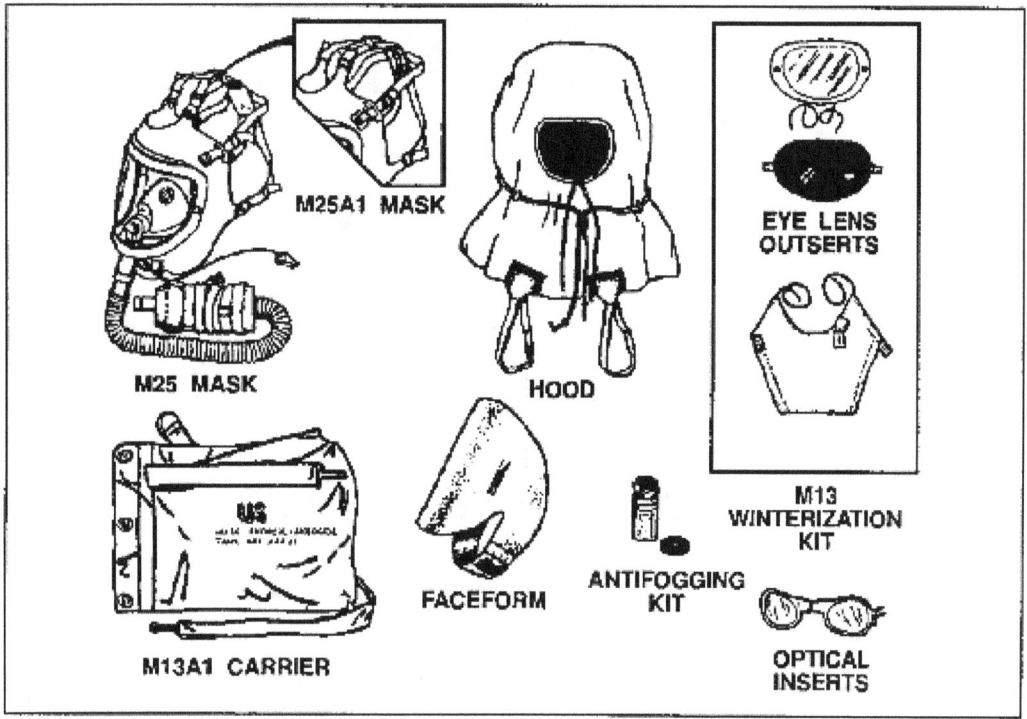

Figure 1-7. M25 and M25A1 chemical-biological masks and accessories.

A microphone assembly in the mask allows communication with other crew members. Communication is through the vehicle communications system. In addition, crew members can communicate with other vehicles having FM receivers.

TMs 3-4240-280-10 and 3-4240-280-23&P give instructions on the care and maintenance of these masks.

M42 Combat Vehicle Crewman Mask

The M42 chemical-biological mask has the same components (Figure 1-8) as the M40, In addition, though, the M42 combat vehicle crewman mask has a built-in microphone for wire communication. The canister on the M42 mask is attached to the end of a hose and has an adapter for connection to a GPFU. Just as the M40 mask, the filter canister is designed with NATO standard threads.

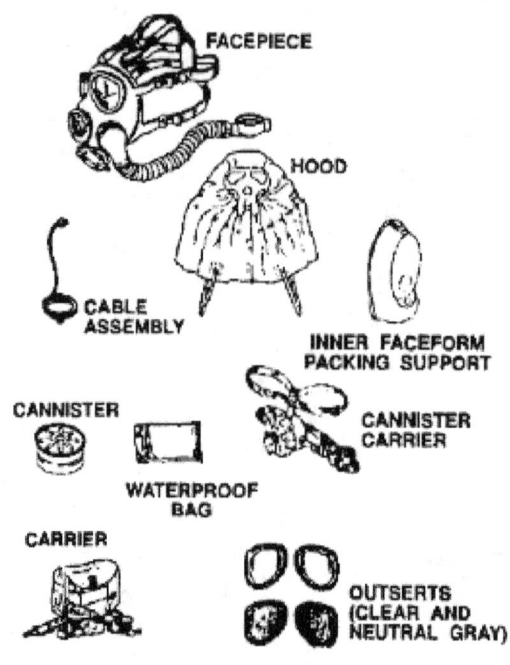

Figure 1-8. M42 chemical-biological mask and accessories.

TMs 3-4240-300-10-2 and 3-4240-300-20&P give instructions on the care and maintenance of the mask.

ABC-M24 Aircraft Protective Mask

The ABC-M24 aircraft chemical-biological mask (Figure 1-9) protects, both in the aircraft and on the ground, against all known chemical and biological aerosols and vapors. The wearer can attach it to the aircraft oxygen supply system by using an M8 adapter kit. The facepiece is not force-ventilated. A microphone element and bracket assembly are in the nose cup for communication.

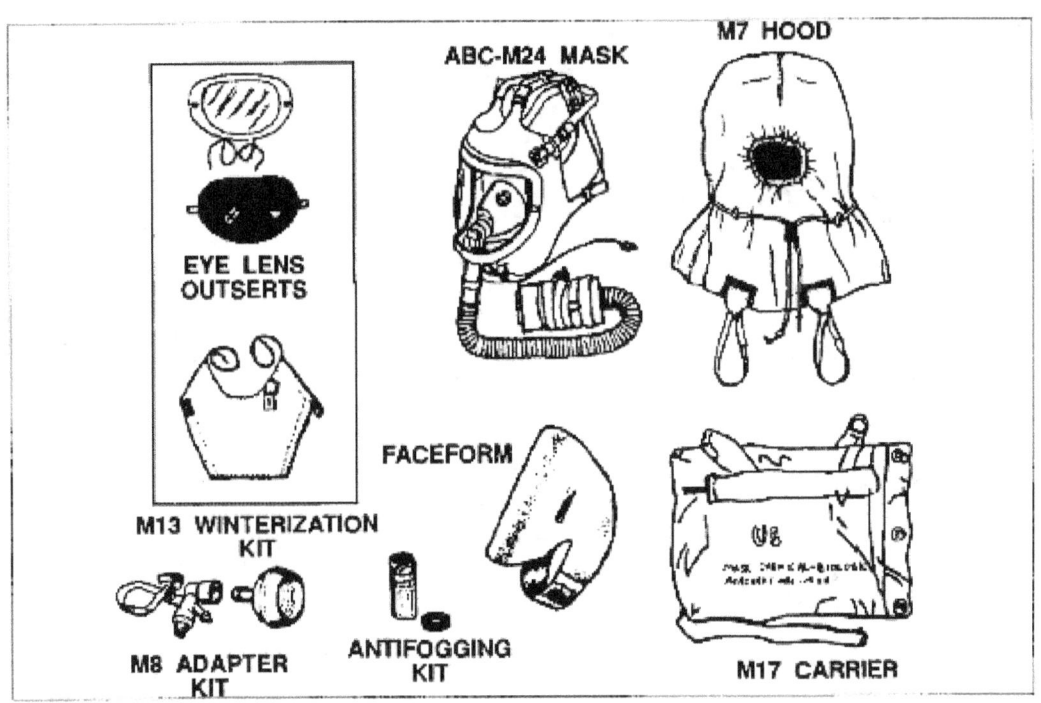

Figure 1-9. ABC-M24 aircraft chemical-biological mask and accessories.

TMs 3-4240-280-10 and 3-4240-280-23&P give instructions on the care and maintenance of this mask.

M43 Aircraft Protective Mask

The M43 mask is a form-fitting butyl rubber facepiece with lenses that mount close to the eyes; an integrated hood with a skull-type suspension system; a portable blower/filter system that operates on battery or aircraft power to maintain positive pressure in the facepiece; and an inhalation air distribution assembly for regulating the flow of air (Figure 1-10). The M43 Type I has a notched eye lens to allow interface with the integrated helmet and display sighting system (IHADSS) equipment. The mask was specifically designed for compatibility with subsystems of the AH-64. The M43 Type II has unnotched lenses for use by non-AH-64 aviators. Both types of masks provide face, eye, and respiratory protection from concentrations of CB agents, toxins, and radioactive fallout particles; however, they do not have the capability of mounting eye lens inserts. Additionally, the mask provides for external voice or wire communications and a drink tube assembly.

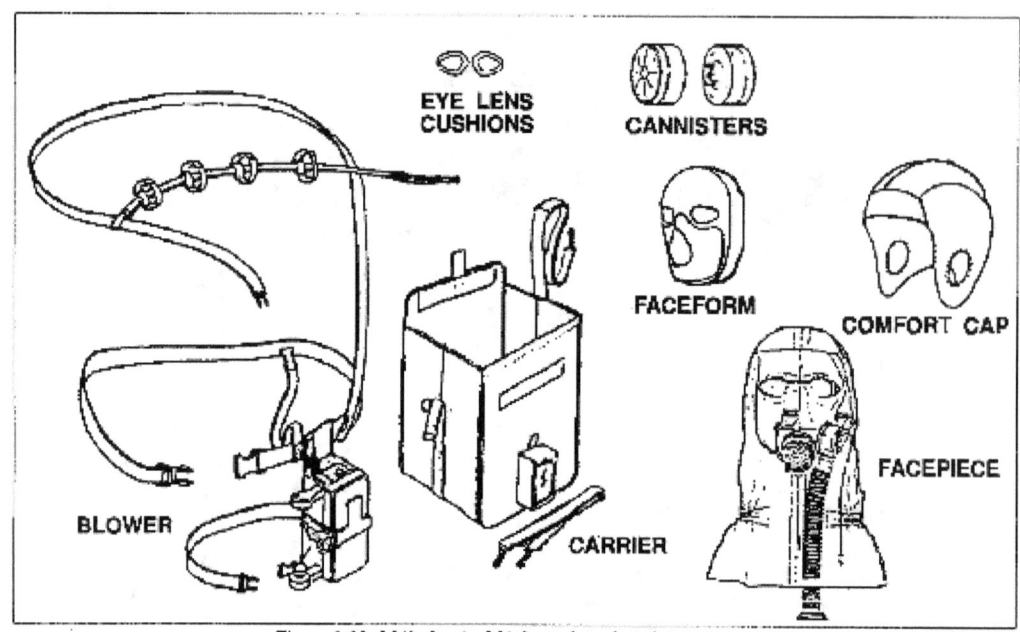

EYE LENS CUSHIONS

CANNISTERS

FACEFORM

COMFORT CAP

BLOWER

CARRIER

FACEPIECE

Figure 1-10. M43 chemical-biological mask and accessories.

TM 3-4240-334-10 gives instructions on the care and maintenance of the mask.

Special Purpose Masks

Several masks are special purpose masks. The present M9A1 field protective mask is in the field and is designed to be used with the M3 toxicological agent protective hood. The M40 special purpose mask will replace the M9A1. The M40 special purpose mask consists of an M40 with an additional canister and a special purpose hood of heavy weight, butyl-coated fabric with a double skirt, M3A1. These masks are primarily used with the toxicological agent protective outfit. It protects specially trained personnel performing duties when liquid agent exposure is expected.

Decontamination Equipment

When skin becomes contaminated, decontaminate it immediately, that is, neutralize or remove contamination from all exposed skin. Do this by using the M258A1 skin decon kit (Figure 1-11) or M291 skin decon kit (Figure 1-12), which are issued to each soldier. If a soldier is incapacitated, a buddy must perform the decon, using the kit issued to the victim.

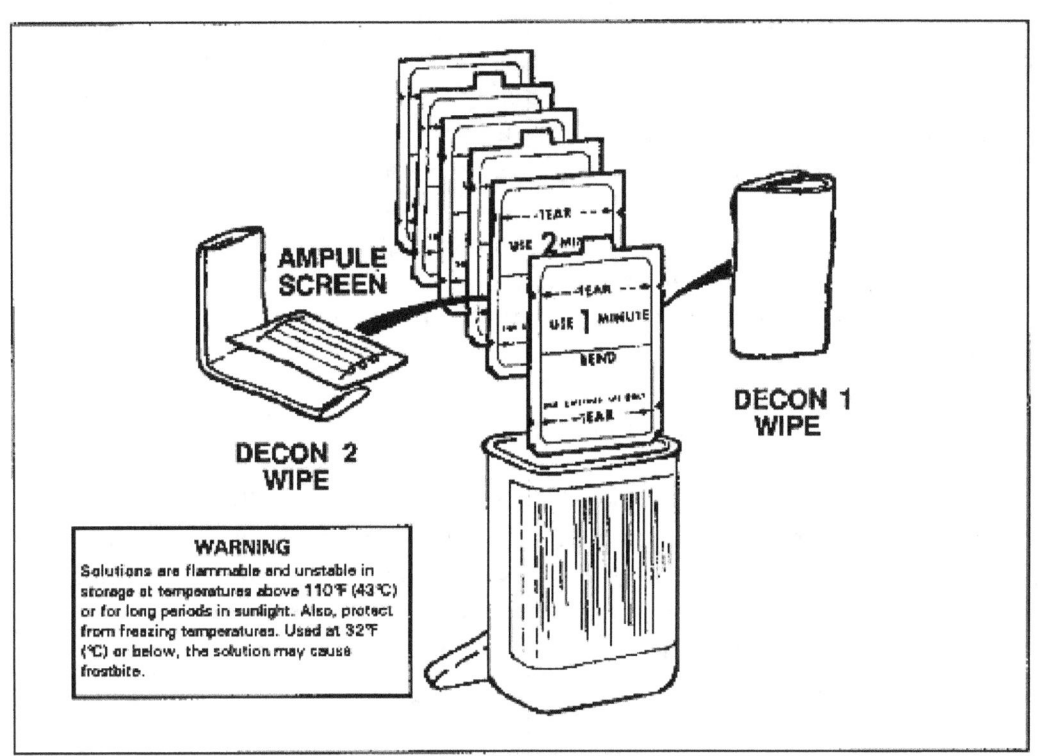

Figure 1-11. M258A1 skin decontamination kit.

Inside the figure:

AMPULE SCREEN

DECON 2 WIPE

DECON 1 WIPE

TEAR
USE 2 MIN

TEAR
USE 1 MINUTE
BEND

TEAR

WARNING
Solutions are flammable and unstable in storage at temperatures above 110°F (43°C) or for long periods in sunlight. Also, protect from freezing temperatures. Used at 32°F (°C) or below, the solution may cause frostbite.

Figure 1-12. M291 skin/equipment decontamination kit.

M258A1 Skin Decontamination Kit

The M258A1 skin decon kit is designed for chemical decon. It comes in a hard plastic case containing three sets of foil-packaged decontaminating wipes. These wipes contain solutions that neutralize most nerve and blister agents. Attach the kit to the protective mask carrier or LCE. Protect it from temperatures above 110F(43°C) and below 32F (0°C). Cold weather operations in Appendix B gives further details.

The substance in the packets leave a residue on the mask that when checked with M8 paper causes a color change similar to GB. The Soldiers Manual of Common Tasks provides step-by-step procedures on the use of the kit. For details on the maintenance and care of the kit, See TM 3-4240-216-10.

M291 Skin Decontamination Kit

The M291 skin decon kit as it becomes available replaces the M258A1 for skin decontamination. It consists of a flexible outer pouch containing six individual skin decontaminating packets. Each packet consists of a foil-packaged, laminated fiber material containing a reactive resin. Its use is very similar to that of the M258A1. It decontaminates the soldier's hands, face, ears, and neck. The M291 kit should be stored in the large cargo pockets of the BDO trouser for easy access. The M291 is capable of operation in temperatures ranging from -50°F to 120°F.

Detection Equipment

On the battlefield, soldiers need to help measure radiation and detect chemical agents. They may use radiacmeters (dosimeters) to record cumulative gamma and neutron radiation dosages received and detector papers to detect and identify liquid chemical agents.

Individual Dosimeter

The new DT236/PD individual dosimeter looks like a wristwatch without a face. Wear it on the wrist to measure the cumulative dose of gamma and neutron radiation received. It is designed to augment the IM93 dosimeter. Selected trained personnel use the CP696/UD radiac computer-indicator to read this dosimeter (Figure 1-13). Data obtained form the basis of radiation dose exposure records. Units will maintain one DT236 per individual assigned plus 10 percent for loss or damage. During periods of heightened tension when other contingency items are issued to soldiers, the DT236/PD will be issued to each individual. Once issued, each soldier will wear the DT236/PD on his wrist at all times except when being read and cleaned. The readings obtained from DT236/PD dosimeters in a unit will be averaged and used to determine the radiation exposure status (RES). The RES determined from existing dosimetery equipment and the RES based on the DT236/PD will be compared and the higher of the category (worst case) will be used. When the unit assumes MOPP, the DT236/PD will be worn underneath the MOPP suit. A DT236 may be decontaminated with the M258A1 and the M291 skin decon kits. However, if a chemical agent soaks into the wristband, it must be replaced. The DT236 is not designed to replace existing dosimetry equipment and specifically is not designed to replace the film badge worn by medical personnel. The DT236 is designed to be worn by tactical personnel only. TM 11-6665-236-12 gives instructions on the care and maintenance of the DT236/PD.

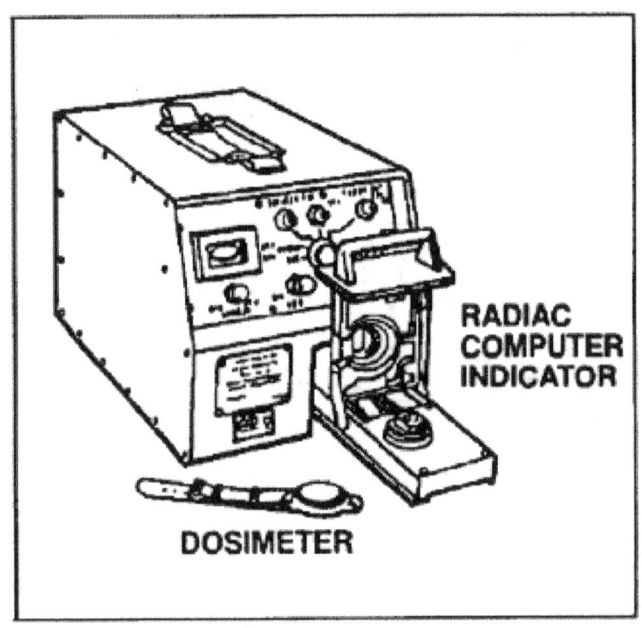

Figure 1-13. DT236/PD individual dosimeter and CP696/UD radiac computer-indicator.

Chemical Agent Detector Paper

Soldiers receive two types of chemical agent detector paper. The ABC-M8 VGH chemical agent detector paper is called M8. It detects and identifies liquid agents. The M9 chemical agent detector paper detects the presence of liquid agent. The M9 does not identify agents.

M8 detector paper (Figure 1-14) comes in booklets of 25 sheets. Use the M8 paper to detect and identify liquid V-or G-type nerve agents or H-type blister agents. The sheets are impregnated with chemical compounds that turn dark green, yellow, or red upon contact with a liquid chemical agent. A color chart in the booklet helps determine the type of agent contacted. The paper must touch liquid agent; it does not detect vapor. It is best suited for use on nonporous materials. Because some solvents also cause it to change color, the paper is unreliable for determining the completeness of decon: for example, DS2 mimics a positive V agent reaction, a black/green color change (see FM 3-5). M8 paper is also in the M256/M256A1 chemical agent detector kit.

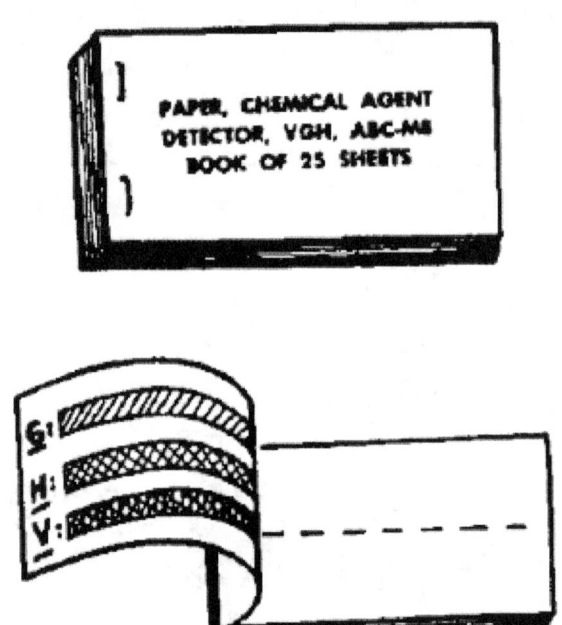

Figure 1-14. ABC-M8 chemical agent detector paper.

Use M9 chemical agent detector paper (Figure 1-15) to detect the presence of liquid chemical agents. It does not detect chemical agent vapor. The paper indicates the presence of a nerve agent (G and V) or a blister agent (H and L) by turning a red or reddish color. Because of this, read M9 paper with only a white-light source.

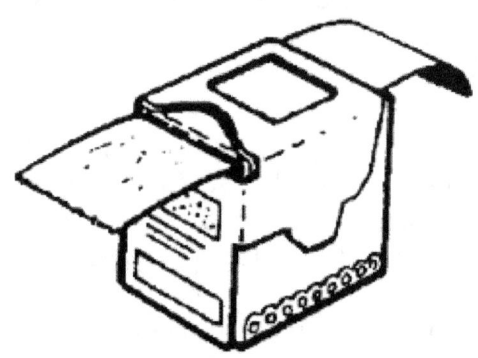

Figure 1-15. M9 chemical agent detector paper.

The self-adhesive M9 paper attaches to most surfaces. When attaching it to clothing, place it on the upper portion of your right arm, left wrist, and either your left or right ankle to allow adequate representation of contamination encountered. When placing it on a piece of equipment, ensure the location is free of dirt, oil, and grease, and place the paper where it will not be stepped on. It is advised that M9 paper that has been placed on equipment be removed before DS2 is sprayed over it; if that is not done, it becomes almost impossible to remove the paper. The M9 paper is usable in any weather, in temperatures above 32°F (0°C). However, exposure to extremely high temperatures may produce false readings. Scuffs, certain types of organic liquids, and DS2 also cause false readings. DS2 turns M9 paper blue. If the paper shows spots or streaks of pink, red-brown, red-purple, or any shade of red, assume it has been exposed to a chemical agent. See TM 3-6665-311-10 for further information.

M256-Series Chemical Agent Detector Kit

The M256-series chemical agent detector kit (Figure 1-16) is issued at squad, crew, or section level. It provides a squad-level ability to detect and identify field concentrations of nerve blister, or blood agent vapors. It differentiates between classes of agents and helps determine when unmasking may be safe after a chemical attack. The kit consists of 12 individually packaged samplers/detectors, a set of instruction cards, and a packet of ABC-M8 VGH chemical agent detector paper. These components come packed in a small, compact, plastic case. Each sampler/detector detects harmful vapor concentrations of nerve, blister, and blood agents. It changes color upon contact with chemical agents at concentrations hazardous to an unmasked person. See TM 3-6665-307-10 for further information.

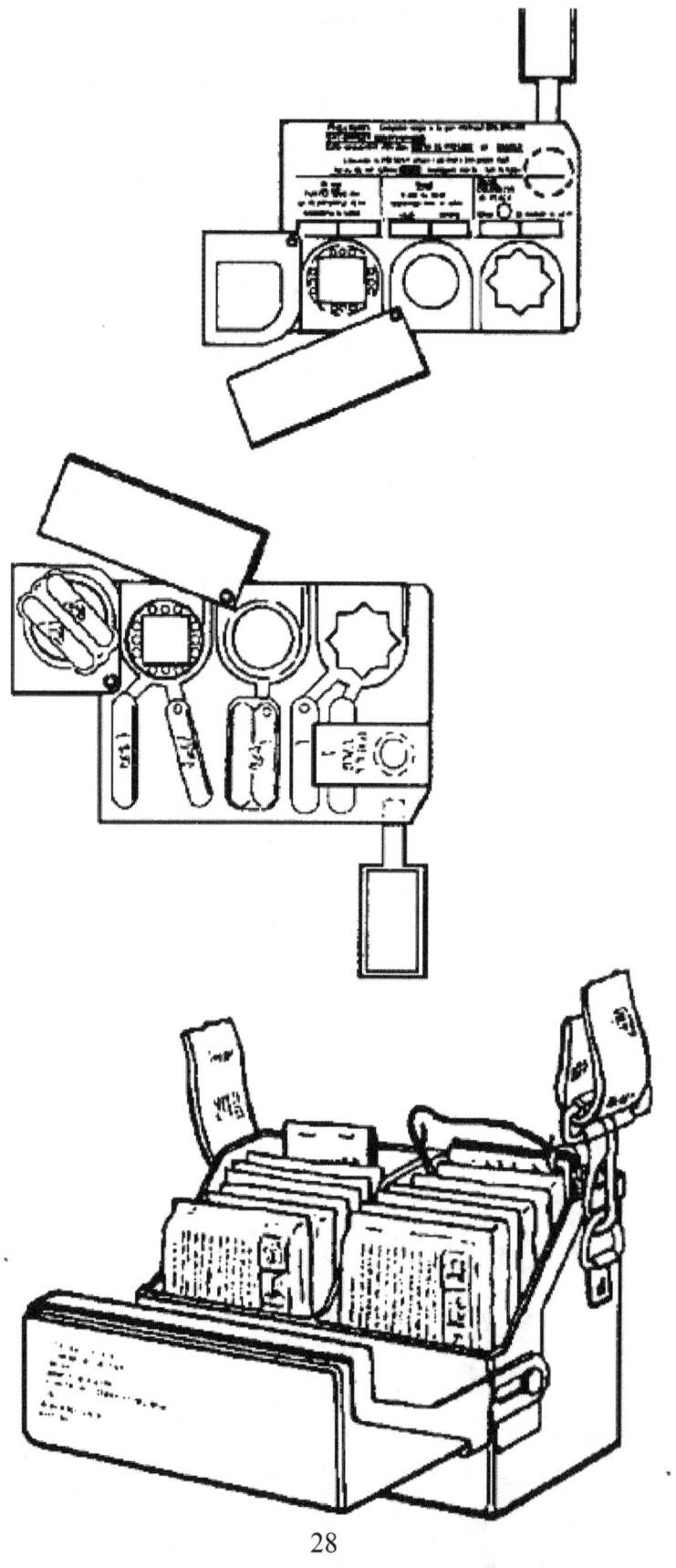

Figure 1-16. M256/M256A1 chemical agent detector kit.

First-Aid Equipment

Nerve agent poisoning requires immediate first-aid treatment. Soldiers receive three NAAKs, Mark I (Figure 1-17), for this purpose.

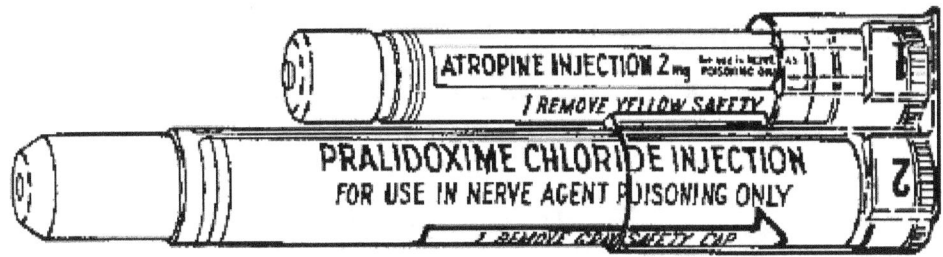

Figure 1-17. Nerve agent antidote kit, Mark I.

Soldiers may become subjected to nerve agent poisoning on the battlefield. Immediate treatment with the NAAK is required if they are to survive. The NAAK consists of one small autoinjector containing atropine and a second autoinjector containing pralidoxime chloride. A plastic clip holds the two injectors together. Store the NAAK in the accessory storage pocket inside your mask carrier. Protect the NAAK from freezing. Cold weather operations in Appendix B gives details.

Nerve Agent Pretreatment Pyridostigmine

The nerve agent pretreatment pyridostigmine (NAPP) (Figure 1-18) is an adjunct to the NAAK. When used in conjunction with the NAAK this pretreatment enhances the survivability of the soldier in a nerve agent chemical environment. Each soldier is initially issued one NAAK, which he is responsible for carrying and safe-guarding against loss. He will secure the NAPP in the sleeve or breast pocket of the BDO. Soldiers will begin taking their NAPP tablets when ordered by their commander based on his assessment of possible agent exposure within the next few hours or days. One tablet is to be taken on a continuous basis once every eight hours until all 21 tablets have been taken or the soldier has been directed to discontinue taking the tablets. NAPPs should be stored/refrigerated in temperatures ranging from 35°F to 46°F. If the medication is removed from the refrigerator for a total of six months, it should be assumed that it has lost its potency and should not be used.

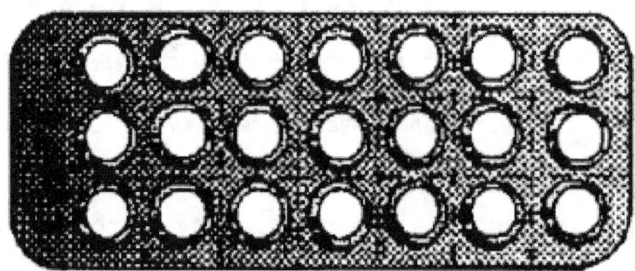

NERVE AGENT PYRIDOSTIGMINE PRETREATMENT TABLET SET

(NAPP)

1. COMMENCE TAKING ONLY WHEN ORDERED BY YOUR COMMANDER.
2. TAKE 1 TABLET EVERY 8 HOURS AS DIRECTED.
3. IT IS DANGEROUS TO EXCEED THE STATED DOSE.

30-MG PYRIDOSTIGMINE BROMIDE X 21 TABLETS.

OUTER WRAPPER

PYRIDOSTIGMINE BROMIDE TABLETS

Figure 1-18. Nerve agent pyridostigmine pretreatment tablet set.

Convulsant Antidote for Nerve Agents

The CANA (Figure 1-19) is similar to existing autoinjectors but modified to hold a 2-milliliter volume of diazepam. The exterior of the autoinjector will be distinguishable from the NAAK kit by two flanges on the length of the barrel. The autoinjector is packaged in a chemically hardened material. The CANA is a disposable device for intramuscular delivery of diazepam to a buddy who is incapacitated by nerve agent poisoning. It is administered by buddy aid only and is an adjunct to the NAAK kit. The CANA is an individually issued item. See TM 8-288 for further information.

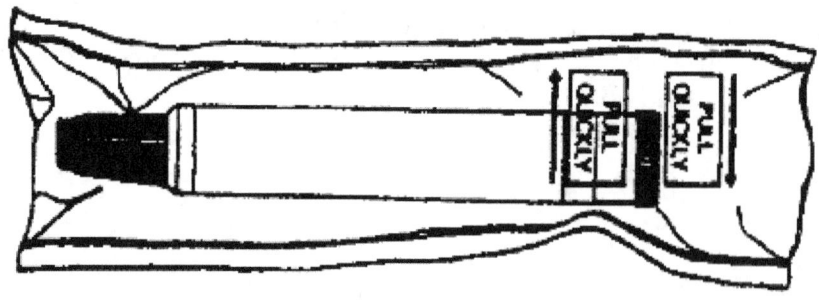

Figure 1-19. Convulsant antidote for nerve agents.

30

RELATED EQUIPMENT

Commanders must ensure that the appropriate section, squad, or platoon has personnel trained to operate and maintain the assigned NBC defense equipment. Operation and maintenance of individual and unit NBC equipment are both a leadership and individual responsibility. Not everyone in the unit will be provided these items of NBC equipment, but any soldier may become responsible for them or need to use them. The items include the M256/M256A1 chemical agent detector kit, IM93/UD dosimeter, M11 decontaminating apparatus, and M13 decontaminating apparatus. Skills applicable to these items can be found in STP 21-24.

Chemical Agent Monitor

The chemical agent monitor (CAM) (Figure 1-20) is designed to be used to detect chemical agent vapor and provide a readout of the relative concentration of vapor present. It can be employed to monitor--

- Personnel or vehicles prior to decontamination and after.
- The inside of collective protection shelters.
- Relative concentrations of agents to assist in the selection of the appropriate level of protective posture.
- The completeness of decontamination.

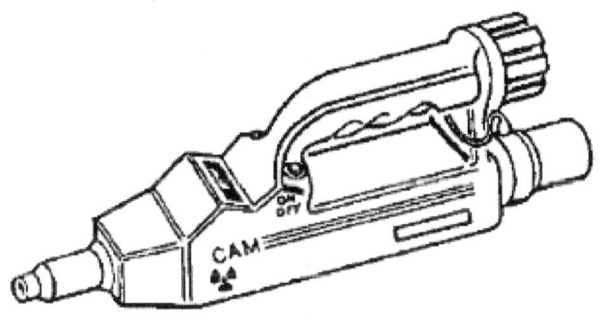

Figure 1-20. Chemical agent monitor.

The CAM draws in air and samples it for contamination. It indicates the level of contamination on a bar graph indicator. When very light concentrations are present, the CAM samples for a longer period of time to reduce the possibility of false indications. When an agent vapor is detected, the CAM will provide a bar graph indication of the relative concentration of the sample (Figure 1-21). Although very close to what is actually there, the indication is only an approximation of the concentration. If vapor is not present, the instrument will not provide an indication. If vapors are transient, the CAM would provide intermittent indications. This is primarily a function of weather, time of exposure, and the challenge presented. See TM 3-6665-327-13&P for instructions on care and maintenance.

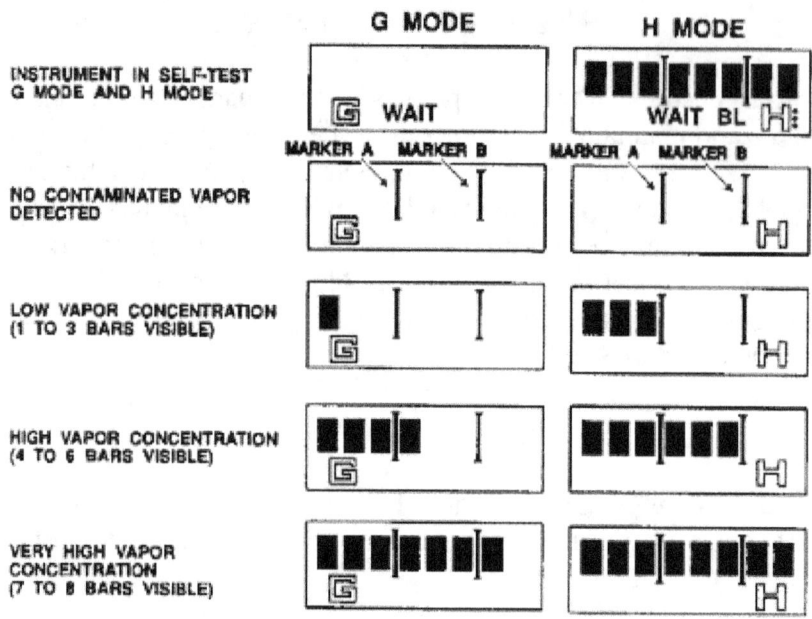

Figure 1-21. Description of CAM displays.

M34 Soil Sampling Kit

The M34 sampling kit (Figure 1-22) is intended for use by authorized NBC personnel to perform sampling of soil, surface matter, and even water. The primary use though is to gather soil samples for processing at laboratories in the rear.

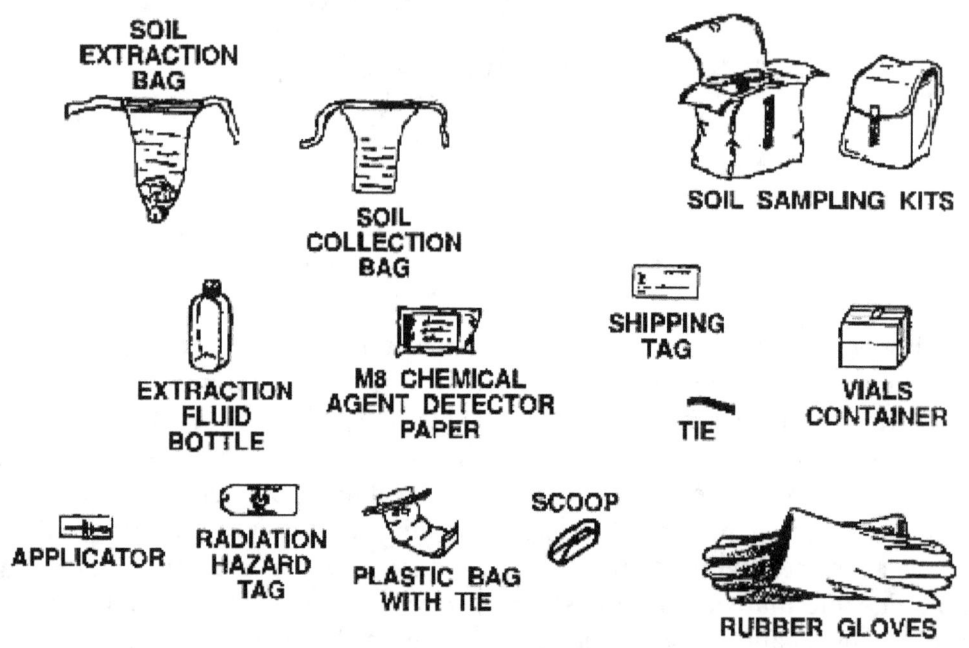

Figure 1-22. M34 soil sampling kit.

The sampling kit consists of a carrier, a plastic scoop, 2 extraction fluid bottles, 2 soil extraction bags, 16 individually wrapped ampules, 6 soil collection bags, 10 plastic-covered wire ties, M8 paper, 3 radiation hazard tags, and 8 shipping tags with envelopes.

*The components are used in the field to collect soil and water samples, samples from contaminated surfaces, munition fragments, material fragments, small objects, and dead animals. The carrier is used as a shipping container for transmitting samples to the laboratories. See TM 3-6665-2608-10 for further information.

IM93/UD Dosimeter

The Army standard tactical instrument for reading total radiation dose is the IM93/UD (Figure 1-23). It is a tubular device, about the size of a fountain pen. It allows the user to read the accumulated gamma total dose simply by looking through the lens while pointing the instrument toward the sun or another bright light source. One end has a dust cap to keep dirt from the charging contacts.

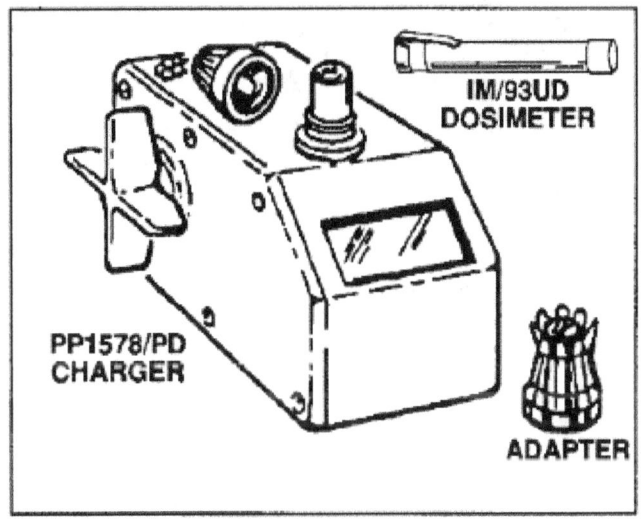

Figure 1-23. IM93/UD dosimeter and PP1578A/PD radiac-detector charger.

This dosimeter requires a charging unit--the PP1578A/PD radiac-detector charger. This charger is a small, electrostatic-charge generator. It is designed to serve all US and certain NATO combat dosimeters. The charger has its own NATO adapter stored within the case. The major operating features of the charger are the charging knob, charging pedestal, and window. Reading the unit requires direct sunlight or another bright light source, such as vehicle headlights or a flashlight. See TM 11-6665-214-10 for instructions on care and maintenance.

M272 Water Testing Kit

The M272 (Figure 1-24) kit will detect and identify dangerous levels of common chemical warfare (CW) agents in water sources. It can be used by non-chemical corps personnel who are required to collect and check any water source such as wells, lakes, rivers, and city water systems. The M272 is a lightweight kit that will detect and identify harmful amounts of CW agents when those are present in raw or treated water. See TM 3-6665-319-10 for further information.

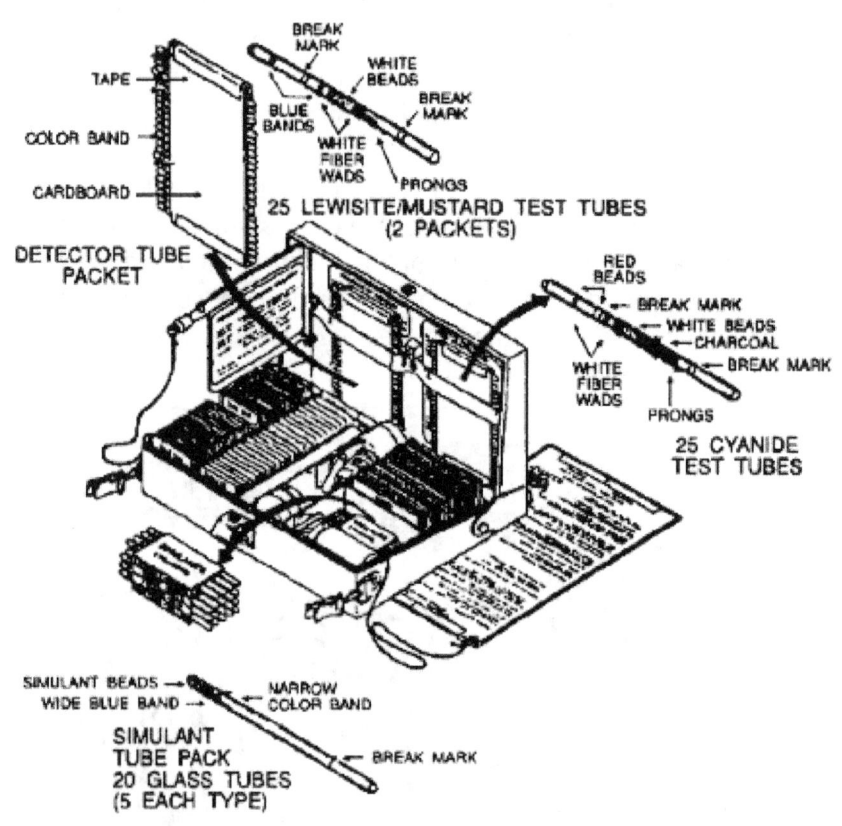

Figure 1-24. M272 water testing kit.

AN/VDR2 Radiac Set

The AN/VDR2 is used to locate and measure radioactivity in the form of gamma rays and beta particles (Figure 1-25). It displays dose rates and total accumulated dose resulting from fallout.

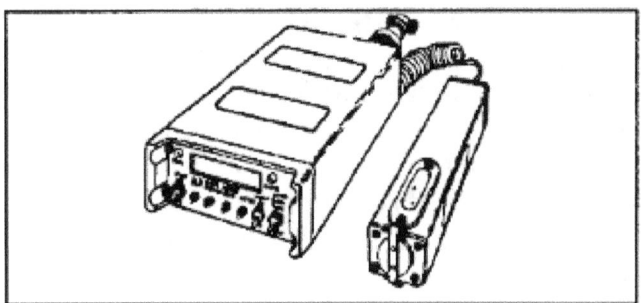

Figure 1-25. AN/VDR2 radiac set.

The AN/VDR2 has the following capabilities:

- It detects, measures, and displays level of gamma radiation dose rate from 0.01 uCyph to 100 Gyph.
- It detects and displays level of beta particle dose rate from 0.01 uGy to 5 cGyph.
- It measures, stores, and displays accumulated dose from 0.01 uGy to 9.99 Gy.

The AN/VDR2 will replace the IM174/PD and the AN/PDR27 as the standard radiac instrument. See TM 11-6665-251-10 for further information.

IM174/PD Radiacmeter

The IM174 series (Figure 1-26) is a portable tactical survey instrument designed to measure gamma radiation dose rates from 0 to 500 cGyph. The IM174 series is primarily used by NBC personnel to determine gamma radiation levels from radioactive contaminants while performing survey and monitoring tasks. Procedures for using the IM174/PD are discussed in FM 3-3. TM 11-6665-213-12 provides further information.

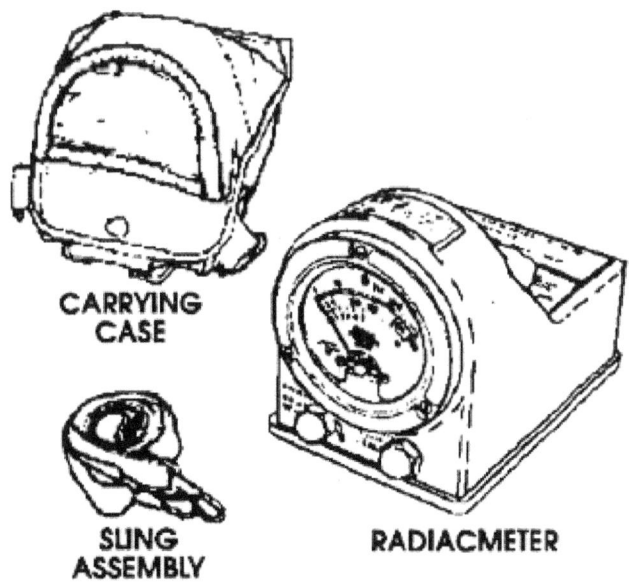

CARRYING
CASE

SLING
ASSEMBLY

RADIACMETER

Figure 1-26. IM174/PD radiacmeter.

AN/PDR27 Radiac Set

The AN/PDR27 (Figure 1-27) is designed to detect beta radiation and measure and detect gamma radiation. The AN/PDR27 is used as a point source instrument to monitor low levels of radiation contamination on personnel, supplies, and equipment. It is portable, watertight, lightweight, and rugged. It is issued on a one per divisional company-size combat and combat support unit and as required for medical, maintenance, and bath units and water supply points.

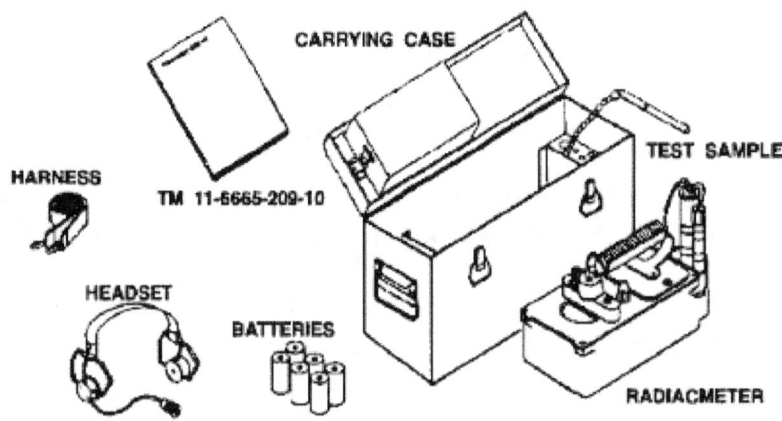

Figure 1-27. AN/PDR27 radiac set and components.

See TM 11-6665-209-15 and TM 11-6665-230-15 for further information.

DS2 ABC-M11 Portable Decontaminating Apparatus

The M11 apparatus (Figure 1-28) decontaminates small areas, such as the steering wheel or other equipment that soldiers must touch. It is a steel container with aluminum spray-head assembly and a nitrogen gas cylinder that provides the pressure. It is filled with 1-1/3 quarts of DS2, which is sufficient for covering 135 square feet. The effective spray range is 6 to 8 feet. After each use, refill the M11 with DS2 and fit it with a new nitrogen cylinder, and it will be ready to use again. See TM 3-4230-204-12&P for additional information.

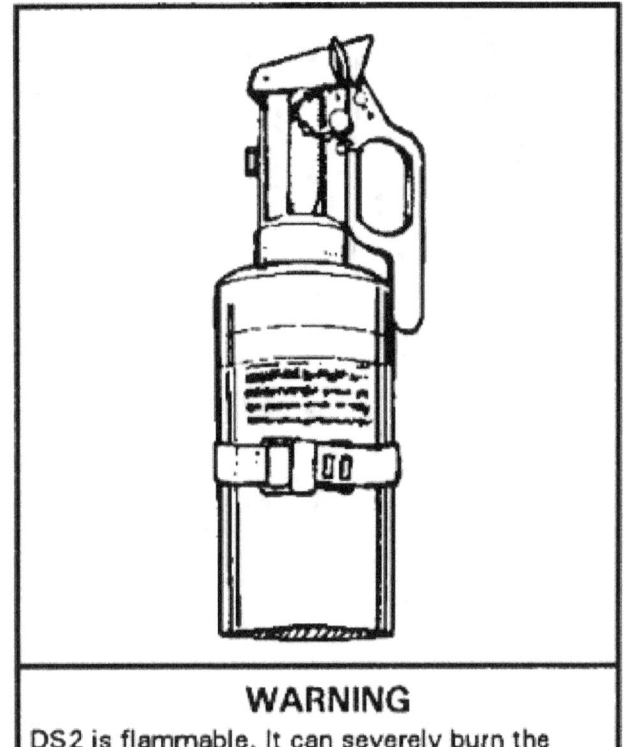

WARNING

DS2 is flammable. It can severely burn the skin, cause blindness, and/or deteriorate the battledress overgarment. Do not use it near an open flame or allow it to touch skin or clothing. Personnel handling DS2 must wear protective

Figure 1-28. ABC-M11 portable decontaminating apparatus.

M13 Portable Decontaminating Apparatus

Use the M13 apparatus to decontaminate vehicles and crew-served weapons larger than .50 caliber. The M13 (Figure 1-29) is about the size of a 5-gallon gasoline can. It comes prefilled with 14 liters of DS2 decon agent. Decon capability is 1,200 square feet. A hose assembly, pump assembly, wand assembly, and brush are attached to the fluid container for disseminating DS2. The brush allows removal of thickened agents, mud, grease, or other material from surfaces. See TM 3-4230-214-12&P for further information.

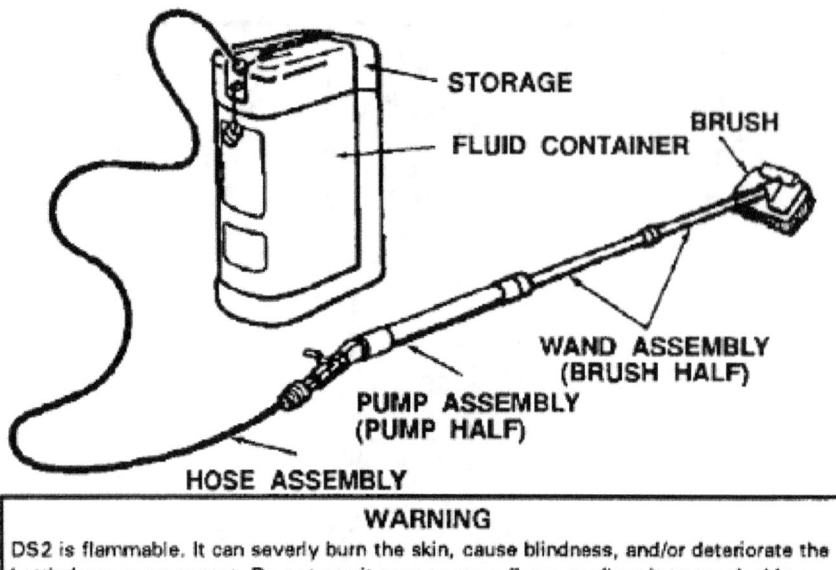

STORAGE

FLUID CONTAINER

BRUSH

WAND ASSEMBLY
(BRUSH HALF)

PUMP ASSEMBLY
(PUMP HALF)

HOSE ASSEMBLY

WARNING

DS2 is flammable. It can severly burn the skin, cause blindness, and/or deteriorate the battledress overgarment. Do not use it near an open flame or allow it to touch skin or clothing. Personnel handling DS2 must wear protective clothing and eye protection.

Figure 1-29. M13 portable decontaminating apparatus.

MOPP Gear Sustainment

To meet sustainment requirements for operations under NBC conditions, commanders must apply the sustainment imperatives of AirLand Battle doctrine. These imperatives include anticipation, integration, continuity, responsiveness, and improvisation. An understanding of these imperatives can ensure prompt delivery of needed items.

At present, units maintain two sets of contingency MOPP gear, commonly referred to as the NBC "A" bag and "B" bag of individual chemical equipment (ICE) packs. In most units, the "A" bag is to be with the soldier as part of his initial deployment gear if there is likelihood of an NBC threat. The "B" bag would be provided if needed. Getting this one or both sets of gear to the soldier must be thoroughly thought out and planned for based on the operational situation using the sustainment imperatives as a guide. For your unit's specific quantities check with your next higher headquarters or use CTA 50-900 for specific quantities.

A forward deployed unit, such as an armored cavalry regiment (ACR), may require both sets of MOPP gear be immediately available based on the threat. The "A" bag is carried by the soldier as part of his individual field gear. The "B" bag can either be part of the troop trains or squadron trains. This is again based on the threat. Other methods can be devised based on unit policy.

Given a low NBC threat situation such as Operations Urgent Fury, deployment to Grenada in 1983, and Just Cause, deployment to Panama in 1989, units deployed at MOPP zero. Unit sets of MOPP gear, including "A" bags, were palletized for immediate follow-on resupply if the NBC threat situation changed.

Resupply of the second set of MOPP gear into combat configured loads can also be accomplished by palletizing the needed individual protective equipment (IPE). This method can be used by both light and heavy units. The intent of palletizing is to create a "push package" that can either be broken down at an arrival airfield or at a unit trains site for immediate issue to company-level units or for further movement forward to units in the field. The method of palletizing and movement is dependent on the type of unit and how they perform their mission. The configuration of the pallets themselves and where they would be kept while in garrison will be dictated by unit SOP. Space will be a crucial factor. In light infantry divisions, pallets must be configured so as to fit on an aircraft that will be resupplying the units. In heavy divisions, pallets need to be configured to fit on whatever prime mover that is designated to haul the pallets.

A possible palletized configuration for use by a light infantry unit that, based on the expected NBC threat, initially does not deploy with either their "A" or "B" bags could be--

- One pallet with the unit's "A" bags and related IPE equipment: M256-series kits, M8 and 9 paper, M258A1/M291 kits, DS2, and M4 winterization kit.
- One pallet with the unit's "B" bags and related equipment.
- Another pallet containing other unit NBC equipment.
- One other pallet containing STB by itself since for safety reasons DS2 and STB cannot be transported together.

Configurations will vary based on a unit's general deployment plan (GDP) or contingency mission and the likelihood of an NBC threat in their area of operation (AO). All this would be integrated and executed through the logistics channels. These items will be moved based on certain time lines dictated by the operation plan (OPLAN) and on events that are expected to occur during the operation.

Chemical Protective Undergarment (CPU)

Description. The CPU is a lightweight two-piece undergarment made of a nonwoven fabric with activated charcoal. The jacket has a zippered front with velcro wrist attachments. The trouser waist has an elastic band for a snug fit to the body. The undergarment weighs two pounds, 11 ounces. NOTE: The CPU primary basis of issue indicates that it will be issued to Special Forces and Combat Vehicle Crews.

Protection Capabilities.

The CPU provides excellent protection against all known chemical agent vapors, liquid droplets; biological agents; toxins; and radioactive alpha and beta particles. The CPU is not a stand alone garment. The CPU is worn under standard duty uniforms such as the Battle Dress Uniform (BDU) or the Combat Vehicle Crewmen coverall. The CPU is not designed or intended to be worn under the BDO or CPOG. The CPU is donned when soldiers are directed to go from MOPP0 to MOPP1. When the CPU is used at MOPP3/4, the protection afforded is equivalent to that provided by a MOPP3/4 ensemble using either the BDO or CPOG. Following exposure to a liquid chemical agent at MOPP3/4, soldiers should exchange their uniform and CPU within 12 hours. Further, CPU the should be disposed of if the exterior uniform has been exposed to a liquid chemical agent.

Do not remove the undergarment from the bag until it is ready for use. When the undergarment is removed from its vapor-barrier bag and worn, its protective qualities last for a minimum of 15 days. The protective qualities for the CPU begins to decline following 15 days; however, any specific decrease in CPU effectiveness has not been determined through test and evaluation. The weartime for the CPU begins when it is removed from the sealed vapor-barrier bag, and stops when the CPU is sealed back in the vapor-barrier bag. If the original vapor-barrier bag is not available to the soldier for undergarment storage, use a replacement storage bag that, as a minimum, is water resistant or water repellent. When any packaging leaks are discovered, seal or repair them with tape as soon as possible.

The CPU can also be laundered once during its 15 day utilization period (Note: During testing, the CPU was only laundered once; it is not known if repeat washing will decrease CPU effectiveness.) and retain its protective qualities. The CPU can be hand-washed in fresh water, or laundered by a quartermaster laundry and bath unit. NOTE: Follow the CPU laundering instructions outlined on the size and care labels

Serviceability.

The CPU becomes unserviceable if it is ripped or torn; however, it can be repaired by following instructions that are provided in CPU use and care manual or TM 10-8400-201-23. The CPU remains serviceable if the vapor-barrier bag suffers damage (i.e., pinholes, rips, tears), provided the undergarment has not been physically damaged or exposed to chemical agents. The CPU comes in a sealed vapor-barrier bag that protects against rain, moisture, and sunlight. The CPU is resistant to rust, rot, and petroleum.

Chapter 2

MOPP Analysis

This chapter addresses the methodology for determining appropriate levels of protection from chemical hazards. Units do this by modifying their protective postures, using chemical agent detectors and alarms, determining automatic masking criteria, and making informed decisions at the right time.

On the battlefield, units will have incomplete intelligence concerning enemy NBC chemical capabilities. However, units use intelligence preparation of the battlefield (IPB) to estimate how many enemy fire support systems are in range, where and what they are, and how they could support probable enemy courses of action (COA). Further, your assessment of the enemy's intent and capabilities is a necessary part of the MOPP analysis and directly affects your recommendations.

However, at higher levels of command, for example, brigade or higher, more data are available to better determine threat capabilities and intent. Estimates provided by these headquarters enable subordinate units to determine appropriate postures.

Subordinate units must be given the flexibility to modify MOPP guidance received from higher headquarters based on local conditions. Units may be granted the flexibility to raise or lower their protective posture from that recommended by higher headquarters by using the techniques described in this chapter. This may be done down to platoon level and by any element that finds itself isolated. If higher headquarters specifically denies this flexibility, then protective postures may only be raised, not lowered, by these units.

This chapter will discuss the use of IPB as it relates to NBC operations, standard MOPP postures, automatic masking, MOPP flexibility, the sources and management of performance problems in MOPP, troop preparation, MOPP analysis procedures, and other procedures regarding the wear of the BDO and other individual protective equipment. Advice on use of MOPP guidance, techniques for use of alarms, and unmasking procedures are included, as well as filter replacement criteria.

Assessing Threat Information

Chemical officers' and NCOs' (battalion/brigade) responsibilities include using MOPP analysis to provide their commander with the best possible NBC estimate. In coordination with the S2 and S3, chemical staff personnel (battalion/brigade) address NBC during all phases of the battle. This is done by using assessment information from higher headquarters (see discussion in Chapter 3) and summarizing that information for their unit's needs.

The IPB process includes evaluation of the threat-the organization, composition, tactical doctrine, weapons, equipment, and their supporting battlefield functional systems of the enemy. It includes evaluating areas of operation and times of interest set by the commander. Terrain and weather analysis are also included in the process. The final step in the process is threat integration. This includes integrating the above mentioned items and enemy doctrine to determine how the enemy will fight. Threat integration is accomplished through development of the doctrine, situation, event, and decision support templates used by the S2 in briefing the commander.

The chemical officer uses the doctrine template in his estimate to address the when, where, why, and how the enemy will employ any NBC hazards in an AO. This provides the commander the information on threat NBC employment required for developing his concept of the operation. Threat chemical barrier production can also be depicted on this template. NBC reconnaissance will be conducted to confirm or deny whether any chemical barriers are present. Procedures to estimate the duration of the hazard are covered in Chapter 3.

Next, the chemical officer applies the situation template to his units' actual AO to provide a detailed assessment of all possible threat NBC actions that have either already happened or are anticipated based on how the battle is taking shape. The situation template helps explain how future events on the battlefield can affect the units' operations.

The events template lays out possible events that could happen as the battle progresses. The chemical officer examines each forecasted event to assess all possible threat NBC interdictions that could impact on his units' mission within-the AO. For example, the chemical officer's/NCO's assessment includes estimating the percentage of friendly chemical casualties that could occur if the enemy employed agents at that particular time. The procedure for estimating chemical casualties is discussed in Chapter 3.

Based on the situation, the events template predicts possible enemy COA at certain times and places on the battlefield. Based on these COA, a decision support template is created.

The decision support template provides the commander with his own COA to counter the threat. These COA are based on certain actions happening on the battlefield, or at a certain time or phase during the battle. The commander may use decision points on the battlefield to initiate certain COA. Based on the NBC threat, these decision points can result in the commander ordering a higher MOPP level based on an increased NBC threat at a particular time or phase of the battle. He may request NBC reconnaissance of critical terrain that templating indicates could be contaminated with persistent agents. These are just a few examples of possible input the chemical officer could provide to the S2's IPB estimate.

Using the IPB process, the chemical officer/NCO provides the commander and staff updates on the NBC situation. The chemical officer provides the following based on the time periods of interest set by the commander:

- Detailed information on enemy NBC capability based on the type of weapon systems that the enemy has available at that period of interest.
- How the enemy would employ chemicals.
- Areas of likely employment based on threat employment doctrine.
- Detailed analysis of terrain and weather in the unit's AO during each period of interest.
- MOPP guidance for each period of interest.
- Templates of predicted fallout data that are updated as conditions change.
- Alternative actions the commander can initiate prior to the time period in question so as to minimize degradation of affected units.
- Continuous monitoring of S2 message and radio traffic for any NBC-related information that could be important to the unit's mission.

Prior planning based on information provided by the chemical officer will help the commander make sound decisions. Regular updates need to be provided to the commander because of rapid changes in the situation.

It is corps and higher-level commanders' responsibility to direct minimum MOPP levels appropriate to the threat. They are aware of the intelligence that might indicate the probable use of NBC weapons. These commanders have the initial responsibility for upgrading unit protective posture. Ordering MOPP2 through MOPP4 is the responsibility of the division and lower commanders. The final responsibility, however, is that of the company commander or platoon leader who is on the spot. At this level there is a better appreciation for what the unit can and cannot do. These leaders increase or decrease their unit's protective posture based on an analysis of the situation and guidance from higher command. Final responsibility at this level retains flexibility of the system. The lower echelon unit's leader should not decrease the protective posture below the minimum level established by the next higher headquarters without prior approval.

Based on the threat assessment, units may be directed to deploy with only their protective masks. During Operation Just Cause in Panama in 1989 and Operation Urgent Fury in Grenada in 1983, several US units, based on intelligence information, determined that the protective mask would meet their NBC defense needs. This represents an example of the flexibility that is inherent in the MOPP system. During Operation Desert Shield/Storm, most US units deployed to Saudi Arabia at MOPP zero and had their MOPP gear readily available. Again, this represents, based on intelligence information and the threat, the flexibility that is inherent in the MOPP system.

Standard Mission-Oriented Protective Postures

All leaders need to be familiar with standard MOPP levels. Knowing these levels will aid the commander or small unit leader in making rapid and educated decisions regarding the level of MOPP to be worn by his soldiers. Standardized MOPP levels allow commanders to increase or decrease levels of protection through the use of readily understood prowords. Commanders determine which protective posture their subordinate units will assume (Figure 2-1), and then direct their units to assume that MOPP level.

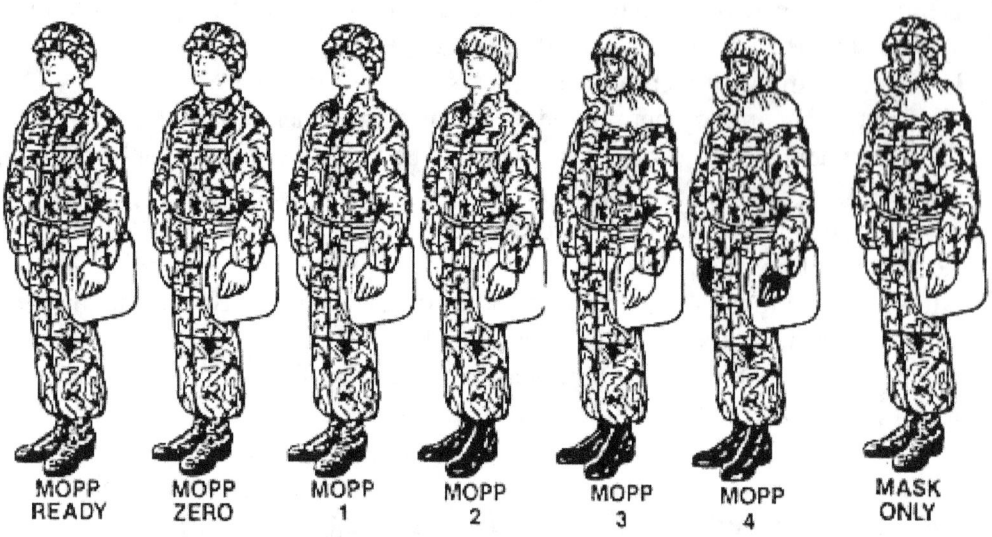

MOPP Equipment	MOPP Levels						Command Mask Only
	MOPP Ready	MOPP Zero	MOPP 1	MOPP 2	MOPP 3	MOPP 4	
Mask	Carried	Carried	Carried	Carried	Worn[1]	Worn	Worn
Overgarment	Ready[3]	Available[4]	Worn[1]	Worn[1]	Worn[1]	Worn	
Vinyl Overboot	Ready[3]	Available[4]	Available[4]	Worn	Worn	Worn	
Gloves	Ready[3]	Available[4]	Available[4]	Available[4]	Available[4]	Worn	
Helmet Protective Cover	Ready[3]	Available[4]	Available[4]	Worn	Worn	Worn	
Chemical Protective Undergarment[2]	Ready[3]	Available[4]	Worn[2]	Worn[2]	Worn[2]	Worn[2]	

[1] In hot weather coat or hood can be left open for ventilation.
[2] The CPU is worn under the BDU (primarily applies to SOF, armor vehicle crewmen).
[3] Must be available to the soldier within two hours. Second set available in 6 hours.
[4] Within arm's reach of soldier.

Figure 2-1. Standardized MOPP levels.

The commander's or leader's directive also can include, based on the threat, the percentage of soldiers that will mask: for example, MOPP1, 50 percent masked. The system is flexible, and subordinate leaders can modify their units' MOPP level to meet mission needs according to the procedures described below. The following standardized protective postures assume that soldiers are also carrying their individual decontamination kit (M258A1 or M291), M8/M9 detector paper, NAAK, and their protective mask, unless the threat assessment indicates a zero percent probability of NBC use.

MOPP Ready

✱✱ Soldiers carry their protective masks with their LCE. The soldier's MOPP gear is labeled and stored no further back than the BSA and is ready to be brought forward to the soldier when needed. Pushing it forward should not exceed two hours. Units in MOPP Ready are highly vulnerable to persistent agent attacks and will automatically upgrade to MOPP Zero when they determine, or are notified, that chemical weapons have been used or that the threat for use of chemical weapons has risen. When a unit is at MOPP Ready soldiers will have field-expedient items identified for use. See Standard MOPP Gear and Field-Expedient Items in Chapter 3 for further discussion.

MOPP Zero

✱✱ Soldiers carry their protective masks with their LCE. The standard BDO and other IPE making up the soldier's MOPP gear are readily available. To be considered readily available, equipment must be either carried by each soldier or stored within arms reach of the soldier; for example, within the work area, vehicle, or fighting position. Units in MOPP Zero are highly vulnerable to persistent agent attacks and will automatically upgrade to MOPP1 when they determine, or are notified, that persistent chemical weapons have been used or that the threat for use of chemical weapons has risen.

MOPP1

✱✱ When directed to MOPP1, soldiers immediately don the BDO. In hot weather, the overgarment jacket can be unbuttoned, and the BDO can be worn directly over underwear. M9 or M8 chemical detection paper is attached to the overgarment. MOPP1 provides a great deal of protection against persistent agent. This level is automatically assumed when chemical weapons have been employed in an area of operations or when directed by higher commands.

MOPP2

✱✱ Soldiers put on their chemical protective footwear covers (CPFCs), GVOS, or a field expedient item (for example, vapor-barrier boots) and the protective helmet cover is worn. As with MOPP1, the overgarment jacket may be left unbuttoned, but trousers remain closed.

MOPP3

✱✱ Soldiers wear the protective mask and hood. Again, flexibility is built into the system to allow soldiers relief at MOPP3. Particularly in hot weather, soldiers can open the overgarment jacket and roll the protective mask hood for ventilation, but trousers remain closed.

MOPP4

Soldiers will completely encapsulate themselves by closing their overgarments, rolling down and adjusting the mask hood, and putting on the NBC rubber gloves with cotton liners. MOPP4 provides the highest degree of chemical protection, but also has the most negative impact on an individual's performance.

Mask Only Command

** The mask is worn. The Mask Only command is given under these situations:

- When RCAs are being employed and no chemical/biological threat exists.
- In a downwind vapor hazard of a nonpersistent chemical agent.

MASK ONLY is not an appropriate command when blister or persistent nerve agents are present.

Automatic Masking

** Automatic masking is the act of immediately masking and assuming MOPP4 when encountering chemical attack indicators on the battlefield.

Before chemical weapons usage is confirmed, soldiers will don the mask only when there is a high probability of a chemical attack. High probability chemical attack indicators are-

- Sounding of a chemical agent alarm.
- Positive reading on chemical agent detector paper or chemical agent monitor.
- Soldiers experiencing symptoms of chemical agent poisoning.

When chemical agents have been employed, commanders at all levels may establish a modified policy of automatic masking by designating additional events as automatic masking criteria. Once this information is disseminated, soldiers will mask and assume MOPP4 automatically whenever one of these events occurs. Automatic masking criteria should be used by the commander as a decision tool and is based on NBC IPB, unit vulnerability analysis, and METT-T. Subordinate commanders may add automatic masking criteria at their discretion. For further guidance on NBC IPB consult FM 3-101, Chemical Staffs and Units.

MOPP System Flexibility

✱✱ MOPP is not a fixed or rigid system. Flexibility is the key to providing maximum protection with the lowest risk possible while still allowing mission accomplishment. Flexibility allows subordinate commanders to adjust the amount of MOPP protection required in their particular situations and still maintain combat effectiveness. Additionally, commanders can place all or part of their units in different MOPP levels or authorize variations within a given MOPP level. For example, based on a high probability of a chemical attack, two soldiers man an observation post/listening post (LP/OP); one soldier wears a mask and the other does not. This ensures that if a sudden attack occurred, one soldier would already be masked and would not become a casualty. The masked soldier would be able to continue the OP/LP mission. This type of risk assessment, initiative, and flexibility is key to survival on today's fast-paced, highly mobile battlefield.

✱✱ Using techniques described in this section (to vary the wearing of MOPP gear) reduces heat stress and soldier performance against the possible risk of contamination and mission accomplishment. Commanders make on-the-spot decisions on whether to modify MOPP. The following paragraphs describe suggested variations.

✱✱ Soldiers may leave the overgarment jacket open at MOPP1, MOPP2, or MOPP3, allowing greater ventilation. Soldiers may leave the hood open or rolled at MOPP3. The various configurations of the MOPP levels with the hood rolled or open are referred to as "MOPP open." Commanders decide which of these variations to use based on the threat, temperature, and unit work intensity.

✱✱ Soldiers wear protective gloves at MOPP1 through MOPP3 when handling equipment that has been decontaminated. This prevents contact with agent that may have been absorbed by equipment surfaces.

Where the hazard is from residual nuclear effects (for example, fallout), the commander modifies MOPP level based on his assessment of the situation and criticality of the mission. MOPP gear does not protect against gamma radiation. This fact is of immediate concern to the commander. Other risks include burns from beta particles and ingestion of alpha particles. Wearing of MOPP gear can reduce the risk of injury from these radiological hazards. A primary concern is to reduce the amount of radioactive contamination that contacts the skin and to prevent ingestion of radioactive particles.

✱✱ Once it has been determined that only a low-level residual radiological hazard exists, the commander may decide to modify the unit's MOPP posture or procedures in fight of mission requirements. For example, soldiers are told to unmask, remove the hoods, and unbutton the BDOS. Soldiers can cover their noses and mouths with handkerchiefs or other material that provides dust protection in lieu of their protective masks. Wearing of full MOPP significantly reduces the beta bum and alpha particle ingestion hazard; performance degradation and heat stress increase. As in the case of protection from chemical hazards, achievement of radiological protection involves a tradeoff against the risk of MOPP: induced performance degration and heat illness.

✱✱ One method of modifying the protective posture allows soldiers to wear the cloth liners from their butyl gloves. This prevents radiological contamination of as much exposed skin as possible. Soldiers issued the M291 kit should use field-expedient substitutes such as a wet handkerchief or commercial "wet-wipes" to remove radiological particles that accumulate on hairy areas of the body. The ration supplement sundries pack, NSN 8970-00-268-9934 for females and 8970-01-175-2509 for general use, contains a supply of the latter items.

Understanding and Managing Performance Problems in NBC Operations

✱✱ Once an accurate assessment of the NBC threat has been made, the key to selecting an appropriate MOPP level lies in understanding factors contributing to performance degradation and heat casualties. MOPP4 protects soldiers by completely isolating them from the NBC environment. However, this encapsulation imposes both physiological and psychological stresses upon the wearer and interacts to degrade individual and unit performance. Other combat stress can further compound the strain of encapsulation. Lower MOPP levels reduce the stress associated with encapsulation but increase the risk of exposure to threat agents. Exposure to low levels of some agents can also lead to performance degradation. Leaders that understand the potential problems and how these problems are countered, are prepared to conduct the MOPP analysis procedures presented below. The successful leader will minimize performance problems and casualties through informed planning and thorough preparation.

Physiological Factors

Adding layers over the BDU (for example, protective overgarment, gloves, and overboots) increases the risk of heat stress, even at moderate environmental temperatures and work intensities. This increases the possibility of heat casualties and degrades performance. Hunger, thirst, and discomfort during sustained periods of MOPP wear can also seriously degrade performance.

Heat Stress in MOPP

Body temperature must be maintained within narrow limits for optimum physical and mental performance. The body produces more heat during work than rest. Normally, the body cools itself by evaporation of sweat and radiation of heat at the skin's surface. MOPP gear restricts these heat loss mechanisms because of its high insulation and low permeability to water vapor. In addition, physical work tasks require more effort when soldiers wear protective clothing because of added weight and restricted movement. This results in more body heat to be dissipated than normal and body temperature tends to rise quickly. The amount of heat acclimatization depends upon the amount of physical activity, the level of hydration, the clothing worn, the load carried, the state of heat acclimatization, physical fitness, and fatigue, as well as terrain and climatic conditions.

Adjusting the MOPP level by opening the BDO jacket, unblousing boots, rolling up the hood, and so forth will reduce barriers to body cooling. The decision process for selecting appropriate adjustments is covered under the section on MOPP analyses.

** Work intensity is a major contributing factor to heat stress that can be managed by leaders. Military work is categorized as very light, light, moderate, or heavy. Table 2-1 provides examples that can be used as a guide in estimating the work intensity for a particular mission or task. The incidence of heat casualties can be reduced if soldiers can be allowed to lower their work intensity and/or take more frequent rest breaks. Tables 2-2 and 2-7 provide information necessary to calculate recommended work/rest cycles for various environmental conditions, clothing levels, and work intensities during daylight and night (or fully shaded) operations, respectively. The work/rest cycles specified in the tables are based on keeping the risk of heat casualties below five percent. Under some operational conditions, work/rest cycles offer no advantage to continuous work (see NL entries in Tables 2-2 and 2-7). There are conditions when work/rest cycles offer no advantage: for example, when the environmental and clothing conditions do not permit any cooling during rest (see NA entries in Tables 2-2 and 2-7); leaders may choose to use the estimated tolerance times such as maximum continuous work times specified in Tables 2-4 (daylight) and 2-9 (night or shade) to limit the risk of heat casualties to less than five percent.

	Table 2-1. Work intensities of military tasks.	
WORK INTENSITY IN MOPP 0-1	**ACTIVITY**	**WORK INTENSITY IN MOPP 2-4**
VERY LIGHT	Lying on Ground Standing in Foxhole Sitting in Truck Guard Duty Driving Truck	**VERY LIGHT**
LIGHT	Cleaning Rifle Walking Hard Surface/ 1m/s No Load Walking Hard Surface/ 1m/s 20 kg Load Manual of Arms Walking Hard Surface/ 1m/s 30 kg Load	**LIGHT**
MODERATE	Walking Loose Sand/ 1m/s No Load Walking Hard Surface/ 1.56 m/s No Load Calisthenics	**MODERATE**
	Walking Hard Surface/ 1.56 m/s 20 kg Load Scouting Patrol Pick and Shovel Crawling Full Pack Foxhole Digging Field Assaults	**HEAVY**
HEAVY	Walking Hard Surface/ 1.56 m/s 30 kg Load Walking Hard Surface/ 2.0 m/s No Load Emplacement Digging Walking Hard Surface/ 2.25 m/s No Load Walking Loose Sand/ 1.56 m/s No Load	The work intensity categories of this table are based on metabolic expenditures. Very Light = 105 to 175 watts Light = 172 to 325 watts Moderate = 325 to 500 watts Heavy = 500+ watts The weight of the chemical protective overboots is a primary contributor to increased workj intensity in MOPP.

Table 2-2. Number of minutes of work per hour in work/rest cycle (daylight operations).

WBGT	Ta	MOPP ZERO				MOPP4 + Underwear				MOPP4 + BDU			
		VL	L	M	H	VL	L	M	H	VL	L	M	H
78	82			NL	25		30	10	5		25	10	5
80	84			40	25		25	10			20	10	
82	87			35	20		20	5			15		
84	89		NL	30	20	NL				NL			
86	91	NL		30	20								
88	94			20	15				na			na	na
90	96			20	10		na	na			na		
92	98			10	10								
94	100		30	10	10								
96	103		10										
98	105		na	na	na	na				na			
100	107	na											

KEY TO TABLE
WBGT - Wet Bulb Globe Temperature (°F)
Ta - Ambient Temperature (Dry Bulb - °F)
VL - Very Light Work Intensity
L - Light Work Intensity
M - Moderate Work Intensity
H - Heavy Work Intensity
BDU - Battle Dress Uniform
NL - No Limit (Continous Work Possible)
na - Work/Rest Cycle Not Feasible (See Maximum Work Time in Table 2-4)

INSTRUCTIONS AND NOTES
This table provides, for four levels of work intensity (see Table 2-1), the number of minutes of work per hour in work/rest schedules tailored to the conditions specified. The remainder of each hour should be spent in rest. This table was prepared using the prediction capability of the USARIEM Heat Strain Model. Assumptions used in generating this table include 1) troops fully hydrated, rested, and acclimatized; 2) 50% relative humidity; 3) windspeed = 2m/s; 4) clear skies; 5) heat casualties <5%. This guide should not be used as a substitute for common sense or experience. Individual requirements may very greatly. The appearance of heat casualties is evidence that the selected work/rest schedule is inappropriate for the conditions.
USARIEM 1/11/91

Table 2-7. Number of minutes of work per hour in work/rest cycle (night operations).

WBGT	T$_a$	MOPP Zero				MOPP4 + Underwear				MOPP4 + BDU			
		VL	L	M	H	VL	L	M	H	VL	L	M	H
60	68	NL	NL	NL	40	NL	NL	30	20	NL	NL	25	15
66	75			NL	40			25	15			25	15
72	82			NL	35		NL	20	15		NL	20	10
78	88			NL	30			15	10			15	10
80	91			NL	25			15	5			15	5
82	93	NL	NL	NL	25	NL	30	10	5	NL	25	10	5
84	95			40	25		25	10			20	5	
86	97			35	20		15	5			10		
88	100			30	20		na	na	na		na	na	na
90	102			25	15								
92	104			20	15								
94	106			15	10								

KEY TO TABLE
WBGT - Wet Bulb Globe Temperature (°F)
T$_a$ - Ambient Temperature (Dry Bulb - °F)
VL - Very Light Work Intensity
L - Light Work Intensity
M - Moderate Work Intensity
H - Heavy Work Intensity
BDU - Battle Dress Uniform
NL - No Limit (Continuous Work Possible)
na - Work/Rest Cycle Not Feasible (See Maximum Work Time in Table 2-4)

INSTRUCTIONS AND NOTES
This table provides, for four levels of work intensity (see Table 2-1), the number of minutes of work per hour in work/rest schedules tailored to the conditions specified. The remainder of each hour should be spent in rest. This table was prepared using the prediction capability of the USARIEM Heat Strain Model. Assumptions used in generating this table include 1) troops fully hydrated, rested, and acclimatized; 2) 50% relative humidity; 3) windspeed ≈ 2 m/s; 4) no solar load; 5) heat casualties <5%. This guidance should not be used as a substitute for common sense or experience; individual requirements may vary greatly. The appearance of heat casualties is evidence that the selected work/rest schedule and/or water consumption guidance (Table 2-3) is inappropriate for the conditions.

USARIEM 1/10/91

Table 2-4. Maximum work times (minutes) (daylight operations).

WBGT	T$_a$	MOPP Zero				MOPP4 + Underwear				MOPP4 + BDU			
		VL	L	M	H	VL	L	M	H	VL	L	M	H
78	82	NL	NL	NL	65	NL	177	50	33	NL	155	49	32
80	84		NL	157	61		142	49	32		131	48	32
82	87			114	56		115	47	31		110	46	30
84	89		NL	99	53		104	45	30		100	45	30
86	91	NL		87	50	NL	95	44	29	NL	93	44	29
88	94			74	45		85	42	28		83	42	27
90	96			67	43		79	41	27		78	41	27
92	98			60	40		75	40	26		74	40	26
94	100		193	55	37		70	39	25		70	39	25
96	103		101	48	33	203	65	37	23	194	65	37	23
98	105		82	44	31	141	62	36	22	140	62	36	22
100	107	261	70	41	28	118	59	35	21	118	59	35	21

KEY TO TABLE
WBGT - Wet Bulb Globe Temperature (°F)
Ta - Ambient Temperature (Dry Bulb - °F)
VL - Very Light Work Intensity
L - Light Work Intensity
M - Moderate Work Intensity
H - Heavy Work Intensity
BDU - Battle Dress Uniform
NL - No limit to Continuous Work
USARIEM 1/11/91

INSTRUCTIONS AND NOTES
This table provides for four levels of work intensity (see Table 2-2), the maximum number of minutes work can be sustained in a single work period without exceeding a greater than 5% risk of heat casualties. This table was perpared using the prediction capability of the USARIEM Heat Stain Model. Assumptions used in generating this table include 1) all troops fully hydrated, rested, and acclimatized; 2) 50% relative humidity; 3) windspeed = 2 m/s; 4) clear skies. The guidance should not be used as a substitute for common sense or experience. Individual requirements may vary greatly. The appearance of heat casualties is evidence that the safe limits of work time have been reached.

Table 2-9. Maximum work times (minutes) (night operations).													
		MOPP Zero				MOPP4 + Underwear				MOPP4 + BDU			
WBGT	T_a	VL	L	M	H	VL	L	M	H	VL	L	M	H
60	68	NL	NL	NL	188	NL	NL	76	42	NL	NL	73	41
66	75				119			66	39			64	38
72	82				90			58	36			57	36
78	88				72			53	34			52	33
80	91				64			50	32			50	32
82	93				60		206	49	32		168	48	31
84	95			139	55		144	47	31		133	47	30
86	97			107	51		121	46	30		115	45	29
88	100			82	46		100	44	28		97	43	28
90	102			71	42		91	42	27		89	42	27
92	104			63	39		83	41	26		82	41	26
94	106			56	36		77	40	25		76	40	25

KEY TO TABLE
WBGT - Wet Bulb Globe Temperature (°F)
T_a - Ambient Temperature (Dry Bulb °F)
VL - Very Light Work Intensity
L - Light Work Intensity
M - Moderate Work Intensity
H - Heavy Work Intensity
BDU - Battle Dress Uniform
NL - No Limit (Continuous Work Possible)
USARIEM 1/10/91

INSTRUCTIONS AND NOTES
This table provides, for four levels of work intensity (see Table 2-1), the maximum number of minutes of work that can be sustained in a single work period without exceeding a greater than 5% risk of heat casualties. This table was prepared using the prediction capability of the USARIEM Heat Strain Model. Assumptions used in generating this table include 1) all troops fully hydrated, rested, and acclimatized; 2) 50% relative humidity; 3) windspeed = 2 m/s; 4) no solar load. The guidance should not be used as a substitute for common sense or experience. Individual requirements may vary greatly. The appearance of heat casualties is evidence that the safe limits of work time have been reached.

✶✶ Although strict adherence to work/rest criteria is possible during training exercises, this may not be possible during combat operations. Tables 2-4 and 2-9 provide guidance on tolerance tunes. For example, the maximum number of minutes of work before the risk of becoming a casualty exceeds five percent (1 of every 20 soldiers). These estimates, representing average expected values within a large population, should be considered approximate guidance and not be used as a substitute for common sense or experience. Individuals will vary in their tolerance. Once the work time limit has been reached, soldiers should rest in the shade (using the guidance provided in Table 2-6) before returning to work. As Table 2-6 clearly shows, reduction of MOPP level during the rest period is the key to maximizing the time troops can spend performing work.

				Table 2-6. Recovery time estimates after maximum work (hours of rest in the shade).
WBGT	**Ta**	**MOPP Zero**	**MOPP4**	KEY TO TABLE
60	68	0.25	1.0	WBGT - Wet Bulb Globe Temperature (°F) As Measured in Shade (If Only Full Sun WBGT Is Available, Subtract
66	75	0.25	1.0	5°F WBGT Before Using This Table)
72	82	0.5	1.5	Ta - Ambient Temperature (Dry Bulb - °F) MOPP Zero - Battal Dress Uniform Only
74	84	0.5	1.5	MOPP4 - Battle Dress Overgarment and Mask (Closed)
76	86	0.5	2.0	NCP - No Cooling Possible Under These Conditions - Seek Cooler Location and/or Remove BDO
78	88	0.5	2.0	NOTES AND INSTRUCTIONS
80	91	0.5	3.0	This table provides the number of hours rest in the shade that should be required after working the maximum work
82	93	0.5	4.0	times specified in Table 2-4 or 2-9. This table was prepared using the cooling capacity equations of the
84	95	0.5	6.0	USARIEM Heat strain Model. Assumptions used in generating this table include 1) troops fully hydrated and
86	97	1.0	15.0	acclimatized; 2) 50% relative humidity; 3) windspeed = 2 m/s; 4) no solar load; 5) recovery of normal body
88	100	1.0	NCP	temperature. This guidance should not be used as a substitute for common sense or experience. Individual
90	102	1.0	NCP	requirements may vary greatly.
92	104	1.5	NCP	
94	106	2.0	NCP	USARIEM 1/11/01
96	109	8.0	NCP	
98	111	NCP	NCP	
100	113	NCP	NCP	

In minimizing heat stress, work/rest schedules may be supplemented by microclimate cooling (MCC) systems in which an air or liquid cooled vest worn under the BDO removes body heat away from skin. MCC systems are available inside certain combat vehicles, but MCC options are not usually available for dismounted soldiers.

Even when work/rest schedules and MCC are used, an increased risk of performance degradation and heat casualties is inevitable when wearing MOPP in hot weather.

Dehydration

Because of higher body temperatures, soldiers in MOPP gear sweat considerably more than usual, often more than 1.5 quarts of water every hour during work. Water must be consumed to replace lost fluids or dehydration will follow. Even a slight degree of dehydration impairs the body's ability to regulate its temperature and nullifies the benefits of heat acclimatization and physical fitness, increases the susceptibility to heat injury, and reduces work capacity (including G-tolerance in pilots), appetite, and alertness. Even in soldiers who are not heat casualties, the combined effects of dehydration, restricted heat loss from the body, and increased work effort place a severe strain on the body's functions, and soldiers suffer from decrements in mental and physical performance.

The difficulty of drinking in MOPP increases the likelihood of dehydration. Thirst is not an adequate indicator of dehydration; soldiers will not sense when they are dehydrated and will fail to replace body water losses, even when drinking water is readily available. Unit chain of command must take responsibility for enforcing regular and timely fluid replacement in their soldiers.

Water requirements should be estimated using the guidelines provided in Tables 2-3, 2-5, 2-8, and 2-10. Base the recommended hourly replenishment on current work intensity, temperature, clothing layers, and light cycle. For example, at a moderate work intensity in MOPP4 (over underwear only) and a daylight wet bulb globe temperature (WBGT) of 80°F (27°C) a soldier should drink approximately 2.0 quarts of water per hour if working continuously or 1.0 quart per hour if working according to the work/rest schedule recommended in Table 2-2 (for example, 10 minutes work, 50 minutes rest). Note that continuous work under these conditions may lead to heat casualties after 49 minutes (Table 2-4).

Table 2-3. Water requirements for work/rest cycles (qt/hr) (daylight operations).													
		MOPP Zero				MOPP4 + Underwear				MOPP4 + BDU			
WBGT	T$_a$	VL	L	M	H	VL	L	M	H	VL	L	M	H
78	82	0.5	1.0	1.5	1.0	1.0	1.0	1.0	1.0	1.0	1.0	1.0	1.0
80	84	0.5	1.0	1.0	1.0	1.0	1.0	1.0		1.0	1.0	1.0	
82	87	1.0	1.0	1.0	1.0	1.0	1.0	1.0		1.0	1.0		
84	89	1.0	1.0	1.0	1.0	1.0				1.0			
86	91	1.0	1.0	1.0	1.0	1.0				1.0			
88	94	1.0	1.5	1.0	1.0	1.5			na	1.5			na
90	96	1.0	1.5	1.0	1.0	1.5	na	na		1.5	na	na	
92	98	1.0	1.5	1.0	1.0	1.5				1.5			
94	100	1.0	1.5	1.5	1.0	1.5				1.5			
96	103	1.0	1.5										
98	105	1.5		na	na	na				na			
100	107	na	na										

KEY TO TABLE	INSTRUCTIONS AND NOTES
WBGT - Wet Bulb Globe Temperature (°F) T$_a$ - Ambient Temperature (Dry Bulb - °F) VL - Very Light Work Intensity L - Light Work Intensity M - Moderate Work Intensity H - Heavy Work Intensity BDU - Battle Dress Uniform na - Work/Rest Cycle Not Feasible (See Water Requirements in Table 2-5) USARIEM 1/11/91	Water requirements listed are for both the work/rest schedules specified in Table 2-2 for support of sustained work (shaded blocks), and work times unrestricted by thermal stress (unshaded, same as Tables 2-4 and 2-5). Work intensities may be estimated using Table 2-1. Drinking should be divided over course of each hour to replace water as it is lost to sweat. The table was prepared using prediction capability of the USARIEM Heat Strain Model; assumptions used in generating estimates include 1) troops fully hydrated, rested, and acclimated; 2) 50% relative humidity; 3) windspeed = 2 m/s; 4) clear skies; 5) heat casualties <5%. This guidance is not a substitute for comon sense or experience; appearance of heat casualties is evidence that safe work limits (<5% casualties) have been exceeded.

| Table 2-5. Water requirements for maximum work times (qt/hr) (daylight operations). | | | | | | | | | | | | | |

		MOPP Zero				MOPP4 + Underwear				MOPP4 + BDU			
WBGT	Ta	VL	L	M	H	VL	L	M	H	VL	L	M	H
78	82	.5	1.0	1.5	2.0	1.0	1.5	2.0	2.0	1.0	1.5	2.0	2.0
80	84	.5	1.0	1.5	2.0	1.0	1.5	2.0	2.0	1.0	1.5	2.0	2.0
82	87	1.0	1.0	1.5	2.0	1.0	1.5	2.0	2.0	1.0	1.5	2.0	2.0
84	89	1.0	1.0	1.5	2.0	1.0	1.5	2.0	2.0	1.0	1.5	2.0	2.0
86	91	1.0	1.0	1.5	2.0	1.0	1.5	2.0	2.0	1.0	2.0	2.0	2.0
88	94	1.0	1.5	2.0	2.0	1.5	2.0	2.0	2.0	1.5	2.0	2.0	2.0
90	96	1.0	1.5	2.0	2.0	1.5	2.0	2.0	2.0	1.5	2.0	2.0	2.0
92	98	1.0	1.5	2.0	2.0	1.5	2.0	2.0	2.0	1.5	2.0	2.0	2.0
94	100	1.0	1.5	2.0	2.0	1.5	2.0	2.0	2.0	1.5	2.0	2.0	2.0
96	103	1.0	1.5	2.0	2.0	1.5	2.0	2.0	2.0	1.5	2.0	2.0	2.0
98	105	1.5	2.0	2.0	2.0	2.0	2.0	2.0	2.0	2.0	2.0	2.0	2.0
100	107	1.5	2.0	2.0	2.0	2.0	2.0	2.0	2.0	2.0	2.0	2.0	2.0

KEY TO TABLE
WBGT - Wet Bulb Globe Temperature (°F)
T_a - Ambient Temperature (Dry Bulb - °F)
VL - Very Light Work Intensity
L - Light Work Intensity
M - Moderate Work Intensity
H - Heavy Work Intensity
BDU - Battle Dress Uniform
USARIEM 1/11/91

INSTRUCTIONS AND NOTES
Amounts listed are required to support maximum work times in Table 2-4; estimate work intensities using Table 2-1. Drinking should be divided over course of each hour. If water requirement is 2.0, sweat loss is greater than maximum water absorption during an hour, and troops will become increasingly dehydrated regardless of amount drunk; leaders should plan for an extended rest and rehydration period at work completion. The table was prepared using prediction capability of the USARIEM Heat Strain Model; assumptions used in generating estimates include 1) troops fully hydrated, rested, and acclimatized; 2) 50% relative humidity; 3) windspeed = 2 m/s; 4) clear skies; 5) heat casualties <5%. This guidance is not a substitute for common sense or experience; appearance of heat casualties is evidence that safe work limits (<5% casualties) have been exceeded.

Table 2-8. Water requirements for work/rest cycles (qt/hr) (night operations).

WBGT	T_a	MOPP Zero				MOPP4 + Underwear				MOPP4 + BDU			
		VL	L	M	H	VL	L	M	H	VL	L	M	H
60	68	0.25	0.25	0.5	1.0	0.25	1.0	1.0	1.0	0.25	1.0	1.0	1.0
66	75	0.25	0.25	1.0	1.0	0.5	1.0	1.0	1.0	0.5	1.0	1.0	1.0
72	82	0.25	0.5	1.0	1.0	0.5	1.0	1.0	1.0	0.5	1.0	1.0	1.0
78	88	0.25	0.5	1.0	1.0	1.0	1.5	1.0	1.0	1.0	1.5	1.0	1.0
80	91	0.5	1.0	1.5	1.0	1.0	1.5	1.0	1.0	1.0	1.5	1.0	1.0
82	93	0.5	1.0	1.5	1.0	1.0	1.0	1.0	1.0	1.0	1.0	1.0	1.0
84	95	0.5	1.0	1.0	1.0	1.0	1.0	1.0	na	1.0	1.0	1.0	na
86	97	0.5	1.0	1.0	1.0	1.0	1.0	1.0	na	1.0	1.0	na	na
88	100	0.5	1.0	1.0	1.0	1.0	na	na	na	1.0	na	na	na
90	102	1.0	1.0	1.0	1.0	1.0	na	na	na	1.0	na	na	na
92	104	1.0	1.5	1.0	1.0	1.5	na	na	na	1.5	na	na	na
94	106	1.0	1.5	1.0	1.0	1.5	na	na	na	1.5	na	na	na

KEY TO TABLE
WBGT - Wet Bulb Globe Temperature (°F)
T_a - Ambient Temperature (Dry Bulb - °F)
VL - Very Light Work Intensity
L - Light Work Intensity
M - Moderate Work Intensity
H - Heavy Work Intensity
BDU - Battle Dress Uniform
NL - No Limit (Continuous Work Possible)
na - Work/Rest Cycle Not Feasible (See Maximum Work Time in Table 2-4)
USARIEM 1/10/91

INSTRUCTIONS AND NOTES
Amounts listed are required to support work/rest schedules in Table 2-7; drinking should be divided over course of each hour to replace water as it is lost to sweat. Use Table 2-10 to determine water required to support maximum work times shown in Table 2-9. The table was prepared using prediction capabilities of the USARIEM Heat Strain Model; assumptions used in generating estimates include 1) troops fully hydrated, rested, and acclimatized; 2) 50% relative humidity; 3) windspeed = 2 m/s; 4) no solar load; 5) heat casualties <5%. This guidance is not a substitute for common sense or experience; appearance of heat casualties is evidence that safe work limits (<5% casualties) have been exceeded (that the selected work/rest cycle and/or water guidance is inappropriate for the conditions).

Table 2-10. Water requirements for maximum work times (qt/hr) (night operations).													
		MOPP Zero				MOPP4 + Underwear				MOPP4 + BDU			
WBGT	Ta	VL	L	M	H	VL	L	M	H	VL	L	M	H
60	68	0.25	0.25	0.5	1.0	0.25	1.0	1.5	2.0	0.25	1.0	1.5	2.0
66	75	0.25	0.25	1.0	1.5	0.5	1.0	2.0	2.0	0.5	1.0	2.0	2.0
72	82	0.25	0.5	1.0	1.5	0.5	1.0	2.0	2.0	0.5	1.0	2.0	2.0
78	88	0.25	0.5	1.0	1.5	1.0	1.5	2.0	2.0	1.0	1.5	2.0	2.0
80	91	0.5	1.0	1.5	2.0	1.0	1.5	2.0	2.0	1.0	1.5	2.0	2.0
82	93	0.5	1.0	1.5	2.0	1.0	1.5	2.0	2.0	1.0	1.5	2.0	2.0
84	95	0.5	1.0	1.5	2.0	1.0	1.5	2.0	2.0	1.0	1.5	2.0	2.0
86	97	0.5	1.0	1.5	2.0	1.0	1.5	2.0	2.0	1.0	1.5	2.0	2.0
88	100	0.5	1.0	1.5	2.0	1.0	2.0	2.0	2.0	1.0	2.0	2.0	2.0
90	102	1.0	1.0	2.0	2.0	1.0	2.0	2.0	2.0	1.0	2.0	2.0	2.0
92	104	1.0	1.5	2.0	2.0	1.5	2.0	2.0	2.0	1.5	2.0	2.0	2.0
94	106	1.0	1.5	2.0	2.0	1.5	2.0	2.0	2.0	1.5	2.0	2.0	2.0

KEY TO TABLE
WBGT - Wet Bulb Globe Temperature (°F)
Ta - Ambient Temperature (Dry Bulb °F)
VL - Very Light Work Intensity
L - Light Work Intensity
M - Moderate Work Intensity
H - Heavy Work Intensity
BDU - Battle Dress Uniform
NL - No Limit (Continuous Work Possible)
USARIEM 1/10/91

INSTRUCTIONS AND NOTES
Amounts listed are required to support maximum work times in Table 2-9; drinking should be divided over course of each hour. If water requirement is 2.0, sweat loss is greater than maximum water absorption during an hour, and troops will become increasingly dehydrated regardless of amount drunk; leaders should plan for an extended rest and rehydration period at work completion (see Table 2-6). This table was prepared using prediction capability of the USARIEM Heat Strain Model; assumptions used in generating estimates include 1) troops fully hydrated, rested, and acclimatized; 2) 50% relative humidity; 3) windspeed = 2 m/s; 4) no solar load; 5) heat casualties <5%. This guidance is not a substitute for common sense or experience; appearance of heat casualties is evidence that safe work limits (casualties) have been exceeded.

Soldiers should drink as much as possible before donning the mask, and frequent drinking while working is more effective in maintaining hydration than waiting until rest periods to drink. The estimates in the tables will also provide the S4 with information he can use to calculate potential drinking water requirements and allocate assets needed to get the water to the soldier. Additional water should be made available for such things as hygiene, cooking, and medical requirements.

Training and Conditioning

Well-prepared soldiers suffer less stress when in MOPP4 than do troops who are less prepared. Well-prepared soldiers are those who are in good physical condition and have trained extensively in protective gear. Physically fit soldiers are more resistant to physical and mental fatigue and acclimatize more quickly to climatic heat or the heat associated with MOPP wear than less fit soldiers.

Units that anticipate deployment to regions where employment of chemical/biological agents is possible should augment physical training programs and increase their state of heat acclimatization. To optimize heat acclimatization, soldiers should progressively increase the duration (reaching two to four hours) and intensity of exercise in the heat over 7 to 14 consecutive days. Finally, when soldiers are required to routinely work in

MOPP gear, it is important to practice good hygiene; keep skin clean to avoid developing heat rash that can dramatically reduce the ability to regulate body temperature.

Inadequate Nutrition

In addition to bodily requirements for electrolyte (salt) replacement caused by sustained and excessive sweating, the higher work intensities typical of operations in MOPP lead to an increased demand for calories. Lack of adequate energy supplies can lead to decrements in both physical and mental performance. The Army has tailored its field feeding menus to provide adequate amounts of both salts and calories to support MOPP operations. All rations served or issued must be consumed, however, and potential contamination of food supplies will make it difficult to maintain adequate nutrition while in MOPP.

The method selected to minimize feeding-related problems depends on availability of safe, uncontaminated areas, as well as other operational constraints. In a contaminated area where there is also a vapor hazard, move troops into a collective-protection facility to eat meals. Since collective-protection shelters have limited capacity, rotate small groups through these facilities. In a contaminated area with no collective protection available, relocate troops to a safe area for feeding by rotating small portions of the unit or by entire unit replacement. If soldiers are in a contaminated area with no detectable vapor hazard or in a clean area where they are under a constant threat of NBC attack, use a rotating method for feeding about 25 percent at any one time and take care to prevent contaminating the food.

Psychological Factors

NBC warfare threat adds to an already stressful situation because it creates unique fears in soldiers and isolates them from their environment. MOPP4 reduces the ability to see and hear clearly and makes it more difficult to recognize and communicate with others. This creates or increases feelings of isolation and confusion. The awkwardness of wearing bulky, impermeable garments, gloves, and boots on top the BDU causes frustration in many soldiers and claustrophobia in some. Long periods of reduced mobility and sensory awareness degrade attention and alertness and create or increase feelings of alienation. Chemical filters in the protective mask make breathing more difficult; this too may create feelings of claustrophobia or panic. The enemy will use the chemical agent threat to exploit these weaknesses and to induce protective postures that reduce combat effectiveness.

The adverse impact of psychological stress during MOPP operations can be minimized by the experience and confidence that realistic training in MOPP4 provides. Wearing MOPP causes physical and emotional stress. Tough, realistic, METL-driven training using MOPP creates a stressful environment for soldiers and units. Successful training helps support unit preparations for battle stress encountered during conflict or war.

Combat Stress

The threat of NBC warfare increases the overall psychological and physiological stress that is an integral part of combat. Because MOPP4 is only worn when the threat of imminent attack is the greatest, encapsulation increases generalized fears and anxiety about combat. Combat stress or battlefield fatigue can cause significant numbers of psychiatric casualties; estimates range from 10 percent to 30 percent depending on the duration and intensity of battle (draft FM 8-51 discusses combat stress in detail). Psychological stress stems not only from the death and destruction that characterize combat, but also from the challenging operational conditions: noise, confusion, and loss of sleep. Challenging operational conditions that create fatigue and cause changes in diet and personal hygiene cause physiological stress as well.

Use of short rest breaks to provide relief from MOPP, combined with adequate sleep (6 or more hours of uninterrupted sleep per 24-hour period is optimum; 4 hours is the minimum for a few days of sustained operations), food, and drink, can sustain performance at an optimal level. During the period of 0100 to 0700, leaders must be aware that the body experiences reduced mental concentration, confusion, nervousness, and lack of clear thinking. Leaders should plan activities to reduce boredom, fatigue, inattention, and discomfort; these are major contributors to ineffective performance.

Leaders can minimize the effects of combat stress by attaining and maintaining a high level of unit cohesion and individual identity. Units must train together frequently under demanding conditions. If soldiers know that they can overcome adversity together, unit cohesion will be high. Leaders must take a true interest in the welfare of their soldiers and build the confidence necessary to withstand the effects of stress. Leaders must keep soldiers informed about the tactical situation so that the adverse effects of ambiguity and uncertainty are minimized. Soldiers who become ineffective as a result of combat stress should be given a period of rest as close to the front as possible and given reassurance and support by all members of their unit.

Psychological Symptoms

Rarely will leaders on the integrated battlefield be able to distinguish between the different types of stress. For example, excessive sweating, nausea, and claustrophobia can be caused by fear and anxiety about combat, by dehydration and heat illness, by total encapsulation in MOPP4, or even by exposure to a chemical agent. Symptoms of stress with a psychological origin could include any of the following:

Mood

- Unusual impatience, frustration, or irritability.
- Unusual fatigue or sleepiness.
- Loneliness, isolation, or alienation.
- Feelings of helplessness.
- Claustrophobia.

Thinking

- Forgetfulness or absentmindedness (especially common are errors in map plotting and message coding).
- Impaired decision making, reasoning, or judgment.
- Disorientation, confusion, or panic.
- Hallucinations or paranoia.

Physical Signs

- Rapid breathing (hyperventilation) or rapid heart rate (tachycardia).
- "Cotton mouth" or nausea.
- Cramps or muscle tension.

Military Task Performance Problems in MOPP

Adding layers to the BDU reduces mobility, agility, coordination, and dexterity. Hundreds of military tasks have been tested to determine the degradation from wearing MOPP gear. Units operating in MOPP1 and MOPP2 generally do not experience significant time increases to perform a given task with one exception, Extensive foot travel in MOPP2 is slowed due to the effects of the overboot and GVOs.

Soldiers wearing MOPP4 will take about 1.5 times longer to perform most tasks. Therefore, leaders can estimate the time it will take to complete most tasks in MOPP4 by multiplying the time normally required to complete tasks by 1.5. Decision-making and precision control tasks are slowed even more than manual tasks. For decision-making and precision control (for example, typing a message or aiming) tasks, the normally expected completion time should be multiplied by 2.5 (or more, if soldiers have been in MOPP4 for an extended period or are overheated).

Soldiers depend on each other to ensure unit performance. Individual degradation will affect the unit as a whole. Unit performance will be significantly degraded due to behavioral changes and leader exhaustion.

Leaders must plan for a slower pace of operations in MOPP if accuracy is to be maintained. Repeatedly practicing critical tasks (for example, training well in excess of the standard) can offer some improvements, but this may or may not be sufficient, depending on mission requirements. Tasks that require manual dexterity and unrestricted hearing and vision should be simplified or modified.

In an NBC environment, command, control, and communications are difficult. Wearing the protective mask degrades hearing, vision, and speech; all are important to effective communication. Individuals are difficult to identify by name or rank, leading to confusion as well as contributing to failures in effective communication. Performance of command functions while in MOPP presents a problem all commanders must consider. A few of these challenges include the following:

- Heat stress causes personnel in leadership positions to tire rapidly and affects mental and physical capability.
- The mask voicemitter makes speech difficult to understand.
- The M17-series mask impairs voice communication in both volume and quality on radios and field phones.
- Eye lenses of the mask narrow the field of vision.

NOTE: The M40-series mask considerably diminishes the last three problems.

- The hood impairs hearing.

The following are ways in which leaders can minimize some of these difficulties. Delegate more responsibilities to reduce the stress of wearing MOPP over extended periods of time. Increase flexibility in MOPP wear as discussed earlier in this chapter. The unit SOP must include specific unit guidelines based on unit mission needs. When using the radio, ensure the microphone is held close to the voicemitter, particularly when wearing the M17-series mask. If possible, wear the microphone-equipped M24/M25-series mask or the M42-series mask, and use the vehicular communication system if operating in a combat vehicle. Enhance verbal communications by speaking more slowly than normal and having orders repeated. Hand and other visual signals can be effectively employed. Issue written orders, if time permits, to ensure instructions are understood. Use collective protection, as much as possible, to eliminate the burden of MOPP.

Identifying soldiers in MOPP by name and rank can be accomplished through various means. One way is to use tape showing the soldier's name and rank. Tape is normally available in some form, and there are advantages to using it. When soldiers are not in MOPP, a strip of tape with all the information already printed on it can be placed on the soldier's overgarment bag, as well as on the mask carrier. When the overgarments are put on, soldiers can pull the tape off the overgarment bag and place it on their overgarment to further increase ease of identification. Other methods can be used as long as they suit the commander's needs in being able to identify his soldiers, do not damage or interfere with the use of other equipment, and allow soldiers to perform the mission unimpeded.

Miosis

Although MOPP gear may be the most common source of performance problems during NBC operations, some chemical agents, primarily the nerve agents, can produce performance decrements at exposure levels below that which would cause casualties. Very small amounts of nerve agent such as vapor or aerosol absorbed through the eyes will constrict the pupils. This condition is called miosis. It may or may not involve pain and/or headache. The pupil is unable to dilate normally, thus reducing night vision and the efficiency of using night vision devices. Miosis can reduce the efficiency of performance of other tasks at night: for example, navigating on foot, identifying and engaging targets, driving vehicles under blackout conditions, and flying that requires pilots to change focus frequently.

Symptoms of miosis range from minimal to severe, depending on the nerve agent dosage. Victims may experience headaches when exposed to bright light. Severe miosis and the consequent reduced ability to see in dim light may persist for 48 hours after onset. The pupil gradually returns to normal over several days. Full recovery may take 20 days or longer. Repeated exposures within this period cause cumulative effects.

Commanders must identify personnel performing critical tasks that are dependent on night vision and initiate certain precautions to minimize miosis. These precautions may include the following:

- Have key personnel mask whenever there is risk of encountering miosis-producing hazards such as when close to ground, equipment, or personnel known to have been contaminated with liquid nerve agent.
- After detailed equipment decon (FM 3-5), allow personnel to move away from their equipment. Have them move to a contamination-free area and conduct unmasking procedures. Residual contamination on decontaminated material may be sufficient to cause miosis. Soldiers should disperse in the open air and use the buddy system to observe for possible miosis symptoms.
- Use collective protection as much as possible.

Troop Preparation

It cannot be overemphasized that soldiers and their leaders must train in MOPP gear, including training in MOPP4 over extended periods of time. Further, soldiers cannot be expected to fight successfully in full MOPP gear if they have not trained as a team with their leaders and equipment. Leaders are critically aware of their key role under NBC conditions and their need to make timely and informed decisions.

Just as infantrymen train extensively with their individual weapon to become proficient in its use, individual soldiers should train in MOPP to become more confident and proficient on individual and team tasks. Training in MOPP4 helps leaders and soldiers understand the problems they will encounter when required to fight in MOPP. During preparation for combat, leaders gain knowledge of individual and unit training status and take actions such as individual training and battle drills to ensure maximum preparation prior to combat.

Leaders can ensure success on the NBC battlefield in many ways.

Train Thoroughly and Realistically

- Build confidence and unit cohesion through realistic training in MOPP4.
- Practice critical visual tasks (like marksmanship) in the protective mask until they become automatic.
- Attain and maintain peak physical fitness and acclimatization.
- Ensure radio telephone operators (RTOs) are trained in recognizing and transmitting NBC reports and know their importance to unit survival.

- Cross-train crews and other critical positions.

Plan Ahead

- Check NBC defense guidance in OPLAN/OPORD; anticipate projected work requirements in the next 24-48 hours.
- Ensure serviceability or shortfalls of equipment through precombat inspections of NBC equipment.
- Know the most current weather data, particularly wind direction.
- Plan work/rest cycles appropriate to the environment and the mission.
- Ensure deployment and mounting of alarms.
- Use SOPs to reduce command, control, and communication tasks.
- Keep plans simple.

Think Teamwork

- Use methods of individual identification (name tags, personal items).
- Encourage "small-talk" while in MOPP.
- Pair an experienced soldier with an inexperienced "buddy" whenever possible.
- Use the buddy system to ensure that all members of the unit are regularly checked for signs of stress and agent exposure.

Work Smart

- Provide relief from MOPP4 as soon as the mission allows.
- Use work/rest ratios, slow work rate, and minimize work intensity.
- Work in the shade whenever possible.
- Enforce command drinking to reduce dehydration and heat casualties.

REMEMBER--the most motivated soldiers and leaders are the most likely to ignore their needs for food, water, and rest. They are the first casualties.

- Use collective protection as much as possible.
- Enforce good eating, drinking, and sleeping discipline.
- Rotate jobs and people during long shifts or periods of inactivity.
- Provide relief from extreme temperatures (hot or cold) as soon as possible.
- Remember that even short breaks from total encapsulation are effective in sustaining performance.
- Augment units or divide work between two units.
- Schedule work for a cooler time of day or at night.

MOPP Analysis Procedures

Commanders must perform situation-based MOPP analysis to determine the appropriate MOPP level. This analysis enhances the probability of mission success by balancing the reduced risk of casualties due to chemical/biological agent exposure against the increased risk of performance decrements and heat strain casualties as MOPP levels increase from zero to MOPP4. Because there is no easy formula to use in deciding an appropriate MOPP level, commanders must consider three situation factors when performing MOPP analysis. The three situation factors are mission, environment, and soldier factors. The contributing factors to these situation factors are subject to complex interactions, and a full analysis is more suited to automated tactical decision aids, such as the Automated Nuclear, Biological, and Chemical Information System (ANBACIS) currently in use by higher echelon planners, than the simplified figures and tables of this manual. At the small unit level this type of comprehensive analysis is not normally required. However, an understanding of the physiological and psychological factors that affect health and performance while in MOPP, coupled with experience gained in training under a variety of environmental conditions and mission work loads, will prepare you for the task.

The commander will need to consider mission, environmental, and soldier factors when performing MOPP analysis.

Mission Factors

Ask the following questions:

- What is the mission? Is it offensive or defensive?
- What is the likelihood of chemical agent employment?
- What agents are likely to be employed?
- What are the likely targets?
- What is the expected warning time for agent employment?
- What additional protection (such as shelter and cover) is available?
- How physically demanding is the work that must be performed?
- How mentally demanding is the work that must be performed?
- How quickly must the mission be accomplished?
- What is the expected duration of the mission?
- What is the likely follow-on mission?
- Are adequate water and food supplies available?

The mission will greatly influence the amount of protection needed by each soldier. How important is the mission, and what risks will it require? The answers to several of the mission-related questions will be provided in the IPB process.

Once commanders understand the nature of the threat and probability of NBC weapons use, they can proceed to weigh the other mission-, environment-, and soldier-related factors that influence selection of an appropriate MOPP level. For instance, is it day or night? The best time to use chemical agents is between late evening and early morning, when stable or neutral temperature gradients prevail. Under these conditions, agents tend to linger close to the ground and move horizontally with the wind. During unstable conditions in the heat of the day, agents rise rapidly. This rapid rise reduces the time on target and the agents' casualty-producing capabilities. Thus, it is more likely that agents will be employed during predawn darkness, and the environmental and other conditions influencing MOPP analysis can be more appropriately selected. For instance, the environmental heat load, as measured by the WBGT index, is lower at night. This implies that the degree of protection can be increased to match the magnitude of the threat, while achieving a lesser risk of performance problems and heat casualties.

Mission-related factors greatly influence the amount of protection needed by each soldier. When the threat of chemical/biological agent employment is high, and expected warning time for the unit is low, a high level of MOPP is dictated to provide adequate protection. However, increased MOPP levels can lead to performance degradation. Additionally, the incidence of heat casualties among soldiers performing physically demanding work becomes greater with increasing MOPP levels, especially in high ambient heat. The more critical the mission, the more thorough commanders must be in their analysis; the impact of decreased performance and heat casualties from MOPP must be weighted carefully against the risk of casualties and potential mission failure due to chemical agents.

MOPP analysis must consider the work intensity the mission will require and how long this work load must be maintained. Is time a critical factor in mission success? What will be required of the troops after achieving the mission objective? Can they rest? Must they dig-in and defend in place? These are some of the critical questions the commander must answer in proceeding with a MOPP Analysis. The commander can first estimate the work intensity required to perform the mission using Table 2-1 as a guide. Then, based on knowledge of the environmental conditions, Table 2-2 (daylight) or Table 2-7 (night or shade) can be used to provide guidance on work/rest cycles that can sustain work over long time periods. The guidance in that table assumes that the commander is unwilling to sustain more than minimal (5 percent) heat casualties.

If the time constraints of the mission are incompatible with the work/rest cycles predicted, the commander can assess the impact of conducting the operation using continuous work (for example, few or no rest breaks) using Table 2-4 (daylight) or table 2-9 (night or shade). In addition, Figures 2-2 and 2-3 graphically portray the impact of continuous work on the risk of expected casualties for MOPP zero and MOPP4 during daylight operations. These figures provide leaders with estimates on how long a unit can be expected to operate under varying work loads and temperatures without sustaining more than minimal (5 percent) heat casualties. For example, in Figure 2-2, heat casualties can be expected to occur after about 90 minutes if soldiers work continuously at a moderate intensity in BDUs with the WBGT at 85°F. For troops working under the same conditions, but in MOPP4, Figure 2-3 indicates that the unit can work for only 45 minutes before the risk of heat casualties exceeds 5 percent and for 60 minutes before the risk exceeds 20 percent.

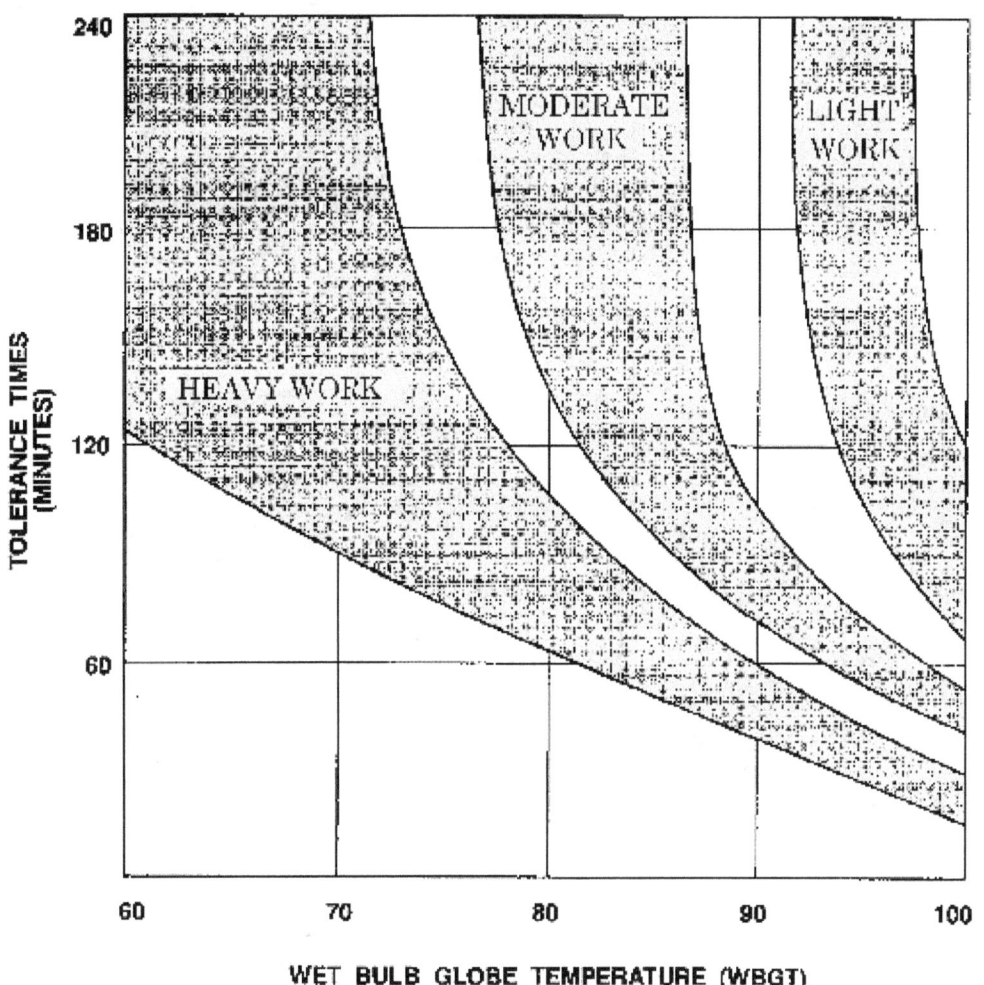

FIGURE 2-2. *Estimated tolerance times at three work intensities in MOPP zero.*

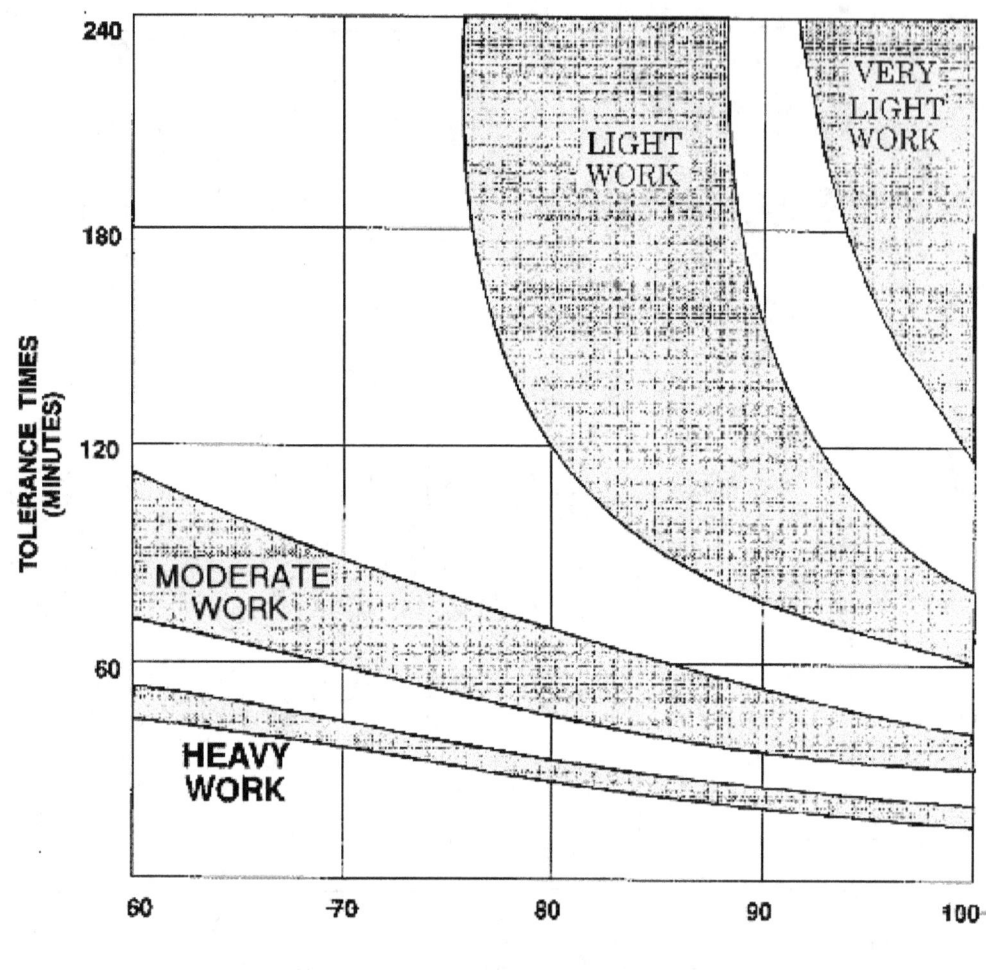

FIGURE 2-3. Estimated tolerance times at four work intensities in MOPP4.

Environmental Factors

Ask the following questions:

- What is the ambient air temperature?
- What is the humidity?
- What is the WBGT index reading for the unit's AO?
- Is it cloudy or sunny?
- Is it windy?
- Is it day or night?

The ambient environmental conditions (outside weather/inside vehicle) must be known before beginning assessment of how these conditions will affect the soldiers' ability to successfully complete a mission. Make sure you have accurate weather information for your location. Check the weather daily; variation in temperature, wind, and humidity can be substantial from region to region. Know what YOUR weather will be. Leaders at all echelons should use and support the extensive weather forecasting resources described in FM 34-81/AFM 105-4. WBGT information can also be obtained from the S2 or staff weather officer (SWO). See Appendix A for further information on operations in special environments.

Most Army guidance for prevention of heat injury and illness is based on WBGT readings (FM 21-10).[1] The WBGT reading provides a single measure of the major determinants of environmental heat stress (for example, air temperature, wind speed, solar load, and humidity). Although the WBGT provides an adequate representation of the heat stress under most conditions, it is not perfect and should be interpreted as approximate guidance. For instance, it was not optimized for conditions commonly seen in environmental extremes, such as the desert. Guidance based on the WBGT is appropriate only for soldiers who are fully acclimatized, optimally conditioned, hydrated, and rested. Additionally, WBGT guidelines do not accurately forecast injury/illness rates under conditions of lower temperatures and high humidity such as may be experienced in the early morning hours; humidity levels over 75 percent substantially increase the risk of heat injury under all work conditions. Other critical items of weather information for the IPB and MOPP analysis are wind direction and speed. When the air temperature is below skin temperature (approximately 92°F), high winds aid in the dissipation of body heat. High winds also make use of chemical agents less effective, and thus decrease the probability of their use. All weather information should be current.

Using tables based on WBGT readings, the commander can better manage personnel resources and minimize the potential for heat casualties. Remember, these tables are only a guide and no substitute for experience.

Soldier Factors

Ask the following questions:

- Are the soldiers well hydrated and nourished?
- Are the soldiers well rested?
- Are the soldiers heat acclimatized?
- Are the soldiers physically fit and well trained?
- Are the soldiers healthy?

The maintenance of full hydration is the most important factor influencing the work performance of soldiers wearing MOPP in warm environments. Dehydration negates the advantages of heat acclimation and high physical fitness. Dehydration impairs the ability to regulate body temperature, reduces mental and physical work performance, and increases susceptibility to heat injuries/illnesses. These adverse effects become increasingly dangerous, as the level of dehydration becomes more severe. Even as little as a 2 percent loss of body weight due to dehydration degrades performance.

Leadership can minimize dehydration by establishing a policy of enforced drinking using the guidelines given in Tables 2-3 and 2-5. Leaders can reduce the likelihood of inadequate drinking in MOPP, especially when masked, by taking advantage of flexible masking policies (MOPP1--25 percent masked), rotating masked and unmasked soldiers often.

The work/rest and maximum continuous work time guidance provided in this chapter assumes that all troops are fully hydrated, heat acclimatized, physically fit, and fully rested. In those cases when the commander is aware that the assumptions of the guidance do not hold, the estimates in the tables must be adjusted upwards or downwards depending on the situation. Dehydration has the greatest impact on performance, but failure to meet the other factors will also impact upon thermoregulation and performance. For instance, going without sleep for more than 30 hours can impair one's ability to regulate body temperature and can reduce task performance.

Thus, the performance degradation factors (1.5 for physical work and 2.5 for mental work) may require upward adjustment. On the other hand, a downward adjustment may be necessary in the cases of overtrained or experienced troops. Following are some examples.

Performance Time Critical. "An engineer unit has been, ordered to construct a river crossing site to provide a retrograde route for a unit that is already contaminated and which is conducting a rearward passage of lines. The threat has employed a persistent agent in the engineer unit's assembly point. The crossing must be completed in two hours, which will require the unit to work steadily at a moderate work load in MOPP4 in full daylight. The WBGT is 75°F."

The task normally takes 90 minutes to complete, but the performance degradation factor for physical work (cited above) is known to be 1.5. Multiplying the performance degradation factor by the normal time (1.5 x 90), the MOPP4 time to completion is 135 minutes. Thus, conducting the mission in MOPP4 will take longer than the commander's guidance permitted. Adjustments required to meet the mission guidance could include--

- Schedule additional engineer units to complete the job.
- Augment the unit with additional manpower.
- If the hazard of liquid contamination is low, adopt a lower MOPP posture. This may reduce the performance degradation factor and allow mission completion within the two-hour target.

Tolerance Time Critical. "Extensive work, estimated to take one hour in MOPP, is required to improve platoon battle position prior to a possible enemy assault within the next two hours of full daylight. The 1st and 2d platoons' assembly areas do not require soldiers to operate in MOPP, but the 3d platoon occupies contaminated terrain that is vital to the unit's defense. The terrain provides for no shade. The WBGT is 80°F."

If the commander considers MOPP4 for the 3d platoon, a review of Table 2-2 indicates that a work/rest schedule is inappropriate (no work/rest cycle is recommended for heavy work in MOPP4 at a WBGT reading of 80°F), and Table 2-4 shows that continuous work of only 32 minutes would be possible before incurring an initial risk (5 percent) of heat casualties.

This does not meet mission guidance, but several options are available. One alternative would be to relieve the 3d platoon with a fresh unit after 30 minutes. If this was not possible, the tables do indicate that MOPP zero would allow mission completion by 3d platoon, however. If the hazard was vapor only, a MOPP1-masked modified posture might provide a balance between the risk of chemical and heat hazards while assuring mission completion. A review of Table 2-6 indicates that if collective protection can be used to provide rest in the shade at a temperature at or below 84°F WBGT, the troops can cool off sufficiently in 30 minutes to repeat the 32 minutes maximum work period. Rest under cooler conditions and at a lower MOPP level can be very effective in sustaining the pace of operations in an NBC environment.

To gain a better appreciation of the risk of heat casualties in the 3d platoon, the commander next refers to the graphic in Figure 2-3. Entering the bottom of the chart at 80°F and reading up until the lower edge of the shaded area for heavy work is encountered, the maximum work time for light (5 percent) casualties can be noted on the right axis. Continuing upward along the 80°F line to the limit of the shaded area, the time at which 20 percent of the unit would be placed at risk for heat illness can be found at about 40 minutes. The analysis indicates the combination of adopting MOPP4 and working continuously at a heavy work load will place greater than 20 percent of the unit at risk of becoming casualties to heat. This risk must be balanced against the risk of becoming a chemical casualty using the procedures in Chapter 3 before deciding on an optimal MOPP level for the 3d platoon

The process is repeated for the 1st and 2d platoons. A very low MOPP level is clearly indicated for these units and a work/rest cycle of 30 minutes work/30 minutes rest, although not ideal, could be implemented to allow the work to be completed with minimal casualties and degradation. If these units did not take any rest breaks, any heat exhaustion casualties might not recover in the remaining hour, even with complete rest and dehydration in the shade, unless cooling systems and intravenous fluids were utilized.

Heat Casualties Critical. "Your platoon has been working at a moderate intensity in MOPP4 for 45 minutes under clear, sunny skies. Hostilities are not imminent, but the task is time sensitive. The WBGT reading is 70°F. Two cases of heat exhaustion have occurred in the past five minutes; many others have slowed the pace of work."

Using the graphic in Figure 2-3, you determine the unit should have been able to work for an additional 15 minutes at this pace before casualties were noted. You remember that one heat casualty is often quickly followed by many others. Realizing that the guidance in the figure is approximate, and not absolute, you call for a rest break. Lack of adequate rest, slight dehydration, individual variance, and an underestimate of the work intensity are among the potential explanations for the mismatch between guidance and reality. If mission success depended on completion of the task, you are confident of the work intensity estimate, and a 20 percent casualty rate is deemed acceptable, you can estimate the time remaining for work from Figure 2-3 by first finding the point where the lower (5 percent) limit of the shaded area crosses the 45-minute line. Reading up from this point (an "effective" WBGT of 85°F) you note that 15 minutes of work may be possible before the 20 percent casualty risk point is reached.

Use Of MOPP Guidance

As stated before, higher headquarters provides directives to each battalion-size element that will include a MOPP level and a percentage of soldiers to be masked at all times. Subordinate units apply flexibility and initiative to this guidance to account for local conditions. Failure to do this exposes units to far greater hazards in the form of heat casualties, direct fire losses, and mission failures. The following techniques are to be used by units in applying guidance received from higher commands to meet their needs.

Once MOPP1 or 2 is established by higher headquarters, subordinate units may not downgrade from this level except for the following reasons:

- Units may temporarily reduce MOPP levels to conduct decontamination operations such as MOPP gear exchange.
- Soldiers inside enclosures may reduce MOPP level at the discretion of the platoon leader or higher commander. The enclosure need not be airtight but should be capable of protecting against the initial liquid hazard.
- Soldiers may reduce MOPP for medical reasons, including such things as foot care, at the discretion of the senior leader present. When possible, complete on a rotating basis.

Increase MOPP in response to direct threats only. The protective posture recommended by higher headquarters is intended to provide an adequate level of protection against the assessed threat of chemical attack. If your unit is at that recommended level, then a chemical attack will probably produce few casualties. Increasing your units' protective posture will increase the time it takes to accomplish your units' mission. Proper MOPP levels based on the assessed direct threat will increase chances of victory.

Increase your protective posture when encountering contamination or before entering an area that is believed to be contaminated (for example, go from MOPP2 to MOPP3). You should have soldiers mask if they are in a downwind hazard area, and they have not deployed detectors. Units should not increase protective postures simply to defend against a perceived, but unconfirmed, chemical attack on their positions.

Battalions and Companies

Many decisions on increasing or modifying MOPP posture are made at squad and platoon level. Squads and platoons frequently conduct independent operations; therefore, the unit leader's training and experience are essential to successful operations under NBC conditions. Directives received by platoons and squads will also indicate a minimum MOPP level and if needed, a percent of soldiers masked. In some cases the guidance received by battalion will be passed unaltered down to squad level.

However, in some circumstances battalion and company commanders may modify this guidance. For example, brigade guidance is for all units to assume MOPP1 with 25 percent of soldiers masked. The battalion commander has three maneuver companies. Two units are in defensive positions, and one is moving to a reserve position. The commander knows that the two companies in defensive positions are well protected (dispersed, covered, concealed) from conventional munitions. From IPB templating, the enemy is expected to attack in our sector with a regimental-size force (in a supporting attack) along two battalion-size avenues of approach within the hour. The battalion commander anticipates that the greatest chemical threat to his two defending companies is the enemy's potential use of lethal, persistent agents; therefore, he decides to place his two companies in defensive positions at MOPP2--25 percent masked. He directs the rest of the battalion to be at MOPP1--0 percent masked. The unit moving into a reserve position remains at MOPP zero--25 percent masked only until they have closed on the designated position. The commander determined that speed was essential; therefore, he did not put the third company into MOPP2 until they were at their position.

Note in the above example that the battalion commander's modification results in fewer soldiers being masked than would have occurred if the brigade guidance had been followed exactly. This is as it should be. In this example, the battalion commander understands the intent of the brigade commander's guidance. Understanding that intent, he then applies sound tactical judgment to the situation. In this case, although fewer soldiers are masked, those units most vulnerable are better protected. The unit that is least vulnerable to chemicals but most vulnerable to other hazards is allowed to operate at maximum effectiveness.

Both battalion and company commanders should implement guidance from their commander in a way that provides greater protection to their most vulnerable units and allows maximum effectiveness for their units that most require it. Units should try to mask a percentage of soldiers close to that directed by brigade, but should the tactical situation dictate modification, sound judgment must prevail. Avoid issuing guidance that uses unworkable masking percentage figures. A platoon leader can easily implement guidance to mask 33 percent, or one in three of his soldiers. Guidance to mask 21 percent of the platoon presents obvious, unnecessary problems.

Platoons and Squads

These units implement guidance from higher headquarters immediately upon receipt and in some cases without modification. Unit soldiers will attain the appropriate MOPP level and establish a rotation schedule that ensures that the proper percentage of soldiers are masked. Sleeping soldiers are not included as a part of this percentage. For example, a squad has ten soldiers, three of which are sleeping. It is directed to mask 25 percent of its soldiers, which means that two of its seven soldiers need to mask. This posture will be maintained unless one of the following events occurs:

- If the unit detects the presence of a chemical hazard, soldiers will automatically mask and attain MOPP4 as soon as possible.
- If the unit witnesses a chemical attack or there are indications one has occurred, then the unit will mask and attain MOPP3 and MOPP4 as rapidly as possible.
- Units in a downwind hazard area will mask if they have no warning system in place.
- Units may unmask whenever they become involved in a, direct fire engagement if no chemical weapons have been used or no contamination hazards exist. This can be done as long as some soldiers are unmasked at the time that the engagement begins.
- Units that masked due to being in a downwind hazard area may unmask if collocated alarm systems have not sounded. For example, an armored unit is advancing within a downwind hazard area. Its crews are masked, but the unit has alarms mounted on their upwind vehicles. None of these alarms have sounded when an enemy force is encountered. This unit may unmask to better fight the battle.
- Units may unmask when it is essential to mission accomplishment. For example, an infantry platoon has been directed to attain MOPP2 with 50 percent of soldiers masked. This platoon is preparing to defend against an enemy force expected within the hour. These preparations are going slowly and efforts to speed the work are frustrated by the high protective posture. The soldiers are becoming exhausted. The platoon leader has his unit unmask. During this time, he requires all soldiers to drink water. He issues instructions and discusses his battle plans with unmasked soldiers who can now hear and speak clearly. After 10 minutes he has 25 percent of the platoon mask. The unit is less fatigued.

As only one in four soldiers is masked, a higher work rate is maintained. As the most labor-intensive tasks are completed, squad leaders order masking for 50 percent of their personnel.

Alarms for Unit Defense

Chemical agent alarms/detectors area critical element of a unit's chemical defense. Without them, a unit cannot be alerted and cannot detect chemical agents until symptoms appear. Once chemical warfare has been initiated, alarms/detectors of some type must either already be in use or ready to be used. The alternative is to have the unit mask. There are numerous types of chemical agent alarms/detectors available to a soldier and a unit. This equipment provides them with that NBC defense necessary to ensure adequate prior warning.

The M8A1 chemical agent alarm is unique in that it is the only automatic chemical agent alarm presently available that provides a unit with an early warning capability of a possible vapor hazard (nerve agents only). Employment techniques and procedures are discussed in detail in FM 3-3. Additional chemical agent detectors are discussed in further detail in Chapter 1.

Once soldiers are under attack, it is important to warn others of the hazard. Early warning gives others more time to react. This additional time saves lives and increases mission effectiveness. The following rules apply when giving the alarm:

- Give the alarm as soon as an attack or a hazard is detected.
- Use an alarm method that cannot be confused easily with normal combat signals or sounds.
- All who hear or see the alarm must repeat it swiftly throughout the unit because of its limited range.
- Supplement the alarm over radio and telephone nets.

The four types of signals for warning personnel of an attack are vocal, sound, visual, and audiovisual. Personnel should warn others, using one or a combination of these signals.

Vocal

The spoken word (vocal alarm signal) is the first way of informing troops of an NBC hazard or attack. The vocal alarm for any chemical or biological hazard or attack is the word gas. The person giving the alarm masks first and then shouts "gas" as loudly as possible. Everyone hearing this alarm immediately masks and then repeats the alarm.

The vocal alarm for the arrival of radiological contamination in a unit, area is the word fallout. The first soldier to detect the arrival of fallout will usually be a radiological monitor operating a radiacmeter at the unit command post (CP). When this radiacmeter records an increase in dose rate to 1 centigray per hour or higher, the monitor should immediately alert unit personnel, using this warning should relay the warning to others, and take cover immediately.

Sound

Sound signals reinforce the vocal alarm to warn of the imminent arrival or the presence of NBC hazards. Sound signals consist of a succession of short signals. The following are examples:

- Rapid and continuous beating on any metal object or any other that produces a loud noise.
- A succession of short blasts on a vehicle horn or other suitable device.
- An interrupted 10 warbling siren sound and vocal alarms in situations in which the sound is lost because of battlefield noises or in which sound signals are not

permitted. The standard hand-and-arm signal for NBC hazards consists of the following steps:

- Put on the protective mask.
- Extend both arms horizontally sideways with double fists facing up.
- Move fists rapidly to your head and back to the horizontal position.
- Repeat as necessary.

Visual and Audiovisual

If the automatic chemical agent alarms are in operation, detected agents will trigger a visual and auditory alarm unit. The person who sees or hears an alarm signal from the alarm unit immediately masks and augments this signal with the vocal signal. Radio/telephone operators who hear the vocal signal immediately mask and relay the signal over the unit radio and telephone nets. Personnel reinforce this signal with other sounds or visual signals.

Unmasking Procedures

✷✷ Unmasking procedures should be conducted after all available methods of agent detection have failed to indicated any agent. Unmasking should be conducted as soon as possible to alleviate soldiers' encapsulation as quickly as possible. The following two unmasking procedures will determine if unmasking is safe.

Unmasking Procedures
Using the M256-Series
Chemical Detector Kit

The M256-series chemical detector kit does not detect all agents. Therefore, use an unmasking procedure also, even if the detector is available. These procedures take approximately 15 minutes. After all tests with the kit, including a check for liquid contamination, have been performed and the results are negative, the senior person should select one or two soldiers to start the unmasking procedures. If possible, move to a shady place. Bright, direct sunlight can cause pupils in the eyes to constrict, giving false signs of nerve agent exposure. It is prudent to have the selected soldiers disarm before instructing them to unmask. The selected soldiers unmask for five minutes, reseal, and clear their masks. Observe them for ten minutes. If no symptoms appear, it is safe to give the all clear signal and unmask. Continue to watch the soldiers for possible delayed symptoms. Always have first-aid treatment immediately available in case it is needed.

Unmasking Procedures
Without an M256
Chemical Detector Kit

✳✳ If an M256-series kit is not available, the unmasking procedures take approximately 35 minutes. Find a shady area. Use M8 paper to check the area for possible liquid contamination. When a reasonable amount of time has passed after the attack, the senior person should select one or two soldiers. The selected soldiers take a deep breath and break their mask seals, keeping their eyes wide open, for about 15 seconds. They then clear and reseal their masks. Observe them for ten minutes. If no symptoms appear, the selected soldiers unmask for five minutes and then remask. If no symptoms appear in ten minutes after remasking, everyone can unmask. Continue to observe the selected soldiers in case delayed symptoms develop.

In both cases, if soldiers display symptoms of agent poisoning, ensure first-aid treatment is available and provided. If agent is still present, the senior person present must make a decision of selecting one of these options:

- Move to a new area and retest.
- If mission dictates that movement cannot be conducted, a retest can be conducted after one hour.
- Use collective-protection equipment if available.

Filter Exchange Criteria

Filter exchange criteria for all NBC filters in the inventory, from the mask filters to the filters on the simplified collective-protective equipment (SCPE), are based on design, physical condition, climatic conditions, and the possible threat agent that could be employed. information in the following paragraphs addresses peacetime, transition-to-war, and wartime exchange criteria.

Peacetime

✳✳ When assessing filter exchange criteria, several factors must be considered. Commanders and NBC personnel must monitor replacement schedules for pieces of NBC equipment having filters. Peacetime exchange criteria for all filters is one year or when the following conditions are applicable:

- Physical damage occurs.
- Filters have become water logged/wet.
- High resistance to airflow is observed.
- Directed by higher headquarters.
- Listed as unserviceable in SB 3-30-2.

Transition to War

Commanders will determine when their units should remove their training filters and replace them with filters from unit contingency stocks. This guidance should be reflected in an SOP or order. Factors for filter exchange consideration are: unit location, unit readiness/deployability alert status, last filters exchange, threat, time available, and stocks available. For example, a forward deployed unit commander, based on an enemy chemical capability in the area of operation, directs by SOP that his unit install its contingency set of filters. Alternatively, a CONUS based unit commander determines that the basis for installing contingency filters would occur upon an increase in unit alert status for deployment to an area with an NBC threat.

✶✶ Before initiating filter exchange, leaders consider the implications for their units. Some considerations are:

- Mission - What is the unit mission?
- Enemy - What is the current NBC threat assessment; is our unit likely to be attacked on arrival in the operational area?
- Terrain - Where should filters be exchanged? At home station, enroute, or in the operational area?
- Time - When should filters be exchanged When will there be adequate time to exchange filters?
- Troops Available - Do we have the right people available to conduct the exchange?

Wartime

The decision to change filters is driven by two considerations: the amount of chemical agent the filter has been exposed to, and the time the filter has been exposed to the atmosphere. These separate considerations are based on the two mechanisms by which the filter provides protection from chemical agents. For all agents, the filter uses mechanical filtration and absorption as the protection mechanism. Additionally for blood agent CK, the filter uses a chemical reaction. The chemical reaction mechanism is degraded by prolonged exposure to CK and the absorption capacity, by exposure over time to air, particularly hot humid air (see table 2-11).

FILTER	COLD HUMID	WARM MODERATE	HOT DRY	HOT HUMID	SYSTEM
C-2/M13A2	52	52	39	10	M40IM42/M43/M17-series protective mask
M10A1	52	52	52	13	M24/M25 protective mask
M18 Gas	52	39	26	4	Filter comp of M13 tank GPFU
M12A1 Gas	52	39	26	4	Fixed site filter used in structure and building
M48 Gas/Particulate	52	52	39	10	MIAI tank overpressure system
MCPE Gas/Particulate	52	39	26	4	Modular collective-protection equipment
HSFC Gas/Particulate	52	39	26	4	Simplified-protection equipment M20IM28
M23 Gas	52	39	26	4	M51 shelter
M10 Gas	52	39	26	4	Fixed-site shelter
C-22 R1 Gas	52	52	52	13	GPFU M48 fixed-site filter

Table 2-11. Wartime climatic filter exchange intervals when blood agent threat is high (given in weeks).

CLIMATE CATEGORY

CLIMATIC DEFINITIONS

CATEGORY	MEAN TEMP (F)	MEAN RELATIVE HUMIDITY (%)
Cold Humid	< -15	<90
Warm Moderate	<60	<70
Hot Dry	<98	<27
Hot Humid	>96	>76

Based on these factors, the following filter change criteria applies:

- In an area of operation with no chemical attacks confirmed and no CK threat, change filters annually.
- In an area of operation with no chemical attacks confirmed and a CK threat, change the filters IAW Table 2-11.
- For units that have received chemical attacks, change all filters every 30 days.

** Information available to the commander to confirm that his unit has been attacked with chemicals would include alarms from chemical agent detectors, positive results from the M256 series chemical agent detector kit, or soldiers experiencing chemical agent symptoms.

---

[1] *If the wet globe temperature (WGT) kit ("Botsball," NSN 6665-01-103-8547) is used, a correction procedure is required (reference message SGPS-PSP, 23 May 1990).*
WBGT = 0.8 x WGT + 0.2 x dry bulb.
Where dry bulb may be measured by removing the dial thermometer from the WGT

Botsball and reading the air temperature after three minutes (shading the sensor from direct sunlight).

Chapter 3

Chemical Vulnerability Assessment and Force Protection

This chapter addresses vulnerability assessment and force protection at the tactical level, brigade through corps, and its integration into the staff estimate process. The assessment provides units with an estimate of the probable impact of enemy chemical attacks on their force. Using this estimate, commanders can help reduce the risks associated with enemy chemical weapons use and maximize force effectiveness under NBC conditions.

The vulnerability assessment is a primary means through which the chemical officer participates in the battlefield assessment process. In the assessment, the chemical officer develops information for integration into the various staff estimates. From the S2, the chemical officer/NCO obtains the following information (but is not limited to)--

- Time periods of interest.
- Weather and terrain data.
- Threat chemical delivery capabilities.
- Threat chemical weapons efficiency information.
- Threat courses of action and intent.
- Named areas of interest (NAIs) and target areas of interest (TAIs).
- Summary of enemy activity, including any NBC attacks.

From the fire support officer (FSO), the chemical officer obtains information on casualty percentages from friendly and threat conventional munitions. Examples of information may include--

- Casualty percentages based on target sizes.
- Casualty percentages based on weapon system.

These are just some of the things that the chemical officer might require from the other staff elements to be able to provide the commander with a chemical vulnerability assessment.

The commander's information needs from the chemical vulnerability assessment include, as a minimum--

- Any reports or threat NBC attacks.
- Higher headquarters NBC defense guidance (minimum MOPP, automatic masking, MOPP gear availability).
- Impact of degradation on mission performance.
- Anticipated chemical casualties and how long persistent agents will remain as a hazard.

Any other pertinent information will just enhance the assessment for the commander.

Coordinating staff officers, with the chemical officer's assistance, use this information to assess the viability of friendly COAs and to decide upon appropriate risk reduction actions. The chemical officer uses the assessment to support the decision-making process in areas such as the development of the concept of chemical defense (for example, MOPP guidance) or chemical unit mission priorities. The simplified data provided by the assessment is also useful in providing the commander information on the enemy chemical capability.

Completion of this assessment requires use of tables and graphs contained in this manual. These items were designed to accomplish two purposes: first, to provide commanders and staffs with an estimate of the likely effects of enemy chemical strikes and second, to provide leaders with a simple, rapid process to support vulnerability assessment on a fast-moving battlefield. Because of rapidly changing situations, units may modify and/or supplement estimates to increase their use under local conditions and to incorporate experience gained through combat. The emphasis on simplicity should remain constant.

At battalion level and below, leaders use MOPP analysis (see Chapter 2 discussion) to conduct their vulnerability assessment. Leaders determine the appropriate protective posture for their soldiers based on the threat and the mission.

This chapter is divided into two parts: assessment procedures and integration of the results into operational plans to achieve appropriate levels of force protection. These procedures apply to brigade-level and higher units. At these levels, there is more information available and time to evaluate and incorporate applicable information into OPLANs. This assessment process results in better synchronization of the battlefield operating systems (BOS) such as fire support, intelligence, command and control, mobility, and survivability. The assessment of chemical vulnerability supports synchronization through improved preparedness for various contingencies such as chemical attacks, improved unit mobility through a more pragmatic approach to MOPP guidance, and improved tactical decision aids to support the commander's information needs.

The end product of the assessment process is information addressing the likely effects of enemy chemical attacks within an AO during specified time periods. This assessment can be conducted prior to or after enemy initiation of chemical warfare. Depending on the commander's concept and the needs of the staff, the assessment can be highly detailed or very brief such as a few lines of information. The assessment process addresses casualty effects estimates, times and locations vulnerable to chemical downwind hazards, chemical barriers, and persistency.

Conduct the assessment in two parts. First, make an estimate of the threat's capability to employ chemical munitions in our force's AO within a specific time period. Second, use this information to generate simplified effects information. The remainder of this second section provides detailed how-to information on how to conduct this analysis. See Figure 3-1 for an overview of the assessment process.

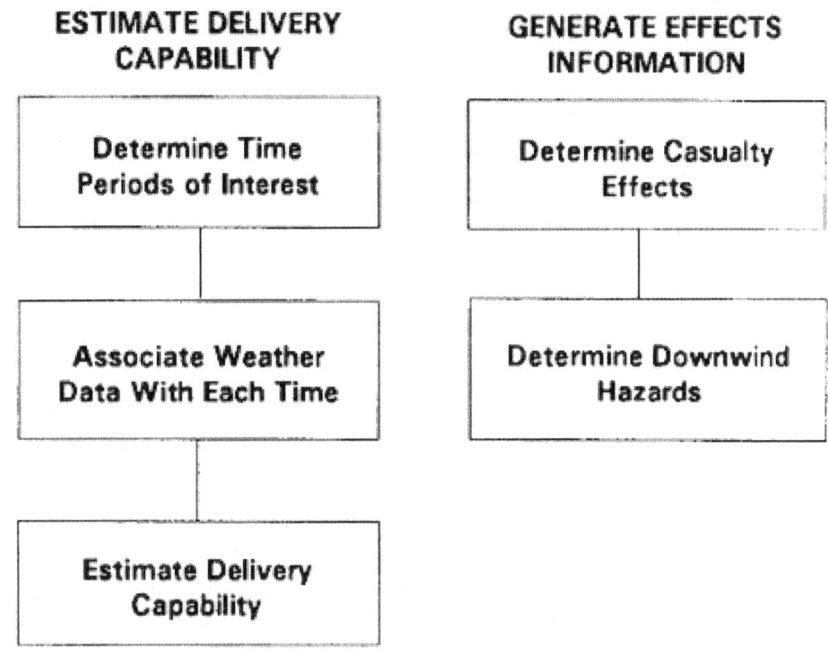

Figure 3-1. Overview of assessment process.

Estimate Delivery Capability

Determine time periods of interest. Time periods of interest are determined based on the commander's concept of the operation and the factors of METT-T. The time period of interest is determined by the chemical officer after coordination with the G2/G3 sections. They will normally conform to phases or the expected duration of an operation, however, it may often be desirable to use other criteria. For example, a light infantry unit may want to use the expected time lag between an anticipated enemy chemical attack and the needed arrival of their protective gear as the time period of interest. A time period could also be based on factors relating to enemy tactics: for example, the expected time of arrival of a second-echelon force. Further, significant weather changes could also influence the selection of time periods.

The time period of interest can range from 6 to 48 hours. The vulnerability assessment process is generally conducted in support of the planning process, and not in support of current operations. A brigade planning window usually focuses on a 12- to 48-hour period and as a rule, time periods of 24 hours or greater are generally used where possible based on the IPB. Time periods of less then six hours are usually not used. For short-term actions, shorter time periods could be used to estimate the effects of initial enemy preparation fires or to estimate the effect of a single chemical attack.

Associate weather data with each time. Associate each time period with a temperature, wind speed, and stability category. All required information can be obtained from the chemical downwind message (CDM). The CDM is generated every six hours and originates from corps and division NBCCs based on information obtained through the US Air Force Weather Service (AWS), SWO, or Fleet Weather Service.

Temperature will impact primarily on agent persistency. For each time period, temperature should be expressed as one of the following: 55°C, 50°C, 40°C, 30°C, 20°C, 10°C, 0°C, -10°C, -20°C, or -30°C. Determine temperature by taking the average of the temperatures from each CDM line applicable to the time period of interest. Use this average temperature for all calculations except for one condition. When estimating persistency for agents expected to last beyond the time period of interest, use the average daily temperature of the day in which the attack occurred.

Wind speed will impact on casualty production, persistency, and downwind agent travel. It should be expressed as one of the following: 3, 6, 9, 12, 15, or 18 kmph. As a rule of thumb, for any wind speed above 18 kmph, use 18 kmph. Calculate wind speed in the same manner you used above for temperature. In some situations it may be necessary to modify this number for casualty estimate purposes. For example, if a 24-hour period contains six hours of expected high wind speeds (very unstable conditions), you will probably elect to disregard those figures and develop a separate (lower) average for casualty estimation. The chemical officer/NCO estimate that an enemy would not employ chemicals for casualty effects during that six-hour period of high winds. Base your decision on whether or not to do this on the magnitude and duration of the wind change and the expected enemy COA.

Stability categories also affect casualty production and downwind agent travel. However, their impact is minor compared to temperature and wind speed.

Expressed as stable (inversion), neutral, or unstable (lapse), determine the stability category in the same way as temperature and wind speed.

Other environmental factors exist that could impact on the assessment. For example, terrain and vegetation could affect the estimate. However, these factors have been incorporated in the persistency estimate process.

Estimate delivery capability. Estimate the number of chemical munitions likely to be employed in your AO for each time period. Coordinate with the S2/G2 to produce this estimate.

The chemical officer will provide the S2/G2 with the time periods of interest. The S2/G2 can, upon request, produce information concerning the threat's capability to deliver chemical munitions in your AO. The estimate should indicate the number of delivery units (by type) and the number of rounds by agent types if available. The S2/G2 also provides estimates on when, where, and what type of agent the enemy will use in your unit's AO. If the situation or event template does not yield needed information, assume that the enemy can optimize his agent mix. For example, to determine the threat's capability to create contamination barriers, we assume they will fire all persistent agents. Likewise, to predict casualty effects, assume that the enemy will fire agents that have the greatest casualty-producing effects.

When the primary threat is covert or unconventional, express enemy delivery capability in terms of agent weight or as agent weight times some expected delivery means: for example, 20--5KG HD field-expedient land mines.

If threat estimates indicate limited agent supply, it will be difficult to estimate how much of that supply will be used each day. As an option for this situation, conduct the assessment for a single enemy attack based on the threat's maximum employment capability during the selected time period.

The S2/G2 will consider a number of factors in making his estimate:

- The number of employment assets within range of your unit.
- Other AOS the enemy force must service. Do not assume that every delivery system within range will be firing into your AO.
- The locations of enemy chemical munitions.
- Threat forces' capability to deliver chemical munitions to the firing units.
- Impact of threat attach on civilians.

The S2/G2 estimate should provide a range of numbers based on estimated threat COA for each time period. For example, the estimate should provide the enemy's maximum capability and its likely delivery capability. Alternatively, different estimates can be provided that would support various enemy COA. Estimates should not be based on friendly COA unless they would significantly impact on enemy delivery capability. It is not necessary to assess every possible situation and enemy option. To do so would result in inefficient use of available time. The goal is to provide estimates to the commander and staff, which can be later refined. Continuously assess the situation and look for events and options with the potential of changing the outcome of the battle.

Generate Effects Information

At this point you have a set of time period/munition delivery estimate combinations. For each of these combinations you can now develop a set of effects information: casualty estimates, contamination barriers, persistence, and times and locations of downwind agent effects. Effects information will provide the following estimates:

- Casualty effects (ten 100-meter by 200-meter targets can be attacked so that troops masking within 15 seconds will suffer 10 percent casualties).
- Contamination barriers (four 200-meter by 400-meter areas can be contaminated to a level sufficient to prevent crossing).

- Persistence (a particular contaminated area can be crossed in mask and summer uniform in four hours; it may be occupied in summer uniform, possibly without mask, in nine hours).
- Downwind agent effects. Subdivide each time period of interest into phases that correspond to specific chemical downwind hazard effects estimates likely to occur during that phase. These procedures do not address the effects of specific attacks. These procedures assist units in determining (based on their AO and weather information) periods of high or low risk from chemical attack. To determine the effect of a specific attack, refer to FM 3-3.

The procedures are brief, unclassified, and generic with respect to both agent type and delivery system. They were designed for use by multiple theaters and levels of command and for applicability across the entire operational continuum.

Determine casualty effects. Tables 3-1, 3-2, and 3-3 provide casualty estimates as a function of temperature and agent delivered expressed in kilograms per hectare (kg/ha). They are valid for wind speeds less than 20 kmph. Other factors such as air stability category, humidity, variations in wind speeds under 20 kmph, and delivery errors were found to have a minimal effect on casualty estimates for a given time period of hours as opposed to a specific instance in time. Figure 3-2 outlines the procedures for determining casualty estimates.

Table 3-1. GB nerve agent casualties.						
Munitions in Rounds per Hectare			Temperature °F			
BM-21/ha	152mm/ha	122mm/ha	10	32	50	68
1	2	4	10%	16%	24%	33%
2	4	7	14%	22%	30%	40%
3	6	10	19%	27%	37%	47%
4	8	14	25%	34%	43%	54%
4	10	17	31%	40%	50%	60%
			Casualty Percentage			

Table 3-2. TGD or VX nerve agent casualties.							
Munitions in Rounds				Temperature °F			
Msl/1000ha	Msl/150ha	Bombs/1000ha	Bombs/150ha	10	32	50	68
6	1	26	4	5%	14%	20%	21%
9	2	40	6	9%	18%	25%	25%
12	2	54	8	12%	24%	31%	31%
15	2	68	10	16%	28%	36%	36%
18	3	80	12	19%	32%	40%	41%
21	3	94	14	21%	35%	42%	43%
24	3	106	16	23%	37%	44%	45%
				Casualty Percentage			

Table 3-3. THD blister agent casualties.			
Munitions in Rounds		**Protective Posture**	
152 mm/ha	122 mm/ha	MOPP zero	MOPP 1
4	7	17%	13%
7	14	24%	18%
11	20	34%	23%
14	27	43%	28%
18	33	51%	32%
21	40	57%	36%
		Casualty Percentage	

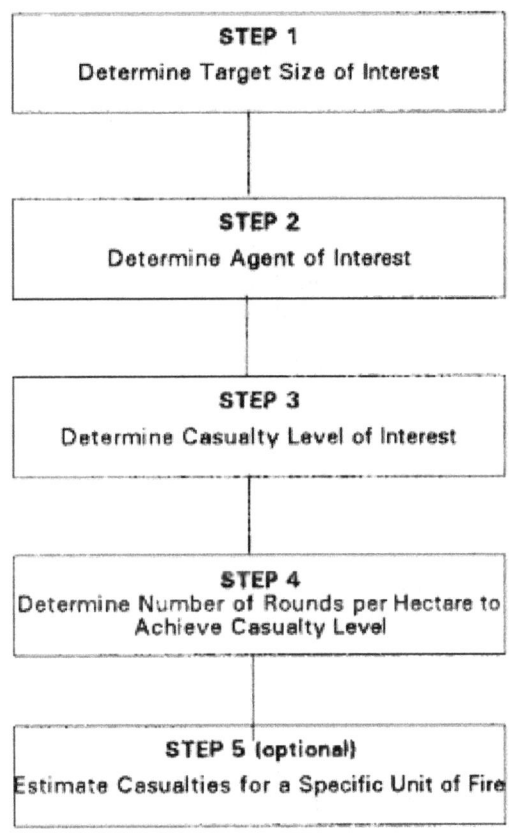

Figure 3-2. Steps in determining casualty estimates.

Step 1. Determine the target size of interest.

a. Based on IPB, select a target(s) that an enemy would target and then determine target size. For example, determine the area occupied by a maneuver company in a defensive

87

position. Use intelligence data concerning enemy targeting methods and priorities at this point. For example, if it is known that our infantry companies are treated as a 400 x 600 meter target by the enemy, then that is the target size that should be used.

b. Calculate the number of hectares in the target size of interest. For example:

Given: 1 hectare (ha) = 10,000 meters square

Target size = 400 meters x 600 meters = 240,000 meters square

Determine the number of hectares in the target area.

$$\text{Number of hectares in the target area} = \frac{240,000m^2}{10,000m^2} = 24$$

Number of hectares in the target area = 24ha

Step 2. Determine agent of interest. The nerve agent table (Table 3-1) is based on a 15 liter per minute breathing rate (rest or light work) and a 15-second masking time. For TGD or VX, the persistent agent table (Table 3-2) is based on MOPP level zero. At higher MOPP levels (for example, MOPP levels 1 to 4), TGD and VX are not effective casualty producers because of the skin protection provided by the overgarment. The blister agent table (Table 3-3) applies to all blister agents. Table 3-3 is based on either MOPP level zero or 1.

Unless it is known which agents the threat will fire, assume that the most effective casualty-producing agent in the threat stockpile will be used. For example, if an enemy can use GB, TGD, or VX, assume the threat will use GB. If the threat has both GB and HD, assume they will use GB.

Step 3. Determine casualty level of interest. Estimate threat courses of action and intent. Coordinate with the S2/G2 to estimate whether the threat attacks would intend to destroy, suppress, or harass our forces. Casualty level of interest estimates using percentages such as 25 percent or 30 percent (suppression) provide an example of this step's application.

Note: Soviet categories of target damage include--

- Destruction. A destroyed target has completely lost its combat effectiveness. A point target is considered destroyed when there is a 90 percent probability that it has suffered serious casualties or damage. An area target is considered destroyed when it is highly probable (90 percent) that no less than 50 percent of the target's subelements (including personnel) or no less than 50 percent of the target area have suffered serious casualties or damage.

88

- Suppression. A suppressed target has suffered sufficient damage or casualties to lose its combat effectiveness temporarily or to restrict its ability to maneuver or effect command and control. An area target is considered to be suppressed when it is highly probable (90 percent) that no less than 25 to 30 percent of the target's subelements or 25 to 30 percent of the target's area or personnel have suffered serious damage or casualties.
- Harassment. Harassment fire is conducted sporadically to prevent troop movement in the open and to lower the morale of the enemy.

Step 4. Determine the number of rounds required to achieve the desired casualty level.

a. Assume MOPP zero for all calculations unless otherwise indicated.

b. Refer, at this point, to Tables 3-1, 3-2, or 3-3. Locate the appropriate temperature and read down until you reach a casualty figure higher then the determined casualty level of interest. Read to the left to find the number of rounds per hectare required to produce that casualty level.

c. Multiply the number of rounds per hectare by the number of hectares in the target. For example:

Given: Casualty level wanted is 30%.

Target size = 24 ha

Present temperature is 50°F

From Table 3-1, extract the following information:

Casualty level – 37%

Weapon system = 152mm

Agent = GB

Rounds per hectare = 6 rds

Rounds required per ha x total number hectares in the target is equal to total number of rounds required: for example, 6rds/ha x 24ha = 144rds.

To achieve greater than 30 percent casualties on the target, the enemy would have to fire 144 rounds of 152-mm artillery.

Note: THD is effective at temperatures down to -30°C (-20°F).

Step 5 (optional). Estimate casualties produced by a specific unit of fire.

a. If intelligence analysis indicates the enemy will engage a specific target with a specific number of rounds, calculations can be performed to estimate the expected casualties on the target. For example:

Required: Determine casualty percentage based on a specific unit of fire for persistent nerve agents.

Given: Target area = 24ha

Agent = GB

Temperature = 50°F

Weapon = 152-mm artillery

Intelligence estimates the enemy will fire 240 rounds at a friendly target. Determine the number of rounds per hectare for the desired casualty effect.

(1) $\dfrac{\text{No. of rds}}{\text{target area}} = \dfrac{240\text{rds}}{24\text{ha}} = 10\text{rds/ha}$

(2) Using Table 3-2, find 10rds/ha and read right to find the casualty percentage based on the 50°F temperature.

Casualty percentage = 50%

b. To determine blister agent casualties, use the same procedures as described before and Table 3-3. However, when reading right to determine casualty percentage, use MOPP zero or 1 rather than temperature.

The above procedures depict an estimated enemy capability to attack a target and/or estimate of casualties if the attack occurred. To estimate the duration of hazards resulting from an enemy attack, see the section on MOPP open/unmasking guidance.

Determine downwind hazards. The purpose of this section on vulnerability assessment is to identify times and locations of vulnerability or relative safety from downwind hazards during a designated time period. Use the CDM as your basic tool during this process. Also use the IPB weather and terrain analysis to determine such things as prevailing winds and type of terrain. This assessment does not focus on specific chemical attacks but identifies potential times and locations of high or low risks from chemical attacks. Hazard prediction for specific chemical attacks is contained in FM 3-3.

Two primary hazards result from downwind agent travel, casualties, and degradation. Downwind agent travel can affect large portions of the force due to the triggering of alarm systems. Activation of alarm systems will cause units to mask. Degradation effects are also enhanced by large area coverage of chemical agent concentrations.

Casualties resulting from downwind hazards should be very few, assuming units make proper use of alarm and warning systems. For the vulnerability assessment, use the CDM to determine whether your unit would fall into one of the following three conditions (see FM 3-6 for stability categories):

High casualty risk. This occurs at wind speeds of 10 kmph or less during stability categories of 5 to 7 (Table 3-4). Agent clouds will produce very narrow, 1 to 4 kilometers wide at 30 kilometers distance, and very long, beyond 20 kilometers, hazard clouds. Dosages over 100 times the lethal levels are possible in the hazard area. Because the cloud is narrow and hugs the ground, it may bypass alarms deployed for area defense. Units located close to the attack mask once they are warned since the potential dosages are too high to be completely mitigated by unit alarm systems. Units further away can be warned only and stand a good chance of being unaffected.

Table 3-4. Atmospheric stability categories.	
Stability Category	**Atmospheric Description**
1	Very Unstable
2	Unstable
3	Slightly Unstable
4	Neutral
5	Slightly Stable
6	Stable
7	Extremely Stable

High degradation risk. This occurs during stability categories of 4 or less and wind speeds less than 10 kmph. Agent clouds will produce wide hazard areas, 2 to 7 kilometers wide at 6 kilometers distance, with lethal effects rarely extending as far as 10 kilometers. The casualty risk to warned, unmasked personnel is low. However, due to the large cloud width it is possible for every unit in the downwind hazard area to be forced to mask for several hours. Alarms may be triggered at distances of 20 to 30 kilometers away.

Low casualty risk. This occurs at wind speeds of 10 kmph or greater at stability category 4 or less. The casualty risk is very low outside the area of immediate effects (see FM 3-3 for downwind hazard prediction). A significant number of units will be forced to mask; however, this effect will be short lived and will not extend as far as in the previous category (2 to 7 kilometers).

The example below shows how all the information obtained can be incorporated into the assessment. Other information can be included and will be discussed later in the chapter. This is only an example and can be modified to best suit the using command.

CHEMICAL VULNERABILITY ASSESSMENT		
1) 240600Z to 252400Z	July 90------70°F	3kmph--neutral(4).
2) 240600Z to 260600Z	July 90------70°F	6kmph--neutral(4).
ENEMY CAPABILITY		
	COA 1	COA 2
	3000rds of 122mm GB/HD 1500rds of 152mm GB/HD 36 bombs 60KG HD	5000 rds of 122mm GB/HD 2500 rds of 152mm GB/HD 54 bombs 60KG HD
Casualties:		
Inf Co. 400x600m area 30% casualties number of munitions required per hectare	17rds/ha-122mm(168rds 15rds/ha-152mm(96rds) 3-bombs/ha 60KG	29rds/ha-122mm(168rds) 26rds/ha-152mm(96rds) 4-bombs/ha 60KG
Barriers:		
HD 200x400m 2 hrs duration	16-122mm(180rds) 16-152mm(92rds) 9-bombs 60KG	27-122mm(180rds) 27-152mm(92rds) 13-bombs 60KG
Downwind hazard:		
240600Z to 240900Z 241000Z to 241300Z 241400Z to 242000Z 242100Z to 250400Z 250500Z to 252100Z 252200Z to 260600Z	high degradation risk low casualty risk high degradation risk high casualty risk high degradation risk low casualty risk	
NOTE: 241000Z to 241700Z--Units at heavy work rates ineffective after 2 hours in MOPP3 or 4. 251100Z to 251600Z--Units at moderate work rates ineffective after hours in MOPP3 or 4		

Standard MOPP Gear and Field-Expedient Items

Standard MOPP gear is used as the primary protection means against liquid droplets. However, field-expedient items such as ponchos and rain jackets also can provide initially (for a period of only minutes) adequate protection against the initial casualty effects of the liquid droplet component of a chemical agent attack. If the following two conditions are met, then casualties resulting from the chemical attack will be less than an equivalent conventional attack:

- Soldiers are at MOPP1 or wearing a field-expedient covering that covers all exposed skin except the face, hands, and feet. This field-expedient covering must be disposed of within 20 minutes.
- Units take protective action against chemical agent vapor by immediately masking.

While effective in protecting against initial liquid effects, field-expedient items are inadequate if an enemy force engages in sustained chemical warfare. Field-expedient items do not allow units to fight dirty or operate in a contaminated environment for extended periods of time. Soldiers will suffer higher sublethal agent dosages if they remain in field-expedient gear too long. Field-expedient overgarments cause significant degradation to our soldiers (for example, heat stress). Operating for long periods while in field-expedient items also greatly increases the risk of the soldier becoming a chemical casualty.

Field-expedient protective gear provides short-term protection. If the threat assessment indicates low risk of chemical agent use, field-expedient protection gear readily available provides a limited backup for the overgarment. Field-expedient items must be quickly replaced by overgarments when the threat assessment indicates the enemy has the capability to employ chemical weapons. The use of field-expedient items is an option during the period between enemy first use and delivery of standard MOPP equipment to subordinate units. However, if a unit is attacked with chemicals, the delay in the receipt of MOPP gear would result in unacceptable casualties to unit personnel. Field-expedient gear could also be used during periods of sporadic small scale chemical attacks or when standard MOPP equipment has been expended.

Use of NBC Reconnaissance Assets

Battalion and higher units use NBC recon and chemical agent alarms as a part of the IPB process and for unit operations.

The chemical officer assists the S2/G2 in developing NAIs that relate to enemy chemical attacks. Based on threat doctrine, likely chemical targets can be identified that support various threat COA.

For example, a brigade identifies potential avenues of approach. For each of these avenues of approach, likely threat countermeasures are identified. Threat doctrine calls for potentially restricting the use of lateral routes with chemical barriers to preclude our timely movement of forces. Also, the detection of chemical barriers along one of our avenues of approach can indicate that the threat could be trying to channelize our forces.

Identification of NAIs along routes for potential chemical attacks helps determine enemy intentions and speeds our response to threat chemical attacks. If a chemical attack was reported in such an NAI, our force could send recon assets to determine the extent of the contamination and identify bypasses if necessary. Decontamination, engineer, or smoke assets can be dispatched to assist in reducing and concealing the obstacle. Finally, the commander can be alerted that his counterattacking force may be delayed in reaching its attack position, possibly requiring him to begin his movement earlier than desired.

Monitor NAIs with a combination of chemical alarms and units (chemical units) in the area. Units in these areas should report the occurrence of chemical attacks or of large scale artillery barrages that impact in their vicinity. Position chemical alarms at key points along the route to cover areas not occupied by units. If an area cannot be continuously monitored, dispatch NBC reconnaissance assets to the area once the threat reaches an NAI that indicates they are committing to a certain avenue of approach.

Consideration is given to area defense against downwind vapor hazards. For example, threat chemical attacks may occur upwind of your unit. By remaining aware of unit situations and weather data, you can determine whether your unit is at a low or high risk (see FM 3-3, CDMs).

To devise a plan, conduct a map reconnaissance to determine likely wind patterns based on the terrain and wind direction. Locate troop concentrations upwind where an enemy can deliver chemical munitions. Select a line between these two locations. Verify the wind directions in this area by a survey of units in the area. Finally, position some means of detection along this line.

Casualty Estimation

The S1/G1 assesses the probability and impact of chemical-related casualties. This assessment addresses whether a net increase in casualties will result from enemy chemical use.

Liquid chemical attacks, artillery or bomb, on our units (see figure 3-3) will create an uneven spread of contamination. Some portions of the targeted area will not receive any contamination. Applying the NBC defense principles of contamination avoidance, protection, and decontamination for our units provides several benefits. Using contamination avoidance techniques and procedures to disperse, harden, or camouflage friendly positions decreases vulnerability. Use of active measures such as NBC reconnaissance and NBC warning and reporting provides detection and identification to determine the presence of clean or contaminated areas. Units maximize use of NBC protection for key facilities and personnel, prioritize use of NBC collective Protection capabilities. Units cover selected high priority stocks and establish priorities for decontamination efforts.

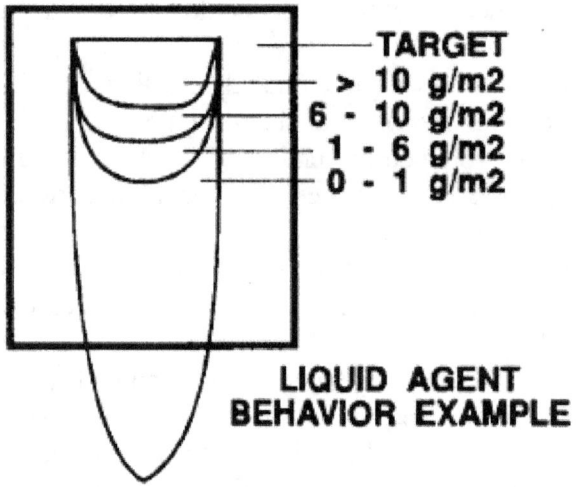

Figure 3-3. Percent target coverage.

If units are wearing protective gear and masks according to doctrine, then no net increase in casualties should result due to threat indirect fire. However, increased casualties will result from the following:

94

- Units in MOPP3 or MOPP4 are less effective in force-on-force battles. This effect is most pronounced if the enemy operates in an undegraded posture. Increased direct fire casualties will probably also result from this degradation.
- Soldiers operating in contaminated areas will make errors, thereby increasing their risk of becoming casualties.
- Increased heat stress casualties can occur. If units in MOPP3 or MOPP4 are worked past the endurance limits (described in Chapter 2), heat casualties are likely. With proper precautions, heat stress should be kept to a minimum.
- Psychological casualties are likely to increase because of encapsulation.

Soldiers may show symptoms associated with chemical agents, such as a runny nose and eye irritation, and believe it is a result of chemical agents.

The effects of the above factors are difficult to predict without the benefit of combat experience.

Chemical Overgarment Risk Assessment

Leaders conduct MOPP analysis to determine what protection level (e.g., MOPP 0, MOPP1, etc) should be used. Decisions are made based on an analysis of mission, threat, and the risk a commander is willing to accept. For example, some commanders in Southwest Asia during Operation Desert Shield made an initial decision that their units should go to MOPP1 and don their initial set of contingency overgarments. Subsequently, they had to decide when to replace these materials, or vehicle parts. Chemical contamination may be detected initially when using chemical detectors. Remember, going to MOPP open or unmasking is a command decision.

MOPP Open Procedure

MOPP open is used to reduce heat stress and prolong soldier endurance when in MOPP3 or MOPP4. MOPP open is used if the vapor on skin has decreased to the ICT5 risk level, but the inhalation and/or liquid-on-skin risk remains above ICTS. The worst case MOPP open times are given in Tables 3-6, 3-9, 3-11, 3-12, 3-14, and 3-16. Local weather conditions may permit going to MOPP open sooner.

**

Table 3-6. Estimated wait times before executing MOPP open procedures (ICTS Risk Level).

AGENT: GA/GF
TERRAIN: SAND
The numbers in the chart represent hours.

WIND SPEED KMPH	STABILITY	TEMPERATURE (F)							
		50	60	70	80	90	100	110	120
0-10	UNSTABLE	60+	53	33	20	13	10	8	5
	NEUTRAL	60+	60+	45	28	18	13	8	5
	STABLE	60+	60+	58	38	23	15	10	8
11-24	UNSTABLE	13	8	5	3	3	2	2	2
	NEUTRAL	20	13	8	5	5	3	2	2
	STABLE	20	13	8	5	5	3	2	2
> = 25	NEUTRAL	2	2	2	2	2	2	2	2

Notes:
1. Worst case MOPP open time—information in the table indicates the time for GA/GF to weather below 5 percent incidence of incapacitation due to vapor-on-skin effects. DO NOT OPEN MOPP WITHOUT FOLLOWING MOPP OPEN PROCEDURES!
2. Opening the MOPP suit—unzip and/or unsnap MOPP clothing; do not remove.
3. When the actual temperature is between two listed temperatures, enter the table with the lower temperature. To get times for grass terrain, multiply numbers in the chart by 0.4. DO NOT INTERPOLATE!
4. See FM 3-6 for definition of stability categories.

**

Table 3-9. Estimated wait times before executing MOPP open procedures (ICTS Risk Level).

AGENT: HD
TERRAIN: SAND
The numbers in the chart represent hours.

WIND SPEED KMPH	STABILITY	TEMPERATURE (F)							
		50	60	70	80	90	100	110	120
0-10	UNSTABLE	60+	60+	60+	60+	48	32	23	15
	NEUTRAL	60+	60+	60+	60+	60+	43	28	20
	STABLE	60+	60+	60+	60+	60+	58	38	25
11-24	UNSTABLE	60+	60+	43	28	18	13	8	5
	NEUTRAL	60+	60+	60+	38	25	18	10	8
	STABLE	60+	60+	60+	40	28	18	13	8
> = 25	NEUTRAL	33	20	13	8	5	5	3	3

Notes:
1. Worst case MOPP open time—information in the table indicates the time for HD to weather below 5 percent incidence of incapacitation due to vapor-on-skin effects. To get times for grass terrain, multiply the numbers in the chart by 0.4. DO NOT OPEN MOPP WITHOUT FOLLOWING MOPP OPEN PROCEDURES!
2. Opening the MOPP suit—unzip and/or unsnap MOPP clothing; do not remove.
3. When the actual temperature is between two listed temperatures, enter the table with the lower temperature. DO NOT INTERPOLATE!
4. See FM 3-6 for definition of stability categories.

Table 3-11. Estimated wait time before executing MOPP open/unmasking procedures (ICTS Levels).

AGENT: HD
TERRAIN: CARC
The numbers in the chart represent hours.

WIND SPEED KMPH	STABILITY	TEMPERATURE (F)							
		50	60	70	80	90	100	110	120
0-10	UNSTABLE	11	7	5	3	2	2	1	1
	NEUTRAL	12	8	5	4	2	2	1	1
	STABLE	13	8	5	4	2	2	1	1
11-24	UNSTABLE	7	5	3	2	2	1	1	1
	NEUTRAL	8	5	3	2	2	1	1	1
	STABLE	8	5	3	2	2	1	1	1
> =25	NEUTRAL	5	3	2	1	1	1	1	1

Notes:
1. Worst case MOPP open/unmasking time—information in this table indicates the time for HD to weather below 5 percent incidence of incapacitation due to vapor on skin and inhalation. DO NOT OPEN MOPP WITHOUT FOLLOWING MOPP OPEN PROCEDURES! DO NOT UNMASK WITHOUT FOLLOWING UNMASKING PROCEDURES!
2. Opening the MOPP suit—unzip and/or unsnap suit; do not remove.
3. When the actual temperature is between two listed temperatures, enter the table with the lower temperature. DO NOT INTERPOLATE!
4. If soldiers are working on vehicles, avoid skin contact with the vehicle.
5. See FM 3-6 for definition of stability categories.
6. For planning, ensure the following steps are taken:
a. Remove as much earth and debris as possible from the CARC painted surface and conduct operator spraydown.
b. Above times are estimated weathering times for CARC painted surfaces; confirm contamination-free status by using detection devices before MOPP reduction.
c. If possible, move equipment from contaminated area.

**

Table 3-12. Estimated wait time before executing MOPP open/unmasking procedures (ICTS Levels).

AGENT: VX
SURFACE: SAND
The numbers in the chart represent hours.

WIND SPEED KMPH	STABILITY	TEMPERATURE (F)							
		50	60	70	80	90	100	110	120
0-10	UNSTABLE	60 +	55	50	46	36	26	17	8
	NEUTRAL	60 +	60 +	60 +	60 +	49	38	26	15
	STABLE	60 +	60 +	60 +	46	51	41	32	23
11-24	UNSTABLE	60 +	55	50	46	35	25	15	5
	NEUTRAL	60 +	60 +	60 +	60 +	48	35	23	10
	STABLE	60 +	60 +	60 +	60 +	49	38	26	15
> =25	NEUTRAL	60 +	60 +	60 +	60 +	47	34	21	8

Notes:
1. Worst case MOPP open/unmasking time—information in the table indicates the time for VX to weather below 5 percent incidence of incapacitation due to vapor on skin and inhalation. DO NOT OPEN MOPP WITHOUT FOLLOWING MOPP OPEN PROCEDURES! DO NOT UNMASK WITHOUT FOLLOWING UNMASKING PROCEDURES!
2. Opening the MOPP suit—unzip and/or unsnap suit; do not remove.
3. When the actual temperature is between two listed temperatures, enter the table with the lower temperature. To get times for grass terrain, multiply numbers in the chart by 0.4. DO NOT INTERPOLATE!
4. See FM 3-6 for definition of stability categories.

Table 3-14. Estimated wait times before executing MOPP open procedures (ICTS Risk Level).

AGENT: TGD
TERRAIN: SAND
The numbers in the chart represent hours.

WIND SPEED KMPH	STABILITY	TEMPERATURE (F)							
		50	60	70	80	90	100	110	120
0-10	UNSTABLE	8	6	4	3	3	3	3	3
	NEUTRAL	8	7	6	5	4	4	3	3
	STABLE	25	22	18	15	13	10	8	5
11-24	UNSTABLE	3	3	3	3	3	3	3	3
	NEUTRAL	5	4	3	3	3	3	3	3
	STABLE	5	4	3	3	3	3	3	3
>=25	NEUTRAL	3	3	3	3	3	3	3	3

Notes:
1. Worst case MOPP open time—information in the table indicates the time for TGD to weather below 5 percent incidence of incapacitation due to vapor-on-skin effects. DO NOT OPEN MOPP WITHOUT FOLLOWING MOPP OPEN PROCEDURES!
2. Opening the MOPP suit—unzip and/or unsnap MOPP clothing; do not remove.
3. When the actual temperature is between two listed temperatures, enter the table with the lower temperature. To get times for grass terrain, multiply numbers in the chart by 0.4. DO NOT INTERPOLATE!
4. See FM 3-6 for definition of stability categories.

Table 3-16. Estimated wait times before executing MOPP open procedures (ICTS Risk Level).

AGENT: TGD
TERRAIN: CARC
The numbers in the chart represent hours.

WIND SPEED KMPH	STABILITY	TEMPERATURE (F)							
		50	60	70	80	90	100	110	120
0-10	UNSTABLE	1.75	1	0.75	0.5	0.25	0.25	0.25	0.25
	NEUTRAL	1.75	1	0.75	0.5	0.25	0.25	0.25	0.25
	STABLE	2	1.25	0.75	0.5	0.25	0.25	0.25	0.25
11-24	UNSTABLE	1	0.75	0.5	0.25	0.25	0.25	0.25	0.25
	NEUTRAL	1	0.75	0.5	0.25	0.25	0.25	0.25	0.25
	STABLE	1.25	0.75	0.5	0.25	0.25	0.25	0.25	0.25
>=25	NEUTRAL	0.75	0.5	0.25	0.25	0.25	0.25	0.25	0.25

Notes:
1. Worst case MOPP open—information in this table indicates the time for TGD to weather below 5 percent incidence of incapacitation due to vapor on skin. DO NOT OPEN MOPP WITHOUT FOLLOWING MOPP OPEN PROCEDURES!
2. Opening the MOPP suit—unzip and/or unsnap suit; do not remove.
3. When the actual temperature is between two listed temperatures, enter the table with the lower temperature. DO NOT INTERPOLATE!
4. If soldiers are working on vehicles, avoid skin contact with the vehicle.
5. See FM 3-6 for definition of stability categories.
6. For planning, ensure the following steps are taken;
a. Remove as much earth and debris as possible from the CARC painted surface and conduct operator spraydown.
b. Above times are estimated weathering times for CARC painted surfaces; confirm contamination-free status by using detection devices before MOPP reduction.
c. If possible, move equipment from contaminated area.
d. Anything not painted with CARC (such as concrete, plastic, and weapons) must be individually checked for contamination.

Procedure With CAM

Designated personnel must survey the suspected contaminated area with the CAM. Since the CAM is designed as a point detector, multiple readings must be taken in and around the unit area. Select areas for sampling that were most heavily contaminated during the attack or low-lying areas where agent vapor may linger. If CAM readings are three bars or less, go to MOPP open. If personnel show any signs of chemical agent poisoning, they should go to MOPP4. If meteorological conditions change, use the CAM to recheck the unit area as described above. See Table 3-5 for allowable MOPP open times based on CAM readings.

Table 3-5. Allowable MOPP open times.				
	(HOURS)			
	CAM BARS			
AGENT	1	2 - 4	5 - 7	8
G	IND	167	17	MOPP4
H	IND	7.5	1.5	MOPP4

Notes:
1. IND—Indefinite, negligible vapor-on-skin hazard.
2. Allowable MOPP open time means the length of time the MOPP suit can be left opened with the given CAM reading and still not exceed 5 percent incidence of incapacitation due to vapor on skin.
3. Remember that the CAM will only tell whether a G-series nerve agent or H-series blister agent is present. It does not identify the specific type of agent, such as GA, GF, or HD.

 **

Procedure Without CAM

Designated personnel must check the area for vapor hazard using the M256-series chemical agent detector kit. If M256 testing indicates a positive reading for blister or nerve agent, going to MOPP open may exceed the ICT5 risk level. MOPP open should not be used due to the vapor-on-skin ICT5 risk unless mission accomplishment is jeopardized. If the M256 results provide a negative reading, initiate action to go to MOPP open and unmasking procedures. If unit personnel show any symptoms of chemical agent poisoning, go to MOPP closed.

Using Worst Case MOPP Open/Unmasking Time Tables

The information in the tables provides planning estimates for unmasking and MOPP open times for chemical agents GA/GF, HD, VX and TGD. The worst case unmasking times are given in Tables 3-7, 3-10, 3-13, 3-15 and 3-17. Tables 3-8 and 3-11 are a combination of MOPP open/unmasking times. Figure 3-5 depicts a MOPP open/unmasking decision flow chart for commanders to use with the MOPP analysis process. The times in the tables assume constant weather conditions. If the weather condition changes, use the following procedures to update time estimates:

99

- Read the worst case time from the current weather conditions directly from the appropriate table. Keep track of how long the current conditions last until the next weather update.
- When weather conditions change, determine the percentage of the original worst case time remaining (remaining time divided by original time).
- Determine the new worst case time for the new weather conditions.
- Multiply percent of original worst case time remaining by the new worst case time. The results are the updated worst case time.

Table 3-7. *Estimated wait times before executing unmasking procedures (ICTS Risk Level).*

AGENT: GA/GF
TERRAIN: SAND
The numbers in the chart represent hours.

WIND SPEED KMPH	STABILITY	TEMPERATURE (F)							
		50	60	70	80	90	100	110	120
0-10	UNSTABLE	60+	60+	60+	55	35	25	15	13
	NEUTRAL	60+	60+	60+	60+	45	30	20	13
	STABLE	60+	60+	60+	60+	55	35	23	15
11-24	UNSTABLE	60+	60+	60+	38	23	15	10	8
	NEUTRAL	60+	60+	60+	43	28	18	13	10
	STABLE	60+	60+	60+	45	30	20	13	10
> =25	NEUTRAL	60+	60+	35	23	15	10	8	5

Notes:
1. Worst case unmasking time—information in the table indicates the time for GA/GF to weather below 5 percent incidence of incapacitation due to inhalation. DO NOT UNMASK WITHOUT FOLLOWING UNMASKING PROCEDURES!
2. When the actual temperature is between two listed temperatures, enter the table with the lower temperature. To get times for grass terrain, multiply numbers in the chart by 0.4. DO NOT INTERPOLATE!
3. See FM 3-6 for definition of stability categories.

✷✷

Table 3-10. *Estimated wait times before executing unmasking procedures (ICTS Risk Level).*

AGENT: HD
TERRAIN: SAND
The numbers in the chart represent hours.

WIND SPEED KMPH	STABILITY	TEMPERATURE (F)							
		50	60	70	80	90	100	110	120
0-10	UNSTABLE	60+	60+	60+	60+	53	35	23	18
	NEUTRAL	60+	60+	60+	60+	60+	48	33	23
	STABLE	60+	60+	60+	60+	60+	60+	45	29
11-24	UNSTABLE	60+	60+	58	38	25	15	10	8
	NEUTRAL	60+	60+	60+	50	33	23	15	10
	STABLE	60+	60+	60+	53	35	23	15	10
> =25	NEUTRAL	53	33	20	13	8	5	5	3

Notes:
1. Worst case unmasking time—information in this table indicates the time for HD to weather below 5 percent incidence of incapacitation due to inhalation. To get times for grass terrain, multiply numbers in the chart by 0.4. DO NOT UNMASK WITHOUT FOLLOWING UNMASKING PROCEDURES!
2. When the actual temperature is between two listed temperatures, enter the table with the lower temperature. DO NOT INTERPOLATE!
3. See FM 3-6 for definition of stability categories.

Table 3-13. Estimated wait time before executing MOPP open/unmasking procedures (ICT5 Levels).

AGENT: VX
SURFACE: CARC
The numbers in the chart represent hours.

WIND SPEED KMPH	STABILITY	TEMPERATURE (F)							
		50	60	70	80	90	100	110	120
0-10	UNSTABLE	8.25	5.25	3.5	2.25	1.5	1	0.75	0.5
	NEUTRAL	8	5	3.25	2	1.25	1	0.75	0.5
	STABLE	9.25	6	3.75	2.5	1.5	1	0.75	0.5
11-24	UNSTABLE	5	3	2	1.25	0.75	0.5	0.25	0.25
	NEUTRAL	5	3.25	2	1.25	0.75	0.5	0.5	0.25
	STABLE	5.75	3.5	2.25	1.5	1	0.75	0.5	0.25
>=25	NEUTRAL	3.25	2	1.25	0.75	0.5	0.5	0.25	0.25

Notes:
1. Worst case MOPP open/unmasking time—information in the table indicates the time for VX to weather below 5 percent incidence of incapacitation due to vapor on skin and inhalation. DO NOT OPEN MOPP WITHOUT FOLLOWING MOPP OPEN PROCEDURES! DO NOT UNMASK WITHOUT FOLLOWING UNMASKING PROCEDURES!
2. Opening the MOPP suit—unzip and/or unsnap suit; do not remove.
3. When the actual temperature is between two listed temperatures, enter the table with the lower temperature. DO NOT INTERPOLATE!
4. If soldiers are working on vehicles, avoid skin contact with the vehicles.
5. See FM 3-6 for definition of stability categories.
6. For planning, ensure the following steps are taken:
a. Remove as much earth and debris as possible from the CARC painted surface and conduct operator spraydown.
b. Above times are estimated weathering times for CARC painted surfaces; confirm contamination-free status by using detection devices before MOPP reduction.
c. If possible, move uncontaminated equipment from the contaminated area.
d. Anything not painted with CARC (such as concrete, plastics, and weapons) must be individually checked for contamination.

Table 3-15. Estimated wait times before executing unmasking procedures (ICT5 Risk Level).

AGENT: TGD
TERRAIN: SAND
The numbers in the chart represent hours.

WIND SPEED KMPH	STABILITY	TEMPERATURE (F)							
		50	60	70	80	90	100	110	120
0-10	UNSTABLE	60	46	32	18	14	10	6	3
	NEUTRAL	60+	53	47	40	33	25	18	10
	STABLE	60+	60+	60+	60	48	36	24	13
11-24	UNSTABLE	25	18	12	5	4	4	3	3
	NEUTRAL	60	45	30	15	12	9	6	3
	STABLE	60	46	30	15	12	9	6	3
>=25	NEUTRAL	18	12	7	3	3	3	3	3

Notes:
1. Worst case unmasking time—information in the table indicates the time for TGD to weather below 5 percent incidence of incapacitation due to inhalation. DO NOT UNMASK WITHOUT FOLLOWING UNMASKING PROCEDURES!
2. When the actual temperature is between two listed temperatures, enter the table with the lower temperature. To get times for grass terrain, multiply numbers in the chart by 0.4. DO NOT INTERPOLATE!
3. See FM 3-6 for definition of stability categories.

**

Table 3-17. Estimated wait times before executing unmasking procedures (ICTS Risk Level).									

AGENT: TGD
TERRAIN: CARC
The numbers in the chart represent hours.

WIND SPEED KMPH	STABILITY	TEMPERATURE (F)							
		50	60	70	80	90	100	110	120
0-10	UNSTABLE	3.25	2	1.25	0.75	0.5	0.25	0.25	0.25
	NEUTRAL	3.25	2	1.25	0.75	0.5	0.25	0.25	0.25
	STABLE	3.5	2.25	1.5	1	0.5	0.5	0.25	0.25
11-24	UNSTABLE	2	1.25	0.75	0.5	0.25	0.25	0.25	0.25
	NEUTRAL	2	1.25	0.75	0.5	0.25	0.25	0.25	0.25
	STABLE	2.25	1.25	1	0.5	0.25	0.25	0.25	0.25
>=25	NEUTRAL	1.25	0.75	0.5	0.25	0.25	0.25	0.25	0.25

Notes:
1. Worst case unmasking time—information in this table indicates the time for TGD to weather below 5 percent incidence of incapacitation due to inhalation. DO NOT UNMASK WITHOUT FOLLOWING UNMASKING PROCEDURES!
2. When the actual temperature is between two listed temperatures, enter the table with the lower temperature. DO NOT INTERPOLATE!
3. If soldiers are working on vehicles, avoid skin contact with the vehicle.
4. See FM 3-5 for definition of stability categories.
5. For planning, ensure the following steps are taken:
a. Remove as much earth and debris as possible from the CARC painted surface and conduct operator spraydown.
b. Above times are estimated weathering times for CARC painted surfaces; confirm contamination-free status by using detection devices before MOPP reduction.
c. If possible, move equipment from contaminated area.
d. Anything not painted with CARC (such as concrete, plastic, and weapons) must be individually checked for contamination.

**

Table 3-8. Estimated wait time before executing MOPP open/unmasking procedures (ICTS Levels).

AGENT: GA/GF
SURFACE: CARC
The numbers in the chart represent hours.

WIND SPEED KMPH	STABILITY	TEMPERATURE (F)							
		50	60	70	80	90	100	110	120
0-10	UNSTABLE	1.25	0.75	0.50	0.25	0.25	0.25	0.25	0.25
	NEUTRAL	1.50	1.0	0.50	0.50	0.25	0.25	0.25	0.25
	STABLE	1.50	1.0	0.50	0.50	0.25	0.25	0.25	0.25
11-24	UNSTABLE	0.75	0.50	0.25	0.25	0.25	0.25	0.25	0.25
	NEUTRAL	0.75	0.50	0.25	0.25	0.25	0.25	0.25	0.25
	STABLE	1.0	0.50	0.50	0.25	0.25	0.25	0.25	0.25
> = 25	NEUTRAL	0.50	0.50	0.25	0.25	0.25	0.25	0.25	0.25

Notes:
1. Worst case MOPP open/unmasking time—information in the table indicates the time for GA/GF to weather below 5 percent incidence of incapacitation due to vapor on skin and inhalation. DO NOT OPEN MOPP WITHOUT FOLLOWING MOPP OPEN PROCEDURES! DO NOT UNMASK WITHOUT FOLLOWING UNMASKING PROCEDURES!
2. Opening the MOPP suit—unzip and/or unsnap suit; do not remove.
3. When the actual temperature is between two listed temperatures, enter the table with the lower temperature. DO NOT INTERPOLATE!
4. If soldiers are working on vehicles, avoid skin contact with the vehicles.
5. See FM 3-6 for definition of stability categories.
6. For planning, ensure the following steps are taken:
a. Remove as much earth and debris as possible from the CARC painted surface and conduct operator spraydown.
b. Above times are estimated weathering times for CARC painted surfaces; confirm contamination free status by using detection devices before MOPP reduction.
c. If possible, move uncontaminated equipment from the contaminated area.
d. Anything not painted with CARC (such as concrete, plastics, and weapons) must be individually checked for contamination.

**

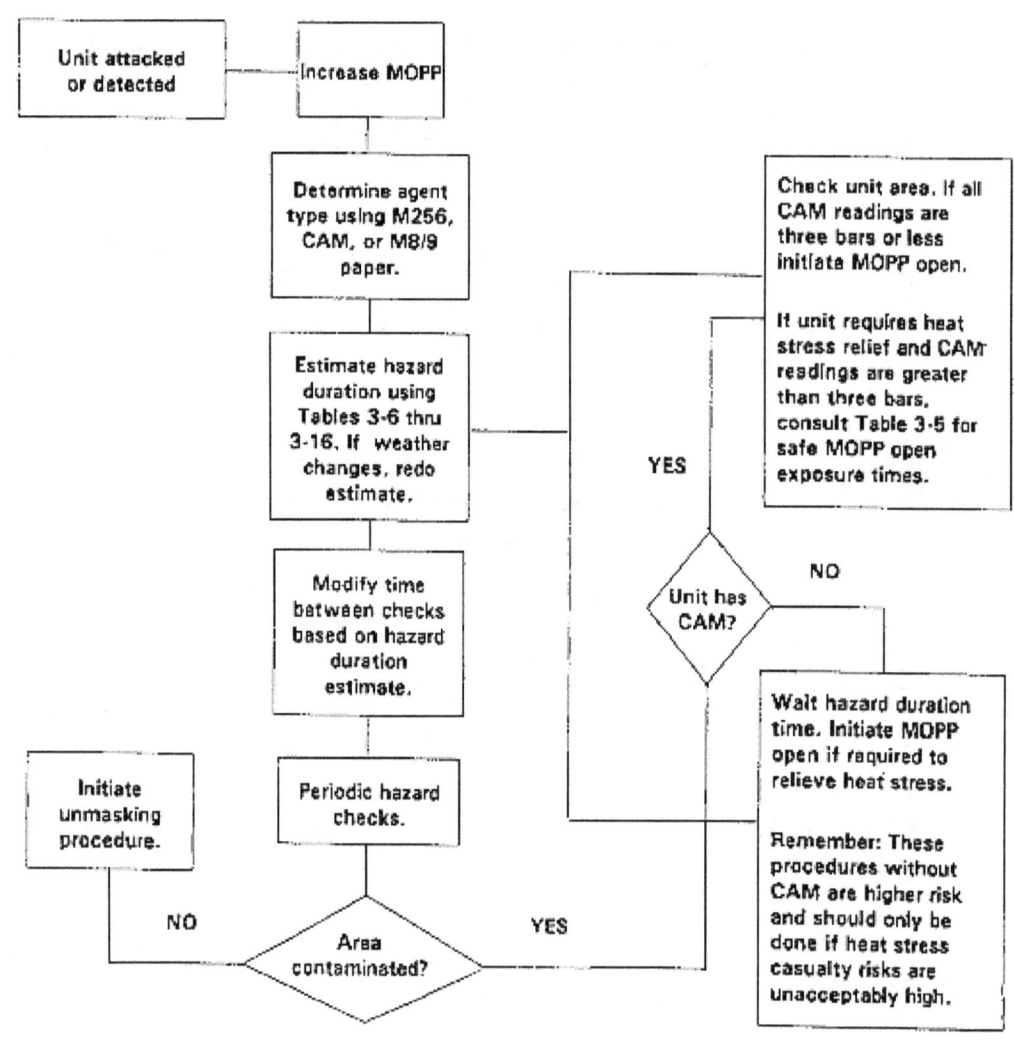

Figure 3-5. Unmasking/open MOPP action/decision flow chart

Example

a. The contamination is HD on sand with initial weather conditions of 90, unstable temperature gradient, and 0-10 kmph wind speed. From Table 3-10 (Sand) the worst case unmasking time is 53 hours.

b. Two hours later the weather changes to a higher wind speed, 11-24 kmph. Percent worst case unmasking time remaining is (53-2)/53 = 0.96.

c. From table 3-10, the worst case unmasking time for the new weather conditions is 25 hours.

d. The updated worst case unmasking time is 25 x 0.96 = 24 hours.

e. After another six hours, the weather changes to 100°F, neutral temperature gradient, and 0-10 kmph wind speed. Percent worst case unmasking time remaining is (24-6)/24 = 0.75.

f. From Table 3-10, the worst case unmasking time for the new weather conditions is now 48 hours.

g. The updated worst case unmasking time is 48 x 0.75 = 36 hours.

h. Repeat the above procedures whenever the weather changes until the hazard is gone or the unit moves away from the contamination hazard.

Formula Procedure

a. Variables.

P = Percent of worst case time remaining
O = Original worst case time from table
N = New worst case time from table
T = Time between original estimate and weather change
U = Updated worst case time

b. Procedure.

(1) Read 0 directly from table.
(2) Weather change:

```
P = (O - T)/O  ←──────────────
U = P x N                     │
Weather changes again:        │
Set 0 = U                     │
Set T = time since last weather change
Repeat as required ───────────
```

group of individuals. Symptoms associated with the ID for a blister agent would include redness, pain and swelling, but no blisters. Symptoms associated with an ID for a nerve agent would include pinpointing of the eye pupils (miosis), dimness of vision, loss of night vision, excessive sweating, runny nose, nausea; headache, tightness in the chest, and shortness of breath.

NOTE: The ID indicated above provides an estimate of the risk of incapacitation to a group of warned/protected individuals from a liquid agent in a targeted area.

CPOG Risk Assessment.

Extending the wear of the CPOG beyond 14 days is an option for the commander, but insufficient information is available from testing to provide an estimated risk of injury or incapacitation associated with extending CPOG wear beyond 14 days. The heavy impregnation of charcoal in the lining of the CPOG serves to continue to provide protection for the soldier against exposure to liquid chemical agents. The chemical protection provided by the CPOG is superior to that provided by any other type of field expedient protection such as wet weather gear.

In summary, the BDO and CPOG are both well designed effective garments, but the preferred chemical overgarment for use is the BDO. The BDO's improved design and capabilities enhance the protection offered to the soldier.

DAYS OF WEAR	RISK OF INJURY
<30	Negligible
>30	30 (approx 5%)
>45	45 (approx 10%)
>60	60 (1 5%)

**   *Figure 3-4 BDO Risk Assessment.*

MOPP Open/Unmasking Guidance

The information in this section is intended to assist the commander, staff, and chemical staff officer/NCO in NBC defense planning efforts concerning MOPP open/unmasking times for agents GA/GF, GD, GB, and HD at high temperatures. Specifically, it provides chemical officers and NCOs a means of estimating the allowable MOPP open times based on CAM readings and the worst case length of time a unit may have to remain in MOPP closed and/or masked. The term MOPP open, as mentioned in Chapter 2, means opening (at MOPP 3/4) the overgarment jacket and rolling the protective mask hood for ventilation to decrease soldier heat stress. The term MOPP closed involves the use of till protection at MOPP4. Additionally, the tables serve as a tool for commanders and staffs to use in conjunction with MOPP open or unmasking procedures. Furthermore, the information in the tables may be used to support commanders' decisions on weighing the risk of chemical casualties against degradation due to time in MOPP. These charts should be used in conjunction with the MOPP analysis process and the commander's judgment on how well his soldiers can tolerate degradation in MOPP4. Following are examples:

If the tables indicate an agent will take too long to weather, based on the commander's estimate of his unit's ability to fight degraded, he may consider moving to a clean area and/or request decontamination. If contamination is encountered, he may use the tables to support his decisions on whether to go through or bypass the contaminated area.

106

The worst case times in the charts are based on the highest contamination levels from a threat use of chemical weapons and bare skin exposure toxicity data. An attacked unit area will most likely have lower levels of contamination, and most soldiers will be wearing some clothing beneath their BDOS. The worst case times given in this section are upper time limits. Periodic monitoring will provide feedback on when the hazard in a particular area has weathered enough to allow MOPP open and/or unmasking. The estimates in these tables are based on the time required for a given agent to weather to an acceptable risk level that is no more than 5 percent incident of mild incapacitation due to vapor on skin and/or inhalation if soldiers open MOPP and/or unmask at the stated time. This risk level is abbreviated as ICT5.

Safety

Based on the MOPP status currently in effect, the MOPP level may have to be upgraded if soldiers undertake tasks that may disturb such things as soil, materials, or vehicle parts. Chemical contamination may be detected initially when using chemical detectors. Remember, going to MOPP open or unmasking is a command decision.

MOPP Open Procedure

** MOPP open is used to reduce heat stress and prolong soldier endurance when in MOPP3 or MOPP4. MOPP open is used if the vapor on skin has decreased to the ICT5 risk level, but the inhalation and/or liquid-on-skin risk remains above ICT5. The estimated wait time before executing MOPP open procedures are given in hours at the ICT5 risk level on Tables 3-6 through 3-17. Local weather conditions may permit going to MOPP open sooner.

Procedure With CAM

Designated personnel must survey the suspected contaminated area with the CAM.. Since the CAM is designed as a point detector, multiple readings must be taken in and around the unit area. Select areas for sampling that were most heavily contaminated during the attack or low-lying areas where agent vapor may linger. If CAM readings are three bars or less, go to MOPP open. If personnel show any signs of chemical agent poisoning, they should go to MOPP4. If meteorological conditions change, use the CAM to recheck the unit area as described above. See Table 3-5 for allowable MOPP open times based on CAM readings.

Procedure Without CAM

Designated personnel must check the area for vapor hazard using the M256-series chemical agent detector kit. If M256 testing indicates a positive reading for blister or nerve agent, going to MOPP open may exceed the ICTS risk level. MOPP open should not be used due to the vapor-on-skin ICT5 risk unless mission accomplishment is jeopardized. If the M256 results provide a negative reading, initiate action to go to MOPP open And unmasking procedures. If unit personnel show any symptoms of chemical agent poisoning, go to MOPP closed.

Using Worst Case MOPP Open/Unmasking Time Tables

The information in the tables provides planning estimates for unmasking and MOPP open times for chemical agents GA/GF, HD, GB, VX and GD. The worst case unmasking times are given in Tables 3-7, 3-10, 3-13, 3-15 and 3-17. Tables 3-8 and 3-11 are a combination of MOPP open/unmasking times. Figure 3-5 depicts a MOPP open/unmasking decision flow chart for commanders to use with the MOPP analysis process. The times in the tables assume constant weather conditions. If the weather condition changes, use the following procedures to update time estimates:

- Read the worst case time from the current weather conditions directly from the appropriate table. Keep track of how long the current conditions last until the next weather update.
- When weather conditions change, determine the percentage of the original worst case time remaining (remaining time divided by original time).
- Determine the new worst case time for the new weather conditions.
- Multiply percent of original worst case time remaining by the new worst case time. The results are the updated worst case time.

Example

a. The contamination is HD on sand with initial weather conditions of 90, unstable temperature gradient, and 0-10 kmph wind speed. From Table 3-10 (Sand) the worst case unmasking time is 53 hours.

b. Two hours later the weather changes to a higher wind speed, 11-24 kmph. Percent worst case unmasking time remaining is (53-2)/53 = 0.96.

c. From table 3-10, the worst case unmasking time for the new weather conditions is 25 hours.

d. The updated worst case unmasking time is 25 x 0.96 = 24 hours.

e. After another six hours, the weather changes to 100°F, neutral temperature gradient, and 0-10 kmph wind speed. Percent worst case unmasking time remaining is (24-6)/24 = 0.75.

f. From Table 3-10, the worst case unmasking time for the new weather conditions is now 48 hours.

g. The updated worst case unmasking time is 48 x 0.75 = 36 hours.

h. Repeat the above procedures whenever the weather changes until the hazard is gone or the unit moves away from the contamination hazard.

Formula Procedure

a. Variables.

P = Percent of worst case time remaining
O = Original worst case time from table
N = New worst case time from table
T = Time between original estimate and weather change
U = Updated worst case time

b. Procedure.

(1) Read O directly from table.
(2) Weather change:

```
P   (O - T)/O  ←──────────────┐
U   P x N                     │
Weather changes again:        │
Set O = U                     │
Set T = time since last weather change │
Repeat as required  ──────────┘
```

Chapter 4

Nuclear Protection

This chapter discusses aspects of nuclear protection that can be accomplished before, during, and after a nuclear attack, enemy or friendly. Soldiers on the battlefield must make defensive preparations to protect themselves. A soldier's NBC defense training is extremely important, as is the use of terrain and shelter.

Terrain Use

By knowing how terrain affects nuclear weapons, soldiers can greatly reduce the risk of becoming casualties. With training and practice, they can learn to recognize defensive positions that will give them optimum protection against a nuclear blast.

Hills and Mountains

Reverse slopes of hills and mountains give some nuclear protection. Heat and light from the fireball of a nuclear blast and the initial radiation tend to be absorbed by hills and mountains. What is not absorbed deflects above the soldiers because of the slope.

Depressions and Obstructions

The use of gullies, ravines, ditches, natural depressions, fallen trees, and caves can reduce nuclear casualties (see Figure 4-1). However, predicting the actual point of an enemy attack of a nuclear weapon is almost impossible. A friendly strike provides the soldier more time to prepare. The best protection remains an area below ground with some sort of overhead cover.

WALLS ARE FAIR PROTECTION

DITCHES ARE GOOD PROTECTION

CULVERTS ARE EXCELLENT PROTECTION

Figure 4-1. Expedient cover against blast and thermal effects.

Obscuration

In an active nuclear environment or when the threat of nuclear weapons use is high, smoke can be used to attenuate the thermal energy effects from nuclear detonations. Chemical smoke units can provide this asset to a commander if they are available. For further information on the application of smoke on a nuclear battlefield see FM 3-50.

Actions Before an Attack

The actions taken before an attack are most critical because they will increase the unit's survivability to the greatest possible extent. These actions range from selecting the right shelters, fortifying those shelters, and protecting vital equipment, to using equipment to increase survivability. These actions and good prior planning will increase unit survivability.

Shelter Selection

Whenever the tactical situation permits, prepare unit defensive positions. These vary from individual fighting positions to improved defensive positions. In a nuclear environment, fighting positions and improved positions protect against nuclear effects. Primary concern should be shielding from gamma and neutron radiation. Gamma radiation protection requires thick layers of dense or heavy shielding material. Examples are lead, iron, and stone. On the other hand, light, hydrogen-based material gives good neutron radiation protection. Examples are water, paraffin, and oil. These materials absorb neutrons, and additional gamma radiation results. Shielding must be provided against this secondary radiation. Generally, the thicker the layers of each type of shielding material, the better the overall radiation protection. The next paragraphs discuss protection against nuclear effects.

Foxholes

Digging in provides the best nuclear defense. This is because earth is a good shielding material. A well-constructed fighting position gives excellent protection against initial nuclear effects. It can also reduce residual radiation (fallout). Figure 4-2 shows examples of fighting positions that give good protection.

PRONE POSITION

OPEN TWO-PERSON FOXHOLE

OPEN ONE-PERSON FOXHOLE

> **Caution:**
> Do not use ponchos or other rubber or plastic
> materials alone as foxhole covers.

*Figure 4-2. Fighting positions that provide
good nuclear protection.*

Soldiers must harden their foxholes/fighting positions against the blast wave as time permits. Lining or revetting foxholes can significantly increase survivability and decrease the size of the opening into the position. Smaller openings allow entry of less initial and residual radiation. However, many metal surfaces are good thermal reflectors. Cover these surfaces to prevent increased danger of burns from the heat of nuclear blasts.

The smaller the foxhole opening, the better. Most of the gamma radiation in the bottom of a foxhole enters in through the opening. The smaller opening of a one-person foxhole reduces gamma radiation two to four times below the amount a two-person foxhole allows to enter.

A deep fighting position or foxhole gives more radiation protection than a shallow one. It places a greater thickness of shielding material or earth between the occupant(s) and the nuclear detonation. Therefore, it provides greater reduction of initial radiation from entering the hole. In a two-person fighting position, radiation reduces by a factor of two for each 16 inches of foxhole depth. Therefore, a fighting position at depth of 4 feet provides six to eight times the protection than a shallow one.

Thermal radiation can reach soldiers in foxholes by line-of-sight exposure or by reflection off the sides. Use dark, rough materials to cover potential reflecting surfaces and as protective cover for soldiers and equipment. Examples are wool (such as blankets) and canvas (such as shelter halves). Remember that thermal exposure may still burn or char these materials. Avoid direct contact with them. Do not use ponchos or other rubber or plastic materials alone as foxhole covers. These items might melt and cause burns. Simply covering a foxhole with ordinary metal screening material blocks the thermal radiation by about 50 percent. Use this screening for thermal protection without entirely blocking soldiers' view through ports. Soldiers must cover exposed portions, and they must keep low. Keeping low reduces thermal exposure just as it reduces nuclear radiation exposure.

Field-Expedient Overhead Cover

An overhead covering of earth or other material reduces exposure to thermal and initial nuclear radiation and fallout. Overhead covering helps prevent collapse. It also provides missile protection.

Beware of poorly constructed overhead cover. The cover must be strong enough to withstand the blast wave. Figure 4-3 shows some examples of good field-expedient overhead cover. Use U-shaped metal pickets, timbers, or certain fabrics, and overlay them with sandbags or earth. Ammunition boxes filled with earth also make good cover. In constructing effective overhead cover, remember the following:

- Choose dense covering materials.
- Cover in depth.
- Provide strong supports.
- Cover as much of the opening as possible.

114

**CUT TIMBER AND SCRAP MATERIALS
AS ROOF SUPPORT SYSTEM**

**U-SHAPED METAL PICKETS AS
ROOF SUPPORT SYSTEM**

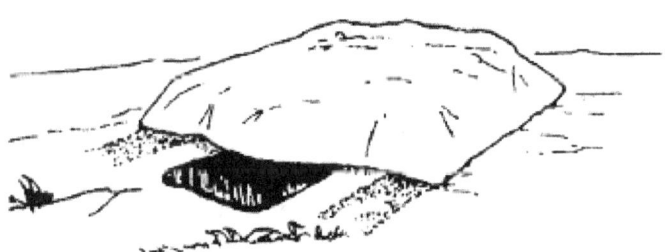

**FABRIC FOXHOLE COVER
OR FIELD PONCHOS**

*Figure 4-3. Examples of field-expedient
overhead cover.*

A vehicle provides expedient overhead cover. A simple and fast method is to drive a vehicle over the top of a foxhole (Figure 4-4). A heavy armored vehicle is better than a wheeled vehicle (of course, being inside an armored vehicle is even better). As with any type of overhead cover, initial radiation can still enter the fighting position through the earth sides or the openings in the sides of the vehicle (between treads, road wheels, and tires). If time allows, use sandbags to cover these openings. Remember, the vehicle is not a good neutron shield. Also, the blast wave may violently displace the vehicle and collapse a foxhole.

Figure 4-4. Tracked vehicle as expedient overhead cover.

Earth-Shielded Positions

Well-constructed fighting positions and bunkers can provide excellent protection against all effects of a nuclear detonation. Radiation is still the greatest concern, though, because of its great penetrating power. Radiation scatters in all directions after a burst. Most, however, travels directly in a line-of-sight route from the fireball.

It is important that as much earth cover as possible be placed between the soldier and the burst. The more earth cover, the better the shielding. Table 4-1 illustrates the value of increasing amounts of earth shielding from a hypothetical free-in-air dose. An open fighting position gives a protection factor of eight. It blocks most of the line-of-sight radiation and allows only a fraction of scattered radiation to enter. Each added 6-inch thickness of overhead earth cover reduces the scattered radiation by a factor of two.

Table 4-1. Shielding values of earth cover for a 2,400-centigray free-in-air dose.		
Soldier In	Radiation Protection Factor	Resultant Dose cGy
Open	None	2,400
Open foxhole, 4' deep	8	300
Same with 6" earth cover	12	200
Same with 12" earth cover	24	100
Same with 18" earth cover	48	50
Same with 24" earth cover	96	25

116

Flat earth cover of an underground shelter protects much better than an equivalent thickness of cover on a similar aboveground structure. This is because the underground line-of-sight thickness is greater. (See Figure 4-5.)

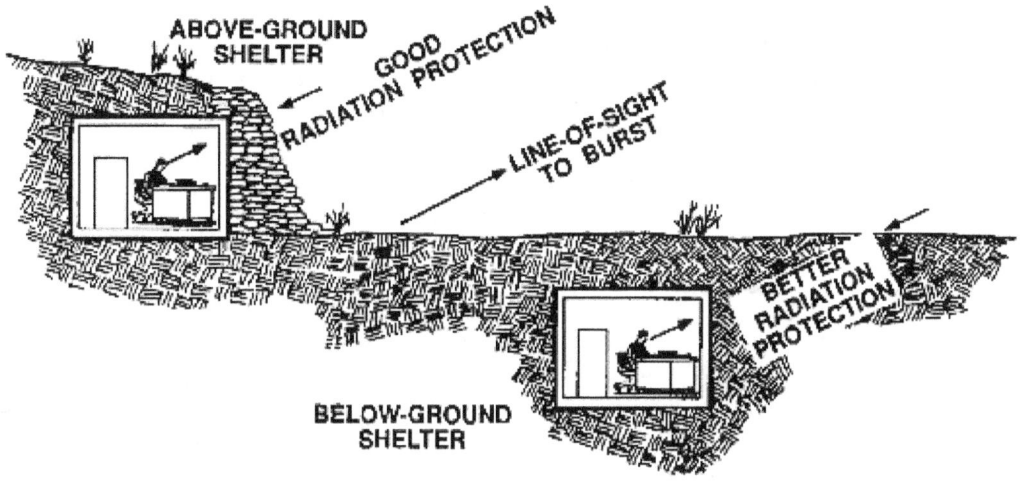

Figure 4-5. Section views of shelters.

A second layer of sandbags gives more protection to fighting positions. Each layer of sandbags, if filled with sand or compacted clay, reduces the transmitted radiation by a factor of two. Table 4-2 shows the payoff for adding layers of sandbags for a hypothetical free-in-air dose of 2,400 cGy.

Table 4-2. Radiation protection factors of sand- or clay-filled sandbags.		
Soldier In	**Radiation Protection Factor**	**Resultant Dose cGy**
Open Open foxhole, 4' deep Same with 1 layer (4 inches) Same with 2 layers (8 inches) Same with 3 layers (12 inches)	None 8 16 32 64	2,400 300 150 75 38

Sand or compacted clay gives better radiation shielding than earth because it is denser. Each layer of sand-or clay-filled sandbags can give up to 66 percent more radiation protection than the same thickness of soil or soil-filled sandbags. For example, Table 4-1 shows that 12 inches of earth gives a protection factor of 24 (100 cGy) for a hypothetical 2,400 cGy dose, and Table 4-2 shows that 12 inches (three layers) of sand-or clay-filled sandbags gives a protection factor of 64 (38 cGy) for the same dose. Generally, heavier sandbags protect better than lighter ones. Avoid cracks between sandbags to prevent radiation leakage.

Neutron radiation can be stopped. Water delays and absorbs neutrons, but since some gamma radiation is given off in the process, dense shielding is still required. Damp earth or concrete protects from both forms of radiation. For example, only 12 inches of

117

concrete or 24 inches of damp earth reduce neutron radiation exposure by a factor of 10. Wet sandbags achieve a reduction factor of two for every 4-inch layer. Other expedient neutron-shielding materials include containers of water, fuel, or oil. Remember that radiation scatters in all directions, and shielding must provide all-around protection.

Protect sandbags from exposure to thermal radiation. Sandbags can burn and spill their contents, which can then be moved more easily by the blast wave. Cover sandbags with a small amount of earth and/or sod (see Figure 4-6) to eliminate this problem. Covering sandbags also enhances camouflage and provides valuable additional conventional fragmentation protection.

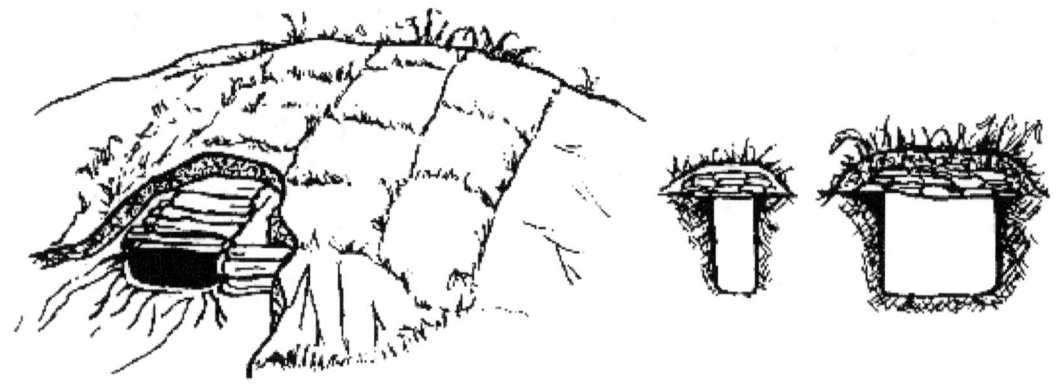

Figure 4-6. Sandbags protected with sod and earth cover.

Buildings

Certain types of buildings offer excellent shelter from nuclear hazards and require a minimum of time and effort to adapt for use. Choose buildings carefully. The stronger the structure, the better the protection against blast effects. The strongest are heavily framed buildings of steel and reinforced concrete. The worst choices are the shed-type industrial buildings with light frames and long beam span. Even well-constructed frame houses are stronger than the latter. Figure 4-7 shows some examples of typical structures that provide good protection. Ammunition storage bunkers also give exceptional protection. These are usually large enough for most vehicles and equipment.

REINFORCED-CONCRETE
STRUCTURE

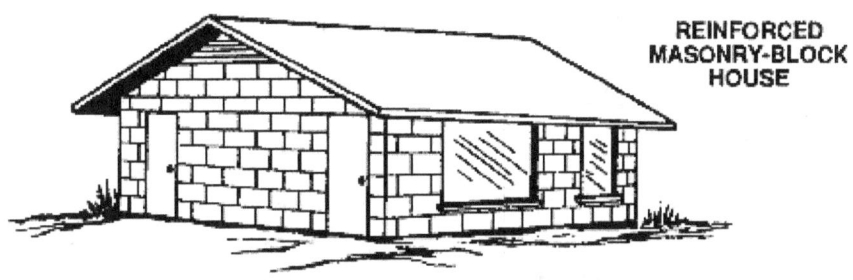

REINFORCED
MASONRY-BLOCK
HOUSE

Figure 4-7. Typical structures that provide good nuclear protection.

Many European rural and urban structures can provide good protection. Many types of pre-World War II European buildings provide good blast and radiation protection. Examples are farmhouses, churches, and municipal buildings. See Figure 4-8 for typical European rural and urban structures that provide such protection. Characteristics to look for include the following:

- Pre-World War II design and construction. These have thick, full-span floor and ceiling beams; heavy roofing tiles; dense, reinforced walls; and, in most cases, a full basement.
- Full basements constructed of concrete or stone. Make sure there is an exit directly to the outside as well as through the upper floors in case of emergency.
- Thick-walled, masonry structured. A thickness of 36 centimeters (greater than 1 foot) is an indication of good, pre-World War II wall construction. In areas, particularly southern Germany, where construction details are typically concealed by stucco finish, desirable features underneath are noticeable when the outside walls are wet. These features include diagonal supports and blockworks.
- Buildings with the least amount of glass. European windows and doors typically are protected by roll-up or folding shutters. These coverings provide some additional blast and thermal protection.

119

Figure 4-8. Typical European structures that provide good nuclear protection.

A shielded building is best. Exterior rows of buildings in closely arranged groups (towns) shield buildings in the interior. These shielded structures suffer less blast overpressure and structural damage than exposed structures. However, debris and rubble problems and fire hazards may increase toward the center of town. Commanders should consider using shelters located two or three rows of buildings from the edge of town to avoid serious hindrance to postattack maneuver.

Soldiers should get belowground level. The basement, because it is below ground, provides increased blast protection and much more line-of-sight radiation protection than aboveground floors. This additional protection results from the surrounding earth fill. Add additional radiation protection by placing a layer of earth or sandbags on the floor above. This additional dead weight will be significant and may require shoring up the floor. Alternately, more protection can be gained by sandbagging a smaller shelter in the basement (such as a sturdy table) without increasing the possibility of the entire floor collapsing. Block windows with sandbags, and enhance the radiation protection and structural strength of any aboveground exterior walls by piling dirt and sandbags against the walls. Generally speaking, soldiers can reduce radiation by a factor of 10 in basements as compared to levels in aboveground floors.

Positions inside of the building can make a difference if sufficient time is available to properly prepare it. On floors above ground, the center of the building offers the greatest protection from both initial and residual radiation. Below the ground, the corners of the building give the greatest protection. In either case, the dose to a prone soldier would be about one-half the dose to a standing soldier. The lesson here is to seek shelter in an underground structure and lie in a corner. If an underground shelter is not available, lie in the center of a shelter under a sturdy table (see Figure 4-9). Other options include lying inside a fireplace, under a stairway, or in a bathroom where the plumbing and relatively close spacing of walls might provide increased structural strength.

Figure 4-9. Shelter in a building.

Tents

Tents are not a preferred shelter against the effects of nuclear weapons. Personnel routinely conducting activities in tents, such as medical, maintenance, and supply personnel, are particularly vulnerable.

A tent does provide some protection. It initially provides good thermal radiation protection. The secondary fire hazard is serious, however, and in most cases, the blast wave will not blow the smoldering tent far enough away to prevent damage and injury from subsequent fires.

You can increase protection inside the tent. If the situation requires continuing operations in a tent--such as may be the case for some field hospital situations--achieve some degree of protection by piling dirt and sandbags as far up the sides of the tent as possible. Lying on the floor is still the safer profile for personnel and may be preferable for bed patients.

A tent offers essentially no resistance to blast winds. Ensure that equipment and glassware are secure. All loose pieces of equipment, such as small instruments, chairs, clipboards, and bottles, will be propelled by the blast and can cause serious injuries.

Beware of tent pole breakage. A broken and splintered tent pole can cause serious injuries. Piling sandbags around the center pole gives some additional support. It also

121

helps ensure enough clearance to the ground to allow soldiers to evacuate the smoldering tent after the initial flash.

Armored Vehicles

Armored vehicles give good NBC protection. In most situations, tanks provide the best vehicular protection available. Lightly armored vehicles also give good protection. These vehicles include infantry fighting vehicles, armored personnel carriers, self-propelled artillery, and some heavy engineer equipment. If time is available, improve this protection with any of the following seven actions.

Get as low as possible inside an armored vehicle. Crew members normally elevated in a tank turret should get on the floor of the armored vehicle. This applies to the tank commander, gunner, and loader. Assuming such a low position reduces the radiation received by a factor of four.

Keep all hatches shut. Obviously, an open hatch will expose the crew unnecessarily to explosion effects. It could also subsequently allow the entry of fallout particles and scattered gamma radiation. Close any other openings, such as the main gun breech.

Prevent injury while inside an armored vehicle. The blast wave will throw soldiers violently about inside an armored vehicle. Wear combat vehicle crew (CVC) helmet or kevlar helmet with chin strap secured to help prevent head injuries.

Secure all loose equipment inside the vehicle. The force of the blast can throw about unsecured, loose equipment inside the vehicle, such as tools, weapons, and helmets, and cause injury or death.

Dig in armored vehicles (hull defilade) or place them in trenches or cuts in roadways (see Figure 4-10). This provides some limited line-of-sight radiation protection and considerable blast protection. A hull defilade fighting position or trench that allows half of the vehicle sides to be covered can reduce gamma radiation by as much as a factor of two.

Figure 4-10. Protection of armored vehicles.

Use sandbags as radiation shielding. A single layer of sandbags placed on top of a tank turret or armored vehicle hull provides valuable overhead gamma shielding. Each layer of sandbags reduces the gamma radiation by a factor of two. Wetting the sandbags enhances the neutron radiation shielding and protects the sandbags from thermal damage.

Although blast damage is generally least for head-on orientation, rear-on orientation may be preferable. This places the mass of the vehicle's engine between the potential radiation source and the crew. This rear-on orientation can reduce potential radiation exposure to half that of a head-on or broadside exposure. At distances above the median lethal dose to the crew in a rear-on orientation, significant damage to the tank is not expected.

Wheeled Vehicles

Avoid using wheeled vehicles as shelter. Generally, wheeled vehicles provide little or no protection from the effects of nuclear explosions. Worse still, they are particularly vulnerable to overturning. This exposes drivers and passengers to increased risk.

The percent of casualties from blast effects is dramatically greater for personnel in wheeled vehicles than for those in the open (see Table 4-3). The percent of casualties expected from radiation is the same for both.

Table 4-3. Comparison of blast casualties from a 10-kiloton fission weapon.								
Range (Meters)	200	300	400	700	800	900	1,000	1,400
Personnel in Open (Percentage)	100	80	41	11	8	5	4	0
Personnel in Wheeled Vehicle (Percentage)	10	100	100	99	80	62	43	1

123

Soldiers should protect themselves as much as possible inside vehicles. If they must accomplish mission-essential activities, such as communications, command, and control, in a wheeled vehicle, they should wear their kevlar helmets with chin straps secured. This precaution helps prevent head injuries if the vehicle is overturned.

Secure all loose equipment inside the vehicles. Inadequately secured equipment, such as weapons, radios, desk, file cabinets, field safes, racks, and generators, can tip over or slide across a van floor and cause serious injuries. Such items can also be thrown to the ceiling and cause injuries when the vehicle turns over. Tying down, blocking, and bracing the equipment will help.

Plan for and prepare adequate field shelters immediately adjacent to facilities that require soldiers to continue operations in wheeled vehicles. Parking the vehicle inside or under a shelter gives some protection to soldiers inside. Existing or natural structures such as ammunition bunkers, underpasses, tunnels, and caves, are in this category.

Aircraft Ground Operations

Revetments give little protection against blast overpressure. However, revetments and barricades protect aircraft from damage by dynamic wind. These also protect aircraft from other hazards, such as the impact of rocks, sand, and other aircraft or aircraft debris. The tactical situation may require revetting for protection from conventional weapons blast and fragmentation damage. Use overhead cover for aircraft, if it is available. Close doors and windows against damaging overpressure. These openings expose the compartment interior to damaging thermal radiation.

Tiedowns can reduce damage from tumbling of the aircraft. Generally, tiedowns do not produce excessive stress on tiedown points. Aircraft plexiglass windows shatter into fragments. This can happen at low blast overpressure (1.5 pounds per square inch) when there is no other significant damage. Tape the edges and the centers of windows. This reduces the extent of fragmentation and the nuisance fragments may cause to cockpit operations.

Electromagnetic Pulse

Prior to an attack where enough warning has been given to the soldiers, commanders must ensure that any electronic equipment such as radios and computers is turned off and protected. Electromagnetic pulse (EMP) is the high-energy, short duration pulse (similar in some respects to a bolt of lightning) generated by nuclear detonation. It can induce a current in any electrical conductor and temporarily disrupt or overload and damage components of improperly protected or unprotected electronic equipment. Transient radiation effects on electronics (TREE) and EMP are discussed in FM 3-3.

Actions During an Attack

Nuclear attack indicators are unmistakable. The bright flash, enormous explosion, high winds, and mushroom-shaped cloud clearly indicate a nuclear attack. An enemy attack would normally come without warning. Initial actions must therefore be automatic and instinctive. Dropping immediately and covering exposed skin provide protection against blast and thermal effects.

Immediate Actions

An attack occurring without warning is immediately noticeable. The first indications will be very intense light. Heat and initial radiation come with the light, and blast follows within seconds. Time to take protective action will be minimal. If exposed when a detonation occurs, soldiers should do the following:

- Immediately drop facedown. A log, a large rock, or any depression in the earth's surface provides some protection.
- Close eyes.
- Protect exposed skin from heat by putting hands and arms under or near the body and keeping the helmet on.
- Remain facedown until the blast wave passes and debris stops falling.
- Stay calm, check for injury, check weapons and equipment damage, and prepare to continue the mission.

Soldiers in foxholes can take additional precautions. The foxhole puts more earth between soldiers and the potential source of radiation. They can curl up on one side, but the best position is on the back with knees drawn up to the chest (see Figure 4-11). This belly-up position may seem more vulnerable, but arms and legs are more radiation-resistant and will protect the head and trunk. Store bulky equipment, such as packs or radios, in adjacent pits if they prevent soldiers getting low in their foxholes, or place these items over the face and hands for additional radiation and blast protection.

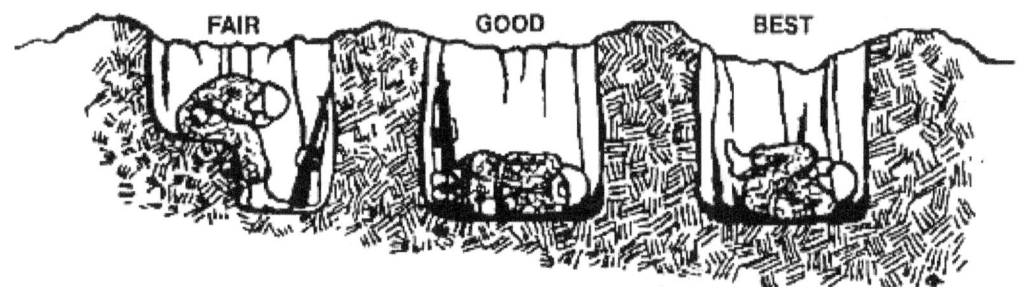

Figure 4-11. Recommended body positions in a foxhole.

Soldiers inside shelters should take protective actions. A blast wave can enter the shelter with great force, and the debris it carries can cause injuries. Lying facedown on the floor of the shelter offers worthwhile protection. However, soldiers should avoid the violent flow of air from doors or windows. Lying near a wall appears safer than standing away from a wall. Near a wall, reflection may increase the pressure wave. This is better,

125

though, than risking being blown out and injured by the blast. Constructing baffles or turns in shelter entrances can prevent overpressure buildups and entry of dust and debris (see Figure 4-12).

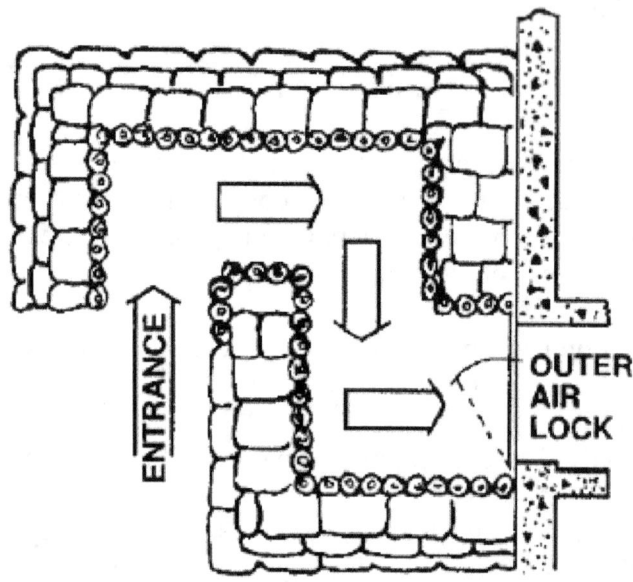

Figure 4-12. Protection from blast flow into shelters.

Nuclear Casualties

Blast, thermal radiation, and nuclear radiation all cause nuclear casualties. Except for radiation casualties, treat nuclear casualties the same as conventional casualties. Wounds caused by blast are similar to other combat wounds. Thermal burns are treated as any other type of burn. First aid cannot help radiation casualties. These casualties will be referred to medical facilities that can handle them.

Actions After an Attack

Protection must not stop when the attack ends. Immediately after an attack, soldiers must check for radioactive contamination, and then must reduce the hazard with basic soldier skills decon. Decontamination techniques to reduce radioactive contamination are to brush, scrape, or flush radiological contamination from surfaces. As a minimum, unit personnel cover foxholes and shelters, and radiac operators begin continuous monitoring. Covering the mouth with a handkerchief reduces the contaminants entering the lungs. This method is generally preferable to masking to avoid trapping contamination in the mask filter. For the commander, poststrike actions include damage assessment and restoration of combat power.

Nuclear Effects in Special Environments

126

The effect of a nuclear attack in different geographic and climatic environments is very distinguishable. The effects of terrain and weather on the use of nuclear devices may cause special problems for commanders having to operate in these extremes. Appendix A discusses these conditions in further detail.

Chapter 5

Biological Protection

✷✷ This chapter discusses aspects of protection that must be accomplished before, during, and after a biological attack. An enemy force could use biological weapons or toxins anywhere on the AirLand Battlefield. Therefore, protection against biological agents could apply to both our close and rear operations. Protection against biological agents and toxins employed against soldiers begins long before the actual attack happens. Biological agents enter the body through the skin, respiratory tract and digestive tract. Key preparations begin with personal health maintenance followed by NBC defensive training, which all soldiers must master.

Leaders conduct defensive planning against possible biological agent attack. Units prepare SOPs that specify their biological defense techniques and procedures. Enemy capabilities and intent are continuously assessed to determine whether an enemy might use biological agents. Disease has been part of the human experience throughout the centuries and has tong been a problem in time of war and peace, affecting both military and civilian populations, often accounting for more casualties than conventional weapons.

Actions Before an Attack

Preparations before an attack can be accomplished long before a biological attack happens. Personal health maintenance and realistic training are just a few ways in which the commander can minimize his biological casualties.

Personal Health Maintenance

All soldiers and leaders must adhere to the basic principles of good health. This applies especially under NBC conditions. Soldiers must continually follow these basic principles such as up-to-date immunizations, good hygiene, area sanitation and physical conditioning so unit efficiency will not suffer severe degradation.

Up-to-Date Immunizations

Immunizations reduce the chances of soldiers becoming biological casualties. Many diseases uncommon in the United States such as cholera and plague are prevalent in other parts of the world. Proper immunizations protect against many known disease-producing biological agents. All soldiers receive basic immunizations. Medical personnel periodically screen these records and keep them up to date. If soldiers or units deploy to areas in which specific diseases are prevalent, readiness preparation may include receiving additional immunizations for needed protection. This prophylactic inoculation should be part of the IPB process and needs to be brought to the commander's attention. Medical and technical intelligence can also furnish information to support assessments. Recommendations may be finished on needed precautions and/or medications that are needed prior to deployment during times of peace or war.

Good Hygiene

Soldiers should protect against the spread of disease by practicing good health habits. The best defense against biological agents is good personal hygiene, keeping the body as clean as possible. This means not only washing the face and hands but also all parts of the body, particularly the feet and exposed skin. Hands need to be cleaned before meals or anytime bare hands are used to help ingest food and liquid or when smoking. Soldiers should brush their teeth, and they must shave. Shaving may seem unimportant in the field, but it is required to achieve a proper seal of the mask. This is important because biological agents and toxins are usually most effective when received via the respiratory system or the skin.

Small nicks, scratches, and cuts are unavoidable in a field situation. Germs, either naturally occurring or intentionally employed as biological agents, enter these breaks in the skin and will cause infections if left untreated. Soldiers should clean any breaks in skin with soap and water followed by first-aid treatment.

Area Sanitation

Another good way to stop the spread of disease is to keep the area clean. Bury all empty ration packets and residue. Locate, construct, and use field sanitation facilities properly. Latrine facilities should include soap and water for washing of hands. Latrines need to be cleaned daily. Avoid leaving such facilities open, and make sure they are properly filled and marked before moving, to help prevent accidental digging in the areas. Control of insects and rodents is also essential in preventing spread of disease. Additional information on field sanitation may be found in FM 21-10 and FM 21-10-1.

Physical Conditioning

Good physical condition requires maintaining the body in a well-rested, well-fed, healthy state. A good physical fitness program will get soldiers in good shape and also increase their emotional health. Soldiers should get as much exercise and rest as the situation permits, and they must remember to eat properly. Good eating habits will help sustain the soldier. If they keep healthy, their bodies will be better able to tight off germs. A high level of physical fitness also reduces the likelihood of heat stress when MOPP gear is worn for extended periods. Physical and emotional energy levels will be high prior to any action, but can quickly decrease if the soldier is not in good physical condition. Continuous operations will require that soldiers learn to sleep in short naps and in MOPP3 or MOPP4. This is also part of the conditioning process. It may also become necessary for soldiers to eat smaller portions at more frequent intervals. Training to mission-essential task list (METL) tasks in MOPP4 supports physical and emotional conditioning. Do not conduct physical training (PT) in MOPP4. Safety constraints dictate sound judgment, which the commander must weigh.

NBC Defense Training

The complexity of the AirLand Battlefield requires commanders to train their units to live, work, and fight in a contaminated environment.

NBC training must be fully integrated into all areas of unit training: individual and collective. A unit that is well-trained and well-equipped is much better prepared to operate successfully. Leader training is especially critical to unit readiness.

Individual Training

Small unit leaders are the key to effective training of our soldiers. Leaders must know their soldiers' capabilities and capacities. Starting with basic training and continuing throughout their military careers, soldiers learn, practice, and train to perform individual NBC survival tasks. Leaders are directly responsible for reinforcing these tasks through continuous training, thereby instilling soldier confidence. These survival tasks are in STP 21-1-SMCT. Leaders should master the NBC knowledge and skills required of them as contained in STP 21-24 or STP 21-111 MQS.

Collective Training

Unit NBC NCOs and officers must provide guidance and help develop training programs for their units. The guidance must include long-and short-range attainable goals. Unit Army training and evaluation programs (ARTEPs) will indicate tasks that are to be accomplished under NBC conditions. Units must train to standard those NBC-specific tasks that are found in the ARTEPS. Units will be severely hampered in mission execution if they have not prepared for operations under NBC conditions. Units train to standard based on their METL. Leaders must plan and conduct tough training in support of their METL and under realistic conditions, including operations of critical collective tasks under NBC conditions.

Actions During an Attack

If threat forces attack with biological agents, there may be little or no warning. This will depend on the S2's and your IPB assessment. We cannot detect or identify biological agents with our currently fielded detector kits and systems. Soldiers in a unit automatically mask when there are high probability indicators of an attack to protect themselves against contamination.

Biological Attack Indicators

✱✱ Biological agents may be disseminated as aerosols, liquid droplets or dry powder. Biological attack indicators fall into two groups to indicate a high probability or possible attack.

High probability.

✱✱ Attacks with biological agents will be very subtle if favorable weather conditions prevail. Symptoms can appear from minutes to days after an attack has occurred. Indicators may be the following:

- Mysterious illness-many soldiers and civilians sick for unknown reasons.
- Large numbers of insects or unusual insects.
- Large numbers of dead wild and domestic animals.
- Mass casualties with flu-like symptoms, fever, sore throats, skin rash, mental abnormalities, pneumonia, diarrheas, dysentery, hemorrhaging or jaundice.

Possibility.

✱✱ Indicators of a possible biological attack are any of the following:

- Artillery shells with less powerful explosions than HE rounds.
- Aerial bombs that pop rather than explode.
- Mist or fog sprayed by aircraft or aerosol generators.
- Unexploded bomblets found in the area.

Immediate Actions

✱✱ Putting on the protective mask and keeping the clothing buttoned up protects adequately against living biological agents. But, an agent can gain entry through clothing using two routes: one, openings such as button holes, zipped areas, stitcting, and poor sealing at ankles, wrist, and neck and two, through minute pores in the fabric of clothing. Putting on one's protective ensemble greatly increases the protection level of the individual soldier. Toxins, however, require the same amount of protection as liquid chemical agents. Since no rapid-warning, biological agent detection device is fielded, consider any known agent cloud as a chemical attack, and take the same actions prescribed for a chemical attack.

For collective protection, personnel must be housed inside a shelter with an efficient air filter system. Many buildings can be converted into temporary shelters if cracks are carefully sealed and a filter system with a ventilating mechanism is installed. Chapter 6 discusses different collective-protection systems that provide the needed protection.

It must be emphasized that in order to counter a biological attack, protective measures must be initiated before an attack. The use of the NBCWRS is ' an effective and established means for giving advanced warning, along with intelligence data provided by the intelligence community.

Actions After an Attack

Actions after a biological attack include taking samples with the M34, M256-series, or CBASK and identifying a casualty by the symptoms they exhibit and treating those symptoms. Early recognition of symptoms and their treatment will increase recovery time and hopefully decrease fatalities.

It is necessary to isolate soldiers showing symptoms of disease. This isolation helps prevent possible spread to others if the disease is communicable. It is also necessary to limit the number of personnel providing care to these casualties. Treatment of live biological agent or toxin casualties requires medical assistance as soon as possible. An indication of a live biological agent attack is a large number of soldiers and civilians with unexplained illness over a short period.

The threat also has a wide variety of . toxins. These can be dispensed alone or with other carriers or agents. Symptoms associated with some toxins mimic other illness or chemical casualty symptoms. Toxin symptoms may include any of the following:

- Dizziness, mental confusion, or double or blurred vision.
- Tingling of skin, numbness, paralysis, or convulsions.
- Formation of rashes or blisters.
- Coughing.
- Fever, aching muscles, and fatigue. *Difficulty in swallowing.
- Nausea, vomiting, and/or diarrhea.
- Bleeding from body openings or blood in urine, stool, or sputum (spit).
- Shock.

These symptoms appear in minutes or hours after the toxin attack. Soldiers should decontaminate immediately after a toxin attack. They should either wash with soap and water or use the M258A1 or M291 decon kits.

Appropriate self-aid and buddy-aid vary, depending on the agent. Soldiers first mask to prevent inhaling or ingesting agents. They then should remove agents from exposed skin, observe each other for early symptoms of a toxic exposure, and request medical assistance.

Operation in Special Environments

Biological protection must be considered when operating in different weather and terrain environments. Biological agents and toxins will be altered depending on where they are employed. Appendix A discusses several types of special operations and how biological agents or toxins affect operations in those environments.

Chapter 6

Collective Protection

Collective protection is required to provide a safe environment for soldiers to carry out tactical functions, such as medical care, command, control, and communications, without being restricted by wearing NBC protective clothing. Collective-protection equipment (CPE) is integrated into some weapon systems to increase their effectiveness in an NBC environment. Planning for collective protection should be an integral part of plans for the AirLand Battlefield. Commanders must examine and accurately plan for the additional manpower and logistics needed to operate in a collective-protection mode. Collective protection does not replace MOPP gear; it only allows the commander to reduce MOPP levels while in a contaminated environment. Collective protection can provide relief from MOPP4 for eating, rest, and hygiene. Understanding entry/exit procedures will greatly impact on the effective use of collective-protection systems.

Types of Collective Protection

CPE provides protection to a group of individuals under NBC conditions that permits relaxation of individual NBC protection. Under NBC conditions, CPE allows soldiers to function effectively. CPE comes to a unit as either a component of a piece of equipment or as a TOE asset. This includes equipment such as the M51 shelter and the M20 SCPE. Used together, these systems enhance a unit's capability to perform its mission in an NBC environment. There are four basic types of CPE: vent ventilated-facepiece, overpressure, hybrid, and total systems (Table 6-1). See Table 6-2 for the advantages and disadvantages of each system.

Table 6-1. Types of collective-protection systems for vehicles and fixed facilities.			
System	Description	Conditions Justifying the Requirement	Example Systems
Ventilated Facepiece	Series of individual respiratory systems (or masks) serviced by a common filter.	• Clean working area subject to inadvertent entry of contamination. • High work rate, reduced breathing resistance. • Frequent entry and exit movements. • Brief inside occupation.	• Infantry fighting vehicles. • Self -propelled howitzers.
Overpressure	A collective NBC filter and overpressure system inside a vehicle or shelter	• Critical manual dexterity skills. • Limited entry and exit movements. • Lengthy inside occupation.	• Air defense. • Communications. • Medical. • Patient evacuation vehicles. • Maintenance and supply sites. • Rest and relief.
Hybrid	Combination of overpressure and ventilated-facepiece systems.	• Flexibility • Lengthy inside occupation. • Emergency entry and exit movements.	• Armored fighting vehicles (tanks). • Helicopters. • Air defense. • Multiple launcher rocket systems.
Total	Hybrid or overpressure plus an environmental control system. Other categories may also incorporate environmental control; for example, ventilated facepiece and microclimatic cooling.	• Same as hybrid. • Extreme climates.	• Same as hybrid.

Table 6-2. Advantages and disadvantages of collective-protection systems.		
System	Advantages	Disadvantages
Ventilated-facepiece	•Reduces stress from breathing resistance. •Reduces eye-lens fogging. •Allows open-hatch operations. •Increases protection level of the mask.	•Requires that users wear MOPP gear. •Is attached by umbilical cord. •Does not protect vehicle interior from vapor contamination.
Overpressure	•Allows reduction of MOPP level. •Reduces vapor contamination inside the vehicle. •Can provide relief from continuous wear of MOPP gear.	•Requires closed-mode operations for safe unmasking. •Requires entry and exit procedures. •Increases logistical support requirements.
Hybrid (overpressure mode)	•Allows reduction of MOPP level. •Reduces vapor contamination inside the vehicle. •Can provide relief from continuous wear of MOPP gear.	•Requires closed-hatch operations for safe unmasking. •Requires entry and exit procedures. •Increases logistical support requirements.
Hybrid (ventilated-facepiece mode)	•Reduces breathing resistance of the masks. •Reduces eye-lens fogging. •Allows open-hatch operations. •Increases protection level of masks.	•Requires that users wear MOPP gear. •Does not protect vehicle interior from contamination. •Is attached by umbilical cord.
Total	•Same as the hybrid system. •Reduces heat-stress casualties.	•Same as the hybrid system. •Increases logistical burden, primarily maintenance.

Ventilated-Facepiece System

Ventilated-facepiece systems supply filtered air to the protective mask canisters (both the M25A1 and M42 masks) of combat vehicle crew members and the M24 and M43 aircrew protective masks. The systems are assigned as GPFUS and are rated by their airflow capacity, in cubic feet per minute. The currently fielded systems are given in Table 6-3. Except for the M13A I GPFU, the components of these systems are similar.

Table 6-3. GPFU fielded systems.	
Number of GPFUs/System	System
1	M60 Tank
1	M60A1 Tank
1	M60A2 Tank
1	M60A3 Tank
1	M728 Combat Engineer Vehicle
1	M1 Tank
1	M1A1 Tank

The filtered, pressurized air supplied to individuals extends the MOPP gear's capabilities. It reduces breathing resistance through masks, and it aids in sweat evaporation. In addition, it can provide warm air to facepieces in cold weather.

Overpressure System

An overpressure system is an enclosure of pressurized; purified air. Gas and particulate filters remove any NBC contamination from the air. The system does not protect against gamma radiation or neutrons. The air pressure precludes leakage of contaminated air into the enclosure. Personnel enter and exit through a protective entrance. This entrance is an air lock, and it prevents contamination from entering the enclosure. Overpressure systems for fixed sites are discussed in detail in FM 3-4-1.

M51 Shelter System

The M51 shelter is a trailer-mounted system (Figure 6-1). It features an overpressure and environmental control system. The shelter is predominately used by battalion aid stations and other medical units. It can also be used as a temporary rest and relief shelter.

Figure 6-1. M51 shelter system.

M20 Simplified Collective-Protection Equipment

The SCPE provides a clean-air shelter for use against chemical and biological warfare agents and radioactive particles (Figure 6-2). It is lightweight and mobile, and it allows

136

unit commanders to convert existing structures into protected command, control, and operations centers. Just as the M51, the SCPE can be used as a temporary rest and relief shelter (for example, as a break area for personnel working in heavy maintenance and supply operations) or as a command and control center. It provides a contamination-free environment in which 10 soldiers can work, eat, or rest without the encumbrance of the IPE. The M20 can be erected without the liner using only the protective entrance and blower compartment. Places such as a bank vault or warehouse freezer are examples of where an M20 without liner can be placed. Any cracks or holes will need to be sealed in the doorway. A bib section is available that will fit between the protective entrance and the frame of any door, and when taped down, seals the entrance from outside contamination. Entry and exit restrictions remain the same. For guidance on maintenance and parts of the SCPE see TM 3-4240-288-12&P.

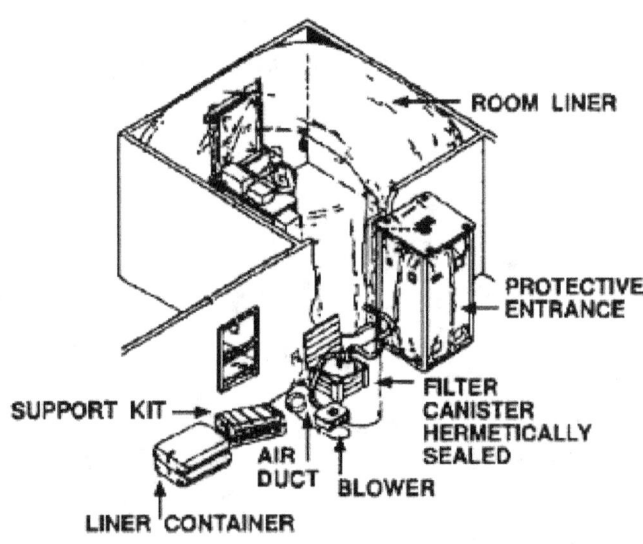

Figure 6-2. Simplified collective-protection equipment.

Modular Collective-Protection Equipment

Modular CPE provides positive pressure NBC protection to a variety of vans and shelters. The system includes a variety of equipment, consisting of GPFUs, protective entrances, and various installation kits (Figure 6-3). An example of MCPE application to weapon systems includes mounting on a wheeled or tracked vehicle, on the M292 expandable van, or on a series of vans linked together (Figure 6-4).

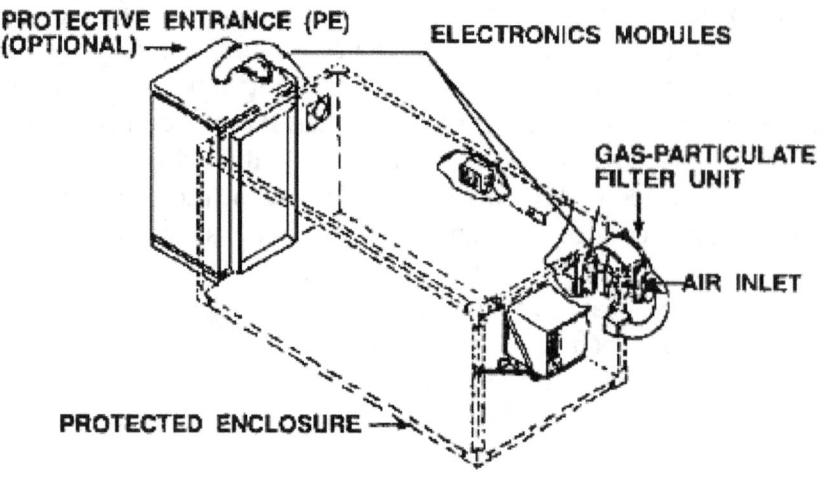

Figure 6-3. Modular collective-protection equipment.

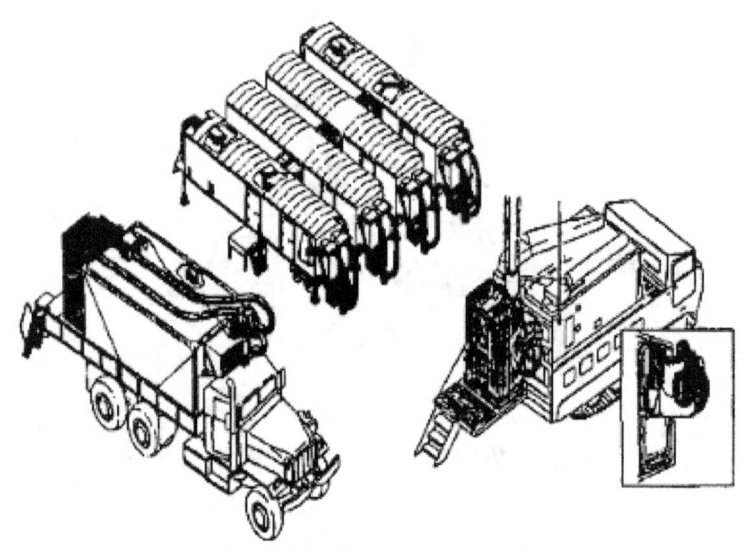

Figure 6-4. Modular CPE examples of application.

Hybrid System

The hybrid system provides protection for personnel in combat vehicles, vans, and shelters. The system combines positive pressure and Ventilated race mask inside the enclosure with the option of using the positive pressure, the ventilated face mask, or both. The system can be used during closed-hatch, positive pressure operations or open-hatch, ventilated face mask operations (Figure 6-5). During open-hatch operations, the positive pressure reduces the amount of vapor contamination that enters. If contamination enters, the system helps purge the interior of toxic vapors. See Figure 6-6 for components of the hybrid system.

138

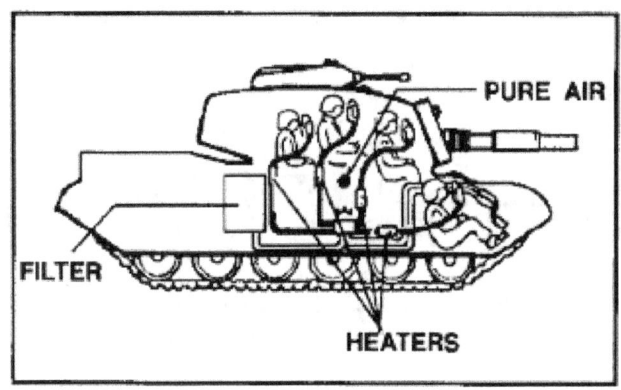

Figure 6-5. Hybrid system.

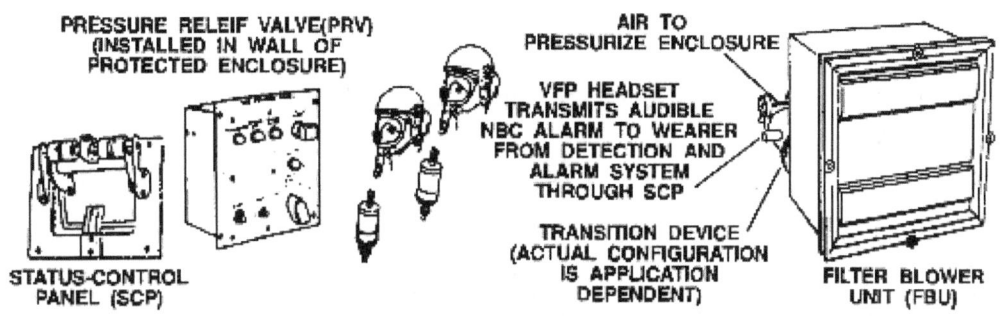

Figure 6-6. Components of hybrid system.

Total System

A hybrid system combines with some form of environmental control to make a total system (Figure 6-7). This system reduces heat-stress casualties; however, it increases the logistical burden, primarily because of maintenance. The M1A1 Abrams main battle tank has a total system. During closed-hatch operations the system provides a positive pressure and crew cooling. During open-hatch operations the system will provide cool, filtered air to the ventilated facepiece and cooling vest. Before initiating open-hatch operations, soldiers must be masked before exiting the M1A1 tank to prevent any possibility of chemical agent exposure. Additionally, the system provides modest overpressure that significantly reduces the amount of contamination infiltrating the crew compartment. Consequently, the time required to purge contamination is reduced.

Figure 6-7. Total system (ventilated facepiece not shown).

Associated Equipment

Collective-protection associated equipment includes cooling and alarm systems and protective entrances.

Cooling Systems

Cooling reduces heat stress in soldiers operating in extremely hot and/or humid conditions. MOPP gear significantly increases the potential for heat stress, making cooling systems desirable. The two basic types are crew compartment and individual. Crew compartment cooling provides air conditioning to the compartment. Individual cooling is more effective when used while MOPP gear is worn. The choice of cooling system depends on the vehicle type and primary mission. The next generation of combat vehicles will provide individual and compartment cooling systems.

Collective-Protection Alarm Systems

Unit TOE chemical detection equipment and warning assets provide area warning to unit positions. These assets will also provide warning to occupants of collective-protection systems. Dedicated alarms are particularly useful for systems that must operate alone and away from supporting units. Unless an alarm is provided, carry out full entry and/or exit procedures whenever anyone enters and/or exits. Even if an alarm is available, occupants must conduct internal monitoring. This can be less frequent than when there is a known external hazard.

Protective Entrances

A protective entrance provides an interface between the contaminated environment and the protected enclosure. It enables shelter users to remove contaminated clothing and perform decontamination procedures, providing a relatively clean environment before entry into the shelter.

In a contaminated environment, overpressure systems not having a protective entrance (air lock) must minimize contamination entering the enclosure. They must establish drills and procedures for this purpose. These systems are usually on smaller, S250-type shelter systems and combat vehicles. An example is a main battle tank. Weight and space constraints make an air lock unfeasible. A system without an air lock consists of a clean shelter area only. During a liquid or vapor chemical attack, the system must remain closed, and soldiers must not enter or exit. Opening the doors allows contamination inside, and the crew must assume a higher MOPP level until the interior is purged or decontaminated.

The disadvantages of systems without an air lock emphasize the need for an air lock in a contaminated environment. An air lock prevents contamination from entering the enclosure. The air lock is pressurized, and contamination is eliminated through the use of filtered air. Air pressure in the entrance is slightly less than that in the protective enclosure, but slightly more than outside pressure. Air passing through the air lock purges contaminants that might enter during entry or exit of personnel or equipment. This air comes from the protective enclosure, the filter unit, or both. Different protective entrance configurations create variations of the overpressure category. These variations are those with a single air lock and those with a two-stage air lock.

Single air lock. In most cases, vans and shelters modified for collective protection use a single-compartment protective entrance. An example is the M12 protective entrance (Figure 6-8). This variation consists of the clean shelter area and an air lock (Figure 6-9). Before entering the air lock from a contaminated area, personnel must remove their MOPP gear except gloves and mask. Minor exposure to chemical agent vapor is possible between overgarment removal and entrance into the air lock. Clothing tends to absorb any chemical agent vapor in the atmosphere during this brief exposure. The amount of agent absorbed depends on agent concentration in the atmosphere, length of exposure, type of agent, type of clothing exposed, and climatic conditions. The air purge in the air lock flushes out the contaminated air brought in. It also reduces the amount of absorbed agent on clothing before the soldier enters the protective shelter. After a soldier and/or piece of equipment enters the protective shelter, monitoring ensures hazardous levels of agent were not carried inside.

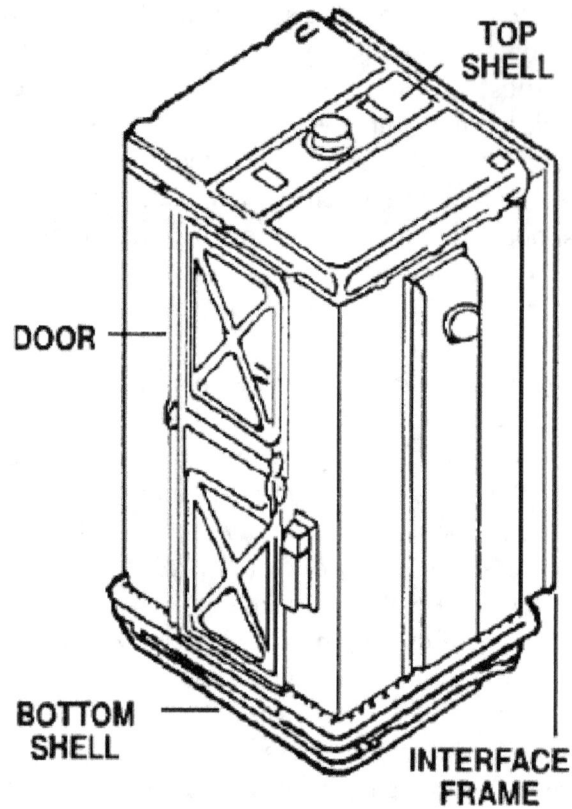

Figure 6-8. M12 protective entrance.

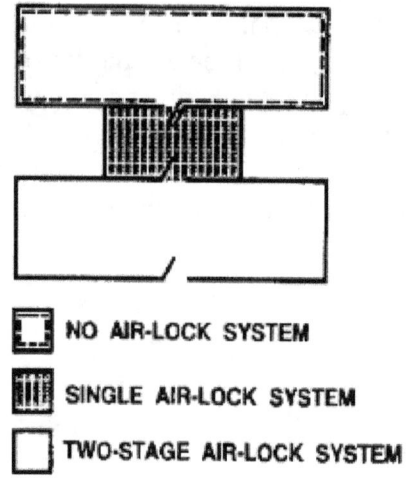

☐ NO AIR-LOCK SYSTEM

▥ SINGLE AIR-LOCK SYSTEM

☐ TWO-STAGE AIR-LOCK SYSTEM

Figure 6-9. Collective-protection entrance configurations.

Two-stage air lock. Adding a contamination control area (CCA) to a single air-lock system creates a two-stage air lock (Figure 6-9). Entering soldiers remove MOPP gear in the CCA. This affords better control of the liquid and vapor hazards of entry and exit.

142

Integral Protective Entrances

Integral protective entrances are designed to offer improved accessibility, more convenient storage and transport, and reduced setup time. There are two types of integral protective entrances: internal and external. Integral protective entrances are smaller than the detachable protective entrances and require less airflow during the purge cycle. The integral protective entrance and the shelter door are provided as a single bolt assembly. Integral protective entrances are currently designed for the S250 and S280 shelters.

Internal integral protective entrance. Deployed internally, the integral protective entrance can remain in its functional configuration and need not be stowed for transport. Since it is contained within the shelter, it is much less vulnerable on the battlefield (Figure 6-10).

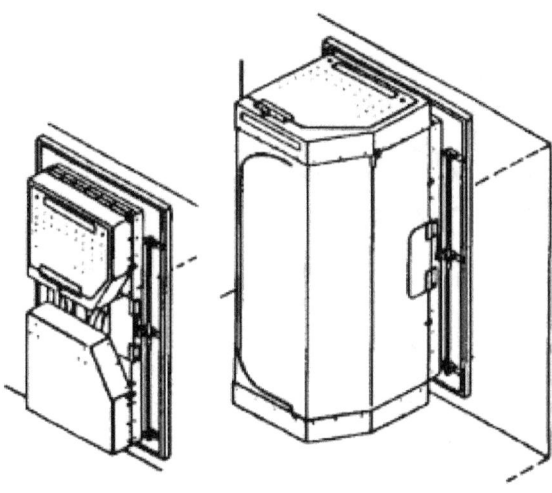

Figure 6-10. Internal integrated protective entrance.

External integral protective entrance. The external integral protective entrance is used for shelters that cannot sacrifice the internal space (Figure 6-11). The self-supporting integral protective entrance must be stowed for transport.

143

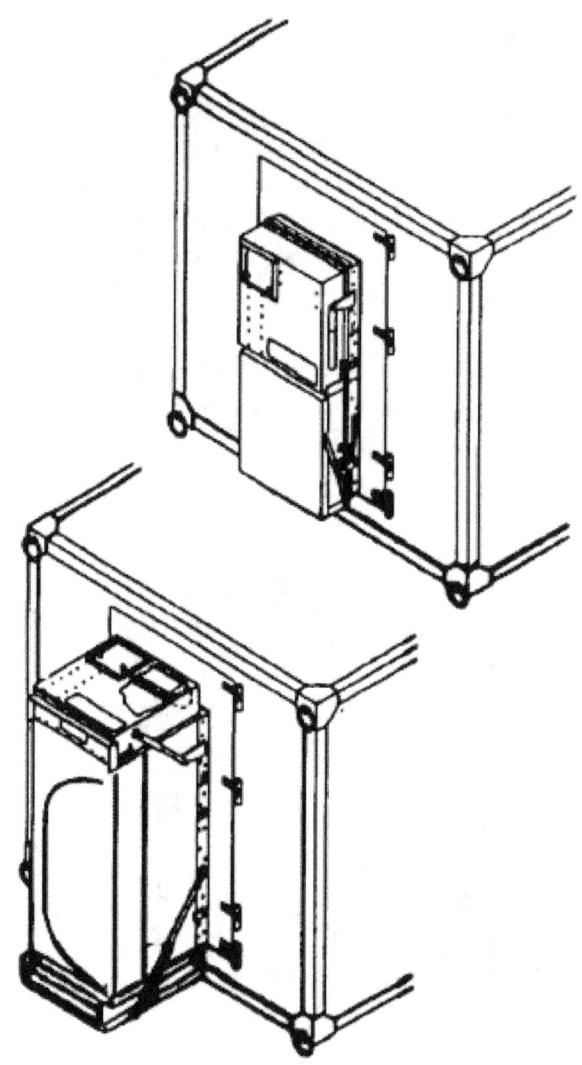

Figure 6-11. External integrated protective entrance.

Field-Expedient Collective Protection

The unventilated shelter is the only type of field-expedient collective protection. Such a shelter has very little value because of the lengthy set-up time and rapid depletion of usable oxygen.

A wide variety of structures may be made into unventilated shelters. Such variety makes specific instructions difficult. Generally, the effectiveness depends largely on the tightness of the seal. The shelter must be airtight, and all openings must remain sealed as long as the hazard exists. Because sealing creates a stagnant air supply inside the shelter, occupancy is limited to a relatively short period.

Collective-Protection Planning

144

Providing for collective protection should bean integral part of plans for the AirLand Battlefield. A protective environment allows soldiers to carry out technical functions without the burden of MOPP gear. Also, soldiers need a protective environment where they can seek relief from MOPP gear. In addition, logistics, manpower, and other considerations enter into the planning for collective protection.

Collective-Protection Uses

Avoiding or displacing from contaminated terrain is desirable. Neither is always possible. It may be necessary to cross, occupy, or remain in contaminated terrain. Otherwise, the enemy could channel our movement and deny us key terrain features that could give our forces a tactical advantage. Every unit is equipped, trained, and conditioned to fight under contaminated conditions when the mission requires. However, individual efficiency and morale may decrease with time, and at some point, relief from wearing MOPP gear is necessary. The best relief method is rotating contaminated soldiers to a known clean area. Even in the worst situations, clean areas exist. Rotation is the least costly in terms of manpower and logistical support. However, the tactical situation may preclude displacement or rotation to clean areas. These situations require collective protection.

Collective-protection systems, like MOPP, are flexible. Flexibility allows the commander to maintain a balance between mission capability and NBC survivability. The commander must consider the threat, mission, tactical environment, and type of collective protection. In assessing a specific situation, the commander must decide if the reduced MOPP levels and relief are worth the additional logistics and manpower burden. For fixed-site collective-protection planning, see FM 3-4-1.

Logistics

Commanders must plan for supplies, maintenance including filter replacement, and transportation to support collective-protection systems.

Supply

Adequate supply planning is a key element in effective use of collective-protection systems. These systems are not supply intensive; however, operation of such systems requires a continuous resupply of consumable and expendable items. Included are items that provide a means of contamination avoidance such as rain gear, ponchos, and plastic bags. These will keep liquid contamination away from the overgarment. Survival under NBC conditions could depend on these items. Therefore, it is not a question of merely maintaining special purpose collective-protection supplies. It is a matter of obtaining needed quantities of existing supplies.

Arrange to have supplies to support extended operations of a shelter kept inside the shelter if possible. Plan for the needed supplies, and stockpile them before an attack. As a minimum, these supplies should include protective clothing, expedient contamination avoidance items, decon kits, detector kits, and filters. These will allow shelter users to conduct an exchange. Provide adequate food and water if the shelter will operate for long periods within the contaminated area. If the shelter requires fuel, ensure it is requisitioned and stored. If the system has an external power supply, store fuel outside and away from the shelter. Plan for supplies to maintain operation of personnel in the shelter. These supplies include pens, paper, batteries, and parts.

Maintenance

In most cases, maintenance of collective-protection systems is minimal at organizational levels. Most systems have little or no operators' maintenance other than before-, during-, and after-operation checks and services. Operators may need to reset circuit breakers or perform system start-up procedures. At the unit level, maintenance is usually limited to troubleshooting and removal and/or replacement of major components or major subassemblies.

Changing expended or contaminated filters is the most significant maintenance task. During GPFU operation, soldiers in charge of protective shelters must be aware of the need for replacing filters. Both the gas and particulate filters require periodic replacement.

Gas filter. The useful life of a gas filter decreases as operating time and exposure increase. As the filter removes contaminants from the air, its residual capacity decreases. Long exposure to moisture also decreases filter capacity for removing chemical agents. Gas filter life expectancy varies. It depends on the size and design of the collective-protection hardware. To determine when to replace a gas filter, the shelter attendant or another responsible soldier must maintain a log of the filter unit operation. Then soldiers should change gas filters according to the system's technical manual. In general, new filters can withstand several chemical attacks. In most cases, missions of 48 to 72 hours can be accomplished in a contaminated environment without a filter change. Given this capacity, filter change during periodic unit maintenance is often advisable. Soldiers should change filters with the same criteria they use for mask filters (see Chapter 2). Coordinate filter change operations with the unit chemical NCO.

Particulate filter. Within the GPFU, a particulate filter collects radiological contamination and other particles from the air. Such accumulation on the filter does not decrease its filtering efficiency. It does decrease the airflow because of the increase in resistance. In most cases, this increase in resistance is very gradual. It is unusual for the airflow resistance to increase to a level that affects the flow rate appreciably. Personnel should replace this filter at the same time they replace the gas filter or when the system drops below the minimum overpressure level specified in the system's technical manual.

Contaminated-filter disposal. Filters do not decontaminate or neutralize contamination; they merely collect and contain it. Therefore, contaminated filters are hazardous. Replacing and disposing of these filters require care to prevent a hazard to personnel or a spread of contamination. Burning does not destroy radiological contamination; therefore, soldiers should bury filters contaminated with radioactive particles, Depth of burial depends on the radiation intensity and soil conditions. Generally, burial under 3 feet of packed earth is adequate. This depth reduces the exposure hazard to less that 1 percent of the initial exposure hazard. (See FM 3-3 for further guidance.) Soldiers must mark burial sites with contamination markers. They must bury or burn filters contaminated with chemical or live biological agents or toxins. If burning is selected, they should place the filters in a pit, soak them with fuel, and ignite them. The heat of combustion kills most biological agents in the filter.

Commanders should establish detailed procedures for filter disposal during peacetime and wartime situations.

Transportation

Collective-protection systems may or may not have organic transportation. For a maneuver unit, the decision to carry a shelter or components is a matter of priority. For example, there may be no indication the threat will employ chemical agents, or the tactical situation may be unsuitable for collective protection; therefore, the maneuver commander may decide not to transport the M51 or SCPE into battle. On the other hand, the threat may be actively employing chemical agents, or the tactical situation may be suitable for employment of collective protection. The commander may choose to accept the transportation burden for the advantage of a readily available shelter system. When the decision is made against having shelter assets in the maneuver units, based on the IPB, these assets should be retained in the unit trains area ready for use. This allows a quick response to changes in the tactical situation.

Manpower

Manpower planning for collective-protection systems encompasses several factors while in MOPP4. These include set-up and tear-down times, lost time from entry and exit procedures, and shelter security. Commanders must estimate these requirements based on information in the next paragraphs.

Set-Up and Tear-Down Times

Table 6-4 shows approximate set-up and tear-down times. These are only estimates. Actual times will vary with the situation and degree of training.

System	Set-Up[1]		Tear-Down	
	Personnel in MOPP4	Time (min)	Personnel in MOPP4	Time (min)
Simplified Collective-Protection Equipment M20	2	30[2]	2	10[3]
Modular Collective-Protection Equipment	2	10[4]	2	5
M51 Shelter	5	30[5]	5	30

Table 6-4. Shelter set-up and tear-down times.

[1] Only set-up time and not fully operational time.
[2] Does not include time to seal a room when the liner is not used.
[3] Based on disposing of the room liner in place.
[4] Protective entrance only.
[5] Site-prep and stake-down times not included.

Entry Times

Commanders should estimate entry processing times for units based on the MOPP gear doffing times in Table 6-5.

Table 6-5. Entry process times.

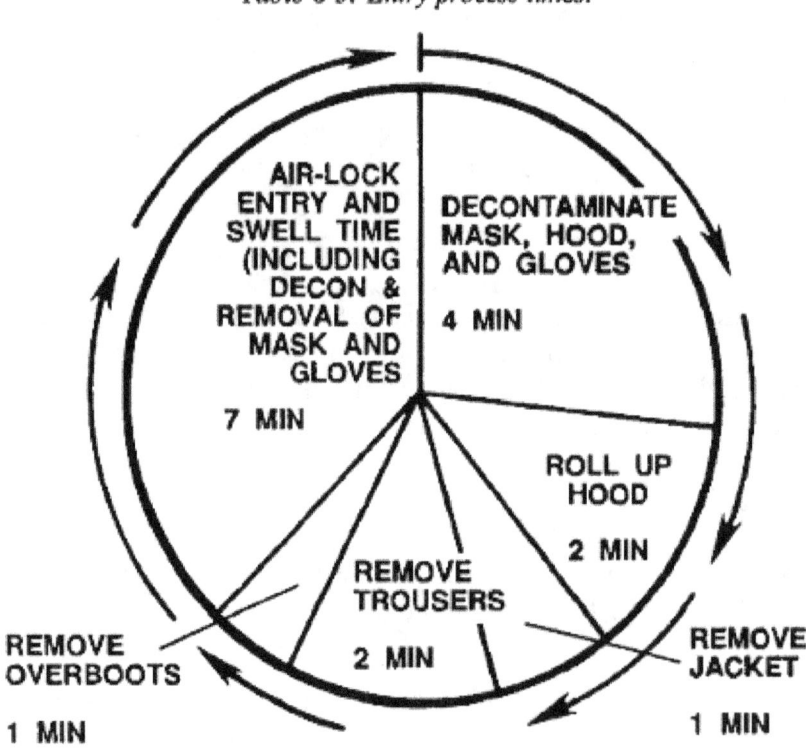

Shelter Security

Commanders must ensure that security is maintained around any protective shelter. Security requirements depend on the tactical situation. Type and strength of a security element depend upon several factors. These are the type of operation being conducted at

148

the shelter, location on the battlefield, and personnel available to protect the shelter. Physical security involves the immediate area around the shelter and shelter entrances.

Patrols, OPs, or both protect the area around the shelter. The best means of physical security are OPs. Position an OP where observers can give early warning to the main shelter area of any unusual activity or an attack. Several OPs provide overlapping observation around the shelter operation area. Where terrain restricts effective observation or the number of personnel prohibits sufficient OPs, patrols can maintain security. Shelters with high entry/exit require attendants. Post attendants at the shelter entrance to control entry, They should also assist in the external operations of the shelter. Exact duties before, during, and after an NBC attack should be outlined in the unit SOP. Soldiers assigned as shelter attendants and their duties will be discussed later in the chapter.

WARNING

Burning filters contaminated with chemical agents or toxins may produce a downwind vapor hazard. Warn units downwind. After burning, cover ashes with the excavated dirt and mark the site with contamination markers, Disposal of any filters after normal maintenance in peacetime also requires special handling and disposal of these as hazardous waste. This includes all mask filters and canisters and collective-protection equipment filters. Material that has been determined to be hazardous waste must be transported, stored, treated, and disposed of as such.

Other Requirements

These requirements are already a part of the commander's planning. However, commanders must readdress each of these to consider the effect of collective protection.

Communications

Personnel use wire communication systems to communicate with those in adjacent shelters or immediately outside the shelter. They may require radios for communications with adjacent units some distance away. If they use radio systems, they should remote the antennas away from the shelter. If possible, they should place antennas so that a hill or other obstacle is between antennas and the enemy.

Latrines

Collective-protection shelters may include sanitary facilities. If the shelter is in a permanent structure, use existing facilities. Consider the location of existing sanitary facilities in selecting a portion of the building for a soldier relief facility. Where water and sewage facilities are not available, provide covered containers or chemical toilets.

Illumination

Have lights installed if power is available, and also always provide battery-operated lights for emergency use. Keep electric light usage to a minimum to prevent excessive heat buildup in the shelter. An alternative would be to use cold light sources such as chemical safety lights (chem-lites). Take blackout precautions where required. Ensure that lights needed to service filter units or generators are shielded from the enemy.

Camouflage

Construct or emplace shelter sites in areas that provide cover and/or concealment. Dense woods or urban areas are best. Commanders must ensure that construction and emplacement actions are well camouflaged.

Water

Have filled canteens or other water containers placed inside the shelter. Provide each occupant at least 3 quarts of drinking water for each day of anticipated occupancy. Even if piped water is available, maintain an emergency reserve of drinking water. Additional water may be needed for hygiene.

Warning and Detection

Plan for warning and chemical detection devices: M8A1, M256-series kits, or a CAM in each protective shelter. These devices serve several purposes. They detect an NBC attack and determine if the shelter interior is contaminated. These devices also monitor soldiers going through decon and determine when soldiers can safely leave the shelter. In addition, they warn of shelter system failure.

Operation of Collective-Protection Systems

Collective protection does not replace MOPP gear nor the MOPP doctrine. For example, the ventilated-facepiece system enhances MOPP gear protection. Overpressure systems create an artificial environment. This changes the nature of the NBC threat and allows the commander to order lower MOPP levels. Commanders and soldiers should be familiar with several actions before, during and after an NBC attack to make the use of collective-protection systems more efficient and effective.

Actions Before an Attack

Before an NBC attack occurs, several actions should make the use of collective protection easier.

Commanders should--

- Determine appropriate MOPP levels.
- Accomplish collective-protection planning.
- Ensure personnel are accounted for and briefed on the threat situation.

Individual soldiers should--

- Assume the appropriate MOPP level.
- Check protection system for proper operation.
- Know entry and exit procedures, but these do not have to be followed until an actual agent attack.
- Accomplish individual protective actions.

Before an attack the shelter attendant should--

- Inspect and maintain the shelter filter system.
- Inspect and maintain the communication system.
- Know entry and exit procedures.

Actions During an Attack

During an attack, suspend or minimize entry into the shelter. Shelter attendant should--

- Don mask and alert shelter occupants.
- Aid in securing air lock doors.
- Prevent unauthorized personnel from entering the shelter.
- Test periodically for contamination.

If entry from a con ted environment is mission essential, internal monitoring becomes critical. Faulty entry and exit procedures may cause hazardous contamination levels inside. Vapor absorbed into clothing can do the same. To minimize this risk, use the following procedures:

- Monitor the shelter interior every 15 minutes using detector/monitoring equipment.
- If hazardous level of agent are detected inside' suspend shelter operations. Soldiers should assume the appropriate MOPP level and evacuate the shelter.

However, if mission dictates, the commander my elect to have soldiers don their protective masks to continue to opeate inside the shelter. This may lengthen the time required to purge the shelter and restore safe conditions. When detector/monitoring equipment no longer indicates the presence of contamination inside, proceed with unmasking procedures and then resume shelter operations.

Further actions during an attack will depend on the type of collective protection. Systems that are components of a weapon system or TOE assets require separate explanations.

✱✱ Weapon-Systems Collective Protection

** Soldiers in weapon systems with collective protection should anticipate the attack. They must be at the same MOPP level as the other soldiers or be protected by having the collective-protection system functioning. Those who are protected by the collective-protection system may continue at the reduced MOPP levels shown in Table 6-5. Those who are not protected by collective protection when an attack occurs should activate the collective-protection system and assume MOPP4. They must remain at that level until the shelter interior is purged. Required purge times vary with the interior shelter volume and the airflow. Check specific technical manuals for each system. When the required purge time passes, soldiers should unmask as outlined in STP 21-24-SMCT. When the all-clear signal is given, soldiers may resume the modified MOPP level shown in Table 6-5.

During an attack, restrict entry and exit. No personnel or equipment should enter or exit except when absolutely mission essential. When an entry must be made, monitor the interior air. Use detector/monitor equipment and determine if the entry introduced contaminants. If the test detects a chemical agent, assume MOPP3 or MOPP4. Purge the air until tests are negative, and then perform the unmasking procedures. After the all-clear signal, soldiers may assume modified MOPP levels.

** TOE Collective-Protection Systems

The commander decides whether or not to use TOE collective-protection assets. Basis for the decision is the determination that more effective command and control, less performance degradation, or relief from MOPP gear is mission essential. If this decision is made in anticipation of an attack, no special set-up procedures are necessary. However, if the decision is made after the attack occurs, soldiers erecting the shelter must carefully avoid transferring liquid contamination to the shelter interior. Also, the interior air must be purged as specified in the TM for the system. Next, the air must be tested continuously with detector/monitoring equipment until the reading is negative. If operations begin before the purge is complete soldiers must maintain mask-onlyposture until they receive the all clear signal.

**

Table 6-6. Collective-protection MOPP levels				
Soldiers Not in Collective Protection			**Soldiers in Collective Protection**	
MOPP Level	MOPP Gear		Ventilated Facepiece	Overpressure
Zero	Overgarment Overboots & Helmet Cover Mask & Hood Gloves	Available Available Carried Available	• Assume MOPP Zero	• Assume MOPP Zero. • Overpressure off.
1	Overgarment Overboots & Helmet Cover Mask & Hood Gloves	Worn Available Carried Available	• Assume MOPP 1	• Assume MOPP Zero or MOPP1. • Overpressure on.
2	Overgarment Overboots & Helmet Cover Mask & Hood Gloves	Worn Worn Carried Available	• Assume MOPP2	• Assume MOPP Zero or MOPP1. • Overpressure on. • Entry and exit procedure not required.
3	Overgarment Overboots & Helmet Cover Mask & Hood Gloves	Worn Worn Worn Available	• Assume MOPP3 or MOPP4 * • When mounted, connect ventilated facepiece to mask	• Maintain MOPP Zero or MOPP1 unless interior is contaminated. • Overpressure on. • Entry/exit procedures required if an attack occurs.
4	Overgarment Overboots & Helmet Cover Mask & Hood Gloves	Worn Worn Worn Worn	• Assume MOPP3 or MOPP4 * • When mounted, connect ventilated facepiece to mask.	• Maintain MOPP Zero or MOPP1 unless interior is contaminated. • Overpressure on. • Entry/exit procedures required if an attack occurs.

* During an engagement, the commander may allow personnel protected for liquid agents to operate temporarily without protective gloves. This option could slightly increase the potential for casualties.

** Limiting entry and exit of collective-protection systems contamination entry. When entry must be performed, soldiers must monitor the interior. This ensures contaminantes have not entered. To minimize entry and exit requirements, the conunander may choose to locate outside the shelter and let the staff operate inside. A liaison officer, appointed by the commander coordinates between the commander, staff, and troops. Direct coordination with troops and staff consumes a large portion of time performing entry and exit procedures.

** When a collective-protection system is used for relief from MOPP gear, the commander must ensure coordination of certain arrangements. These include MOPP-gear resupply and security. Shelters used for soldier relief require a great number of entry and exit cycles. In addition, soldiers must continuously monitor shelter operations. This monitoring ensures the system functions properly and that no contaminants have entered the system.

** Actions after an attack

** Vapor and liquid contamination hazard may remain for some time after an attack. Once it is determined that a hazard no longer exists, con ted soldiers should conduct decon IAW FM 3-5. Soldiers also must take the following actions:

- Ensure contaminated items are not stowed in CPE.
- Acquire decon support if required.

- Resupply expendable, such as IPE, mask and shelter filters, and individual decon kits.
- Continue entry and exit procedures until one hour after detectors indicate the absence of agent vapors outside the shelter.
- Resume before-attack actions, but continue periodic monitoring of shelter interior with detector/monitoring equipment.

After an attack, the shelter attendant will-

- Pass the all clear signal to the shelter occupants when safe to do so.
- Service the filter system if needed.
- Assist entry and exit procedures.
- Continue attendant duties.

Entry and Exit Procedures for Collective-Protection Systems

Entry and exit are slow and risky procedures; therefore, the commander must allow only those soldiers that are mission essential to enter and exit. Entry and exit are the procedures between individual protection and collective protection. Step-by-step instructions allow for safe transition from individual to collective protection and back. Differences between procedures depend on two variables: the type of MOPP gear and the type of collective protection. Two possible MOPP gear ensemble combinations are used in the examples to follow.

- Ground-troop IPE--field protective mask with hood, carrier, helmet with chemical protective cover, individual weapon, armored vest (if worn), and MOPP gear.
- Combat vehicle and aircrew IPE--tank or aircraft mask with hood, combat vehicle crewman or aircraft crewman helmet, individual weapon, armored vest (if worn), and MOPP gear.

Each ensemble and type of enclosure have certain characteristics that dictate different steps. Therefore, procedures for a particular combination are a composite of general guidelines for individual and collective protection. Entry and exit procedures in this chapter illustrate the necessity to modify procedures based on their application and system configuration. Procedures presented here give steps common "to all entry and exit procedures. Actual procedures for a particular system should be more specific. These are in the system's technical manual, and they should also appear in the unit SOP. Guidelines for an SOP are at Appendix B.

Collective-Protection Shelter or Van With an Air Lock

Select a site for shelter erection that is free of liquid contamination. Soldiers setting up the shelter (either M51 or SCPE) should perform steps 1 through 9 of the entry procedures. They should do this before entering the selected set-up site or handling unpackaged liners or support-kit components.

If setting up a shelter where the external agent concentration produces a relative hazard reading of one bar or less on the CAM (indication that no agent is present), entry into the shelter is unlimited. Where the external concentration of agent produces a CAM reading of a seven-bar or more, entries should be discontinued unless they are mission essential.

Soldiers entering the shelter should follow the entry instructions when liquid contamination is detected or suspected on their overgarments, Establish a hot line at least 4 feet from the air lock. Check the floor area between the hot line and the entrance for evidence of liquid contamination. Use both visual check and detector/monitoring equipment. If contamination is present, decontaminate this area; cover it with a plastic sheet, poncho, or similar material; or find another area if possible. If possible, remove overgarments in a room or covered area that is separate from the room in which the entrance is located, and establish the hot line at the doorway between the two rooms. Keep the room with the air lock as clean as possible.

Equipment

Allow no equipment to enter the shelter unless it is known to be free of contamination. Pre-position decon kits, alarms, detector kit samplers, and a CAM inside the air lock. These components require periodic replenishment, depending on the frequency of entries. The CAM will require fresh batteries based on the technical manual guidance.

Entry Instructions for Ground-Troop Ensemble

It is best to doff (remove) items from top to bottom because upper parts of the ensemble overlap lower parts. This order minimizes contamination transfer. Soldiers can perform entry steps with or without assistance from a buddy or shelter attendant. However, soldiers can perform some steps more easily and safely with help. Therefore, the buddy system is strongly recommended. Soldiers in the ground-troop ensemble should use the following 13 steps:

Step 1. Use detector paper to determine areas of gross liquid contamination on your equipment and garments. Give special emphasis to these areas, and use field-expedient absorbents, such as sand, dirt, or rags, to remove the gross liquid contamination. Take special care to avoid touching these areas during overgarment doffing.

Note: If a radiological or biological hazard is present, lightly wipe down the overgarment with hot, soapy water prior to entry into the shelter. This will dampen the overgarment and reduce any secondary aerolization of either radiological or biological contamination while conducting doffing procedures.

Step 2. Remove LCE, mask carrier, and helmet before crossing into the shelter. If the hood is worn over the LCE, loosen the hood straps. Remove your M258A1 or M291 and your M1/M1A1 waterproof bag, and take them with you.

Step 3. Untie the ankle cords, and open the velcro and zippers of both trouser legs.

Step 4. Undo rear snaps of jacket. Leaving top snap closed, undo the remaining two front snaps. Untie waist cords, but leave zipper closed.

Step 5. Undo shoulder straps. Remove them from beneath the arms and reattach them over the shoulder. (Use assistance if possible.) Loosen the neck cord. Decontaminate your mask and hood with your M258A1/M291 skin decon kit. The M258A1 decon kit is a two-packet, two-step process. Use both packets over the same area. Take special care to decontaminate around the eye lenses, inlets, and voicemitter. Decon solutions may leave a residue on the eye lenses. To prevent this, reverse the order of application of the decon packets. Use packet 2 first and then use packet 1. The M291 decon kit replaces the M258A1 and is a single-packet, one-step application. Instructions are included in the M291 packet. Open the packet, slip fingers into the pad, strap, and decon your mask and hood thoroughly.

WARNING

Do not reverse the order of the packets in the M258A1 kit when decontaminating skin. It may cause burns.

The M291 can also be used to decontaminate equipment that needs to be taken into the shelter.

Step 6. Decontaminate gloves before rolling hood. (Use assistance if possible.) Leave the hood zipper closed. Grasp the hood by the straps and lift the hood off your shoulders and partially off your head until most of the back of your head is exposed. Roll the hood. Start at your chin, making sure the zipper and neck cord are tucked into the roll, and work around the entire mask until the rolled hood will stay up, off your shoulders. Roll the hood tightly against your mask without pulling the hood off the back of your head.

Note: If your assistant is also entering the shelter, steps 1 through 6 should be performed on him or her before proceeding to step 7.

Step 7. Undo the top jacket snap, and open the jacket zipper. With one hand, pull the sleeve band over your hand without loosening your glove (make a fist if necessary). Remove that arm from the sleeve. Repeat for your other arm. Place jacket away from the entry path.

Step 8. Stand against a wall or other support for balance, and unsnap and unzip your trousers. (Use assistance if possible.) Pull or have the assistant pull your trousers over the heels of your chemical overboots/GVOs for removal, or "walk" the trousers off. To do this, alternately lift one foot while holding trouser material to the ground with your other foot. Leave the overboots or GVOs on, and place trousers away from the entry path.

Note: Your assistant, if also entering the shelter, should perform steps 7 and 8 now before proceeding to step 9.

Step 9. Air-lock entry.

a. Ground-based shelter with air-lock entry is not applicable to the Patriot. NOTE: Specific reference to the M14 protective entrance (PE) does not appear in this manual.

b. For a van with air lock go up the steps, and loosen your overboot laces or GVO clasps. Open the door. Remove one overboot or GVO at a time, toss it away from the steps, and step into the air lock with your exposed field boot. Do not touch exposed field boots on the exterior platform surface or stairs after removing your overboots or GVOs.

Note: When you are operating an air-lock system in a contaminated environment, the protective entrance and shelter interior must be monitored with detection equipment.

Step 10. Enter air lock and ensure door is closed. When the low pressure indicator light in the PE module goes out, rotate the purge time clockwise to its full extent. Do not set the purge time until after the low pressure light goes out.

Step 11. Decontaminate your gloves again. Then decontaminate the bottom (rolled portion) of your hood. Wait for completion of the purge cycle. When the timer bell sounds, loosen your gloves but do not remove them yet.

Step 12. A trained operator will use the CAM, if available, to detect and indicate the relative level of chemical agent vapor hazard present on personnel/clothing/equipment as well as the interior of the PE/shelter.

When sampling results are negative, stop breathing (hold your breath), remove your mask and hood, and place them in your Ml/M1A1 waterproof bag. Remove

---

WARNING

Suspected false positive reading must be verified with other monitoring equipment such as M8/M9 paper and M256 detector kit before proceeding further.

---

your gloves and drop them to the floor. Carry the M1/M1A1 with you.

Step 13. Enter the shelter and resume breathing.

WARNING

When entries are performed in a contaminated environment, monitor every 30 minutes. If detector/monitoring shows positive, all personnel should mask until the source of the contamination is located and removed and/or further tests indicate the contamination is no

---

Exit Instructions for Ground-Troop Ensemble

Overgarment donning procedures for exiting the shelter are less time-consuming and risky than doffing procedures. Whenever possible, ensure replacement or spare overgarments are pre-positioned inside the shelter. For systems with a high rate of entry and exit, commanders must provide for periodic resupply of spare overgarments. Soldiers should follow these four steps:

Step 1: Put on clean overgarments, overboots, and gloves inside the shelter.

Step 2: Check the compartment control module (CCM) to ensure the air lock (M14 PE) is unoccupied. Stop breathing, and step into the entrance taking your M1/M1A1 bag with you.

Step 3: Open the M1/M1A1 bag, remove your mask by the straps with one hand, and make sure the hood is inside out over the front. Place your mask to your chin and face, and pull the head harness over your head. Tighten cheek straps, clear and seal your mask, and resume breathing. Unroll the hood. Pull the hood over your head, attach the straps, and tighten the neck cord.

Step 4: Exit the air lock and ensure the PE door is fully closed after exiting.

Entry Instructions for Combat Vehicle and Aircrew IPE

Use of the CVC mask (M25-series/M42) or aircraft crewman helmet with a different mask (M24/M43) configuration requires differences in removing and handling the hood. The microphone cord hangs down to the shoulders. It can transfer contamination if not secured to the helmet in some way. The microphone boom must be tucked in well against the helmet; otherwise, it snags the hood. In addition, the main power cord extends beyond the hood. If contaminated, it will be very difficult to decontaminate. To avoid these problems, soldiers should use the following four steps:

Step 1. If you wear your vehicle helmet underneath your hood, the first step is to remove the hood (from back to front) from your helmet. Then remove it from around the eye lenses and then from the filter hose. If you wear your hood underneath your helmet, remove your helmet first. Then remove the hood from your mask in the manner described.

Step 2. With mask and helmet (if applicable) still on, remove your overgarment jacket and trousers. Use the same basic procedures outlined for troops in the ground-troop ensemble, with one exception. When performing the doffing procedure, bend at your waist to prevent the filter canister and hose from touching you when your overgarment is being removed.

WARNING

Ensure the undressing area is well ventilated, and remove contaminated overgarment from the hot line area to avoid buildup of vapor.

Step 3. Proceed to the air lock or hot line. Remove boots as you step into the air lock.

Step 4. Just before entering the protective enclosure, remove your mask, helmet, add gloves. Seal your mask inside your M1/M1A1 bag and enter the enclosure.

Note: For systems without an air lock, remove your mask, helmet, and gloves only after tests indicate the absence of vapor. Place your mask inside your M1/M1A1 bag and seal the bag.

WARNING

Do not touch the eye lens area or the canister hose. These are difficult to decontaminate and are potential transfer hazards.

Exit Instructions for Combat Vehicles and Aircrew IPE

Overgarment donning procedures for exiting the shelter are less time-consuming and risky than doffing procedures. Whenever possible, ensure replacement or spare overgarments are pre-positioned inside the shelter. For systems with a high rate of entry and exit, commanders must provide for periodic resupply of spare overgarments. Soldiers should follow these four steps:

Note: For systems without an air lock, all soldiers don MOPP gear before anyone exits the protective enclosure. After the exit, those remaining reseal and purge the enclosure. When vapor contamination drops below detection levels, the remaining soldiers can follow unmasking procedures.

Step 1. Put on clean overgarment, overboots or GVOs, and gloves inside the shelter.

Step 2. Check to ensure the air lock is unoccupied. Stop breathing, and step into the entrance, taking your M1/M1A1 bag with you.

Step 3. Open the M1/M1A1 bag, don mask, and put on gloves. (Note: A bib section is available that will fit between the protective entrance and the frame of any door, and when taped down, seals the entrance from outside contamination. Entry and exit restrictions remain the same.) For guidance on maintenance and parts of the SCPE see TM 3-4240-288-12&P.

Hatch Vehicular System Without an Air Lock

These procedures are for entering and exiting a tank in a chemical environment. These procedures can be modified for shelters without an air lock. Before exiting for mission-essential tasks, soldiers should don their SCALP or another expedient contamination avoidance item, if available, or rain gear over their MOPP gear. When they complete the tasks, they should remove any expedient contamination avoidance items or rain gear in a top-to-bottom sequence. They must avoid touching clean overgarments with the cover exterior. If heavy liquid contamination is present and/or additional overgarments are available, soldiers must perform two doffing procedures--one for the cover and one for the overgarment.

Entry and exit procedures detailed here assume the following conditions:

- Tank exterior is contaminated.
- Crew is operating "buttoned up" with the NBC overpressure system on.
- Crew is wearing all protective clothing (except mask and gloves).
- Exit is for a mission-essential task, such as corrective maintenance.
- Overpressure system remains on throughout the exit and entry cycle.
- Tactical situation is relatively safe, such as in rearming and/or refueling operations.
- The tank is not under fire.
- Contact with the enemy is unlikely.
- Immediate movement is not anticipated.

Entry Instructions

If you are the loader, perform steps 1 through 8. If you are not the loader, when the loader completes step 8, perform step 1 and then steps 4 through 8. If you are the last soldier in, close the hatch. With hatch closed, the crew performs steps 9 through 12.

Step 1. Mount the tank over the left front road wheel.

Step 2. Decontaminate the hatches and area around the hatch (approximately 4 feet in diameter) using either the M11 or M13 DAP. Acquire the water can from the left bustle rack.

Step 3. After the required stand time, flush the decontaminant from the loader's hatch and surrounding area.

Step 4. Stand next to the loader's hatch and remove any field-expedient contamination avoidance items or rain gear jacket. Take care not to touch the exterior of any field-expedient contamination avoidance items, rain gear, or gloves to your overgarment. Discard the removed items over the side.

Step 5. Loosen the rain trousers, if worn. Roll them with clean side out while pulling them down to your ankles. Do not allow the contaminated side of field-expedient contamination avoidance items, or rain gear, or the contaminated gloves to touch your overgarment. Discard rain trousers over the side.

Step 6. Lift one foot and remove the boot cover. Discard it over the side of the tank, and place that foot with exposed boot inside the decontaminated area. Repeat this procedure for your other foot.

Step 7. Decontaminate your gloves with your personal decon kit, and discard the used wipes over the side.

Step 8. Lower yourself into the tank.

Step 9. Resume operations as if in a contaminated environment.

Step 10. After a purge cycle and as the tactical situation permits, monitor the interior. A crew member should begin sampling with detector/monitoring equipment.

Step 11. If detector results are negative, proceed with unmasking procedures. If no symptoms appear, remove masks and gloves at the tank commander's order. Operate in the normal overpressure buttoned-up mode.

Step 12. If detector results continue positive, remain in MOPP gear. You must remain protected until the mission is complete and further decon can be performed or until further tests are negative.

Exit Instructions

Step 1. Traverse the turret until the main gun is centered over the front slope.

Step 2. Put on mask and protective gloves.

Step 3. If you are the loader, perform exit before any crew member begins.

Put on the SCALP or either a field-expedient contamination avoidance item or rain gear and boot covers. Carrying your personal decon kit, exit through the loader's hatch.

Step 4. If you are not the loader, but are required to exit, move to the loader's station. Put on the SCALP or a field-expedient contamination avoidance item or rain gear and boot covers. Carry your personal decon kit and exit through the loader's hatch. If you are the last to exit, carry the decon apparatus and close the hatch.

Step 5. If you are the loader, determine if the tank and surrounding area are contaminated.

Note: Follow procedures for detecting the presence of chemical agents. For hasty identification, the loader should use M8/M9 chemical agent detector paper for suspected liquid agents. The tank commander can use detector/monitoring equipment to detect any vapor agents. If the need to exit the tank is urgent, skip this time-consuming step and assume this area is contaminated.

Step 6. If no contamination is present, crew members may reduce their MOPP level and perform step 7. If contamination is present, decontaminate the loader's hatch and an area approximately 4 feet in diameter around it.

Step 7. Perform the task(s) that dictated the exit.

Appendix A

Operations in Special Environments

Weather and terrain and how they affect the needs for NBC protection must receive special consideration. Certain weather conditions will greatly influence use of NBC weapons. Likewise, different types of terrain will alter the effects of NBC weapons. Also, the type of operation can directly bear on the need for NBC protection. This appendix discusses several types of operations with emphasis on NBC defense.

Cold Weather Operations

Cold weather and other severe climatic conditions create many new problems in individual protection. Such conditions may exist in the extreme northern United States, Alaska, and northern Europe. Generally, these conditions alter the planning and implementation of individual NBC defensive measures. The following paragraphs explain some of these particular situations and the procedures that soldiers should take to protect themselves.

Nuclear

Blast Effects. At subzero temperatures, the radius of damage to material targets can increase. The increase can be as much as 20 percent. These targets include such items as tanks, IFVs, APCs, artillery, and military vehicles. A precursor wave over heat-absorbing surfaces can increase the dynamic pressure wave. However, tundra, irregular terrain features, and broken ice caps break up the pressure wave. Blast effects can drastically interfere with troop movement. A blast can break up covers and cause quick thaws. The result can be avalanches in mountainous areas. In flat lands, a blast may disturb the permafrost sufficiently to restrict or disrupt movement.

Thermal Effects. Ice and snow have a high reflectivity. This may increase the minimum safe distance as much as 50 percent for unwarned troops and even warned, exposed troops. Reflectivity may also increase the number of personnel whose vision is affected by the brilliant flash, or light dazzle, especially at night.

The pale colors normally used to cover material in cold environment give an advantage. Their low absorption properties may make personnel less vulnerable to thermal effects. Cold temperatures also reduce thermal effects on materials. Snow, ice, and even frost coverings on combustible material greatly reduce the tendency of materials to catch fire. However, thermal effects will dry out exposed tundra areas, and grass fires may result.

Radiation Effects. The number of passable roadways is limited already by weather conditions, and radiological contamination on roadways may further restrict resupply and troop movement. Seasonal high winds in the arctic may present a problem in radiological contamination predictions. These winds may reduce dose rates at ground zero. At the time, they extend the area coverage and create a problem for survey/monitoring teams. Hot spots or areas of concentrated accumulation of radiological contamination may occur in areas of heavy snow and snow drifts.

Monitoring for nuclear radiation requires the use of battery-powered radiac equipment. It is imperative that these instruments be kept warm to maintain maximum efficiency in extreme cold. Radiological surveys normally are limited to those areas or routes occupied or used by large units. Aerial survey is most practical in extreme cold weather areas. Survey and monitoring procedures are covered in FM 3-3.

Protection Against Nuclear Attack

At low temperatures, troops operating in the field are particularly vulnerable to all of the effects produced by a nuclear detonation because of the difficulty in digging foxholes and underground fortifications for protection. Shelters and fortifications constructed from snow and ice provide some protection and, wherever possible, should be constructed to take maximum advantage of the additional protection provided by natural terrain features.

Tents that provide necessary warmth for living will not provide protection from radioactive fallout. Maximum use, consistent with the tactical mission, must be made of natural terrain features to provide protection against fallout. Snow and ice, although not as effective as earth in reducing radiation hazards, are readily available and can be used to provide shielding against radiation effects. Loose snow falling on a contaminated area has a half-thickness of about 60 centimeters (24 inches); that is, 60 centimeters of loose snow covering the contamination will reduce the dose rate to about half the original value. Thirty centimeters (12 inches) of hard-packed snow will reduce the dose rate by about one-half and may be of value when considering constructing radiation shield over contaminated areas or one-half and may be of value when considering around shelter.

Biological

Biological warfare in the arctic is a Possibility. Most vectors will not survive, and it is more difficult to aerosolize live biological agents in freezing temperatures. Toxins, on the other hand, are less susceptible to the cold. It has been found that the survival of microorganisms increased significantly at temperatures below freezing. Temperature inversions that exist over snowfields tend to prolong the integrity of an aerosolized biological cloud. It would thus disperse more slowly and thus remain a threat for a longer period. If an attack with these agents occurs, most likely it will be delivered by covert means It is important, therefore, to be alert at all times to the possibility of sabotage. Personnel are more susceptible to live biological agents in arctic environments. This is because of the rapid rate with which diseases will spread in the warm crowded conditions. It is more difficult to assure the requirement for food, water, rest, and cleanliness in cold weather. Troops suffering from dehydration, or from lack of nourishment or rest, will be particularly vulnerable to a biological attack.

Chemical

In arctic conditions chemical agents act differently according to whether they are blister, nerve, blood, or choking agents.

✱✱ Blister Agents. Usually, blister agents are ineffective as casualty producers, because the temperature is well below their normal freezing points. Liquid mustard agent freezes and becomes solid at 14° C (58° F). However, some blister agents or combinations have very low freezing points. These can be effective as harassing agents, because their vapors produce eye irritation requiring soldiers to mask. Since troops wear additional clothing, the possibility of skin contact is greatly reduced. The greater danger is from blister agents carried inside a heated area. Hence, an attack by blister agents at low temperatures can present a real hazard.

✱✱ Nerve Agents. In arctic operations, nerve agents may play an important role by forcing troops to mask. Agent evaporation takes several hours, and soldiers must remain masked for long periods. Significant contamination at low temperatures and wind speeds may remain several days. Liquid Soman (GD) freezes and becomes a solid at -42° C (-43° F). Except in severely cold conditions, nerve agents will remain liquid, and liquid agents are easily absorbed by outer garments and other porous material. Absorbed agents become a vapor hazard or even a contact hazard if transported into a heated area. and chocking agents require soldiers to mask. Blood and Blood and Chocking Agents. Vapor hazards from blood especially chocking agents remain extremely hazardous and non persistent throughout the low temperature range. These agents may be disseminated as a liquid, solid, or aerosol and require masking whenever they are used. Blood agent AC is extremely hazardous even as low as -65° F (-54° C).

Individual-Equipment Problems

Mask. Soldiers should add the M4 winterization kit to masks for cold weather use. For the M17-series and M40-series masks, pull the hood voicemitter-outlet valve assembly cover opening to below the cover. This prevents moisture from wetting inner clothing. In extreme cold, soldiers wearing masks with winterization kits installed will experience greater breathing resistance. This increases with work load, and it becomes even more pronounced with fatigue. In extreme cold environments the hood may be prone to tearing and the zipper apt to malfunction.

Soldiers should wear their mask carriers beneath their outer garments. This allows body heat to keep the masks warm and flexible. Wearing masks in this manner requires an adjustment to donning time. After each wearing, soldiers must inspect their masks for ice formation, especially in the inlet and outlet valve areas.

To prevent frostbite, soldiers should place a small piece of tape over the exposed metal rivets inside the facepiece. The tape should be just large enough to cover the metal and not so large it interferes with donning.

Fitting the mask requires care. Soldiers must adjust the head harness only tight enough to create a good seal. If the mask is too tight, it will restrict blood flow to certain areas of the face and make those areas more susceptible to frostbite. To don the protective mask in arctic conditions, soldiers should take the following eight actions:

- Stop breathing.
- Remove mask from under parka.
- Remove gloves or mittens as needed to properly don the mask.
- Lower parka hood.
- Don the mask.

NOTE: Do not clear the mask by exhaling a large amount of air into it, as is done in warm weather. A large amount of air exhaled into the mask will frost the cold eye lenses. Instead, exhale steadily and slowly. The outlet valve may stick to the seat. If this occurs, lift the outlet valve cover and rotate the disk with a finger while exhaling only. After freezing the valve, reseat the valve cover.

- Check the mask for leaks by pulling down the cheek flaps of the ice-particle prefilter and covering the inlet valves with your hands.
- Fasten the cheek flaps and resume normal breathing,
- Raise the parka hood and fasten your outer garment.

To remove the mask in arctic conditions, soldiers must take the following five actions:

- Brush snow or ice particles from your mask.
- Remove gloves or mittens as necessary to remove mask.
- Remove mask and immediately dry face and inside of mask.

NOTE: Perspiration collects around the facepiece. Take care when removing the mask to prevent perspiration from freezing on your face and causing frostbite. Use a small towel or cloth to wipe your face and inside of mask. To prevent ice formation, wipe your mask thoroughly before storing it. When possible, further dry the mask by placing it in a warm, heated environment, but avoid placing it in direct heat.

- Store mask in carrier.
- Put on gloves or mittens.

M24125-Series and M43-Series Masks. With these masks, the facepieces become brittle from the cold and can be broken. To prevent this, the mask should be carried beneath outer garments to keep warm. Along with keeping them warn, the face-form is required to prevent creasing and cracking, especially in cold weather.

Battle Dress Overgarment. The BDO is not adversely affected by cold temperatures. Commanders and leaders must be particularly sensitive to the possibilities of their soldiers receiving cold weather injuries, particularly frostbite occurring when soldiers are in MOPP3 or MOPP4. Soldiers are most susceptible to frostbite on their hands, fingers, around the elastic in the arms of the overgarment, and from the buildup of sweat that occurs while wearing the mask and rubber gloves. The chances of hypothermia will increase when the MOPP level is reduced.

The BDO is worn under environmental (cold weather parkas) clothing in keeping with the "layered principle." Overheated soldiers may need to "vent" their chemical protective clothing by opening and cooling down the body core temperature and then reestablishing the protective posture. Before doing this, though, the commander must consider the threat and degree of risk involved. The production of body heat makes the BDO breast pockets particularly well suited for carrying items requiring protection from freezing (for example, M256/M256Al kits and NAAK).

Chemical Protective Overboots and GVOS. Both covers are worn seasonally but do not fit over the vapor barrier (VB) boots required in extreme environments. During winter operations the VB boots provide adequate protection when worn in conjunction with chemical protective clothing. The VB boots are double-layered, natural rubber with an air pocket in between.

Chemical Protective Gloves. Normal procedure when donning the protective gloves is to first put on the cotton liners and then the rubber gloves. During winter operations in a chemical environment, use the wool glove liners (part of the black leather glove set) under the butyl rubber gloves to absorb and wick away perspiration from hand surfaces. Proper glove fit is required to preclude restricting blood circulation and cold weather injury. In an extreme cold environment, the arctic mittens should be worn over the rubber gloves to provide warmth. When mittens are removed, the glove surface should be decontaminated before redonning the mittens.

Nerve Agent Antidote Fit, Mark I & II. Arctic weather affects the Mark I & II kit. When the temperature is below 32° F (0° C) the kit may not function properly. When the temperature dips below 40° F (5° C), remove the kit from the carrier and store it in the shirt pocket. Keep it as close to body temperature as possible. This precludes the danger of severe muscle spasms and/or shock from injecting an extremely cold liquid into a muscle. If the kit freezes, do not use it, but acquire a replacement. In addition, protection from freezing must be provided during transit, storage, and resupply operations because freezing and thawing render the kits unserviceable. Care must be taken during the use of the NAAKs to ensure penetration through winter clothing to the muscle.

M258A1/M291 Skin Decontamination Kit. As with any cold liquid on the skin, the M258A1 must be used when chemical agents contact the skin, even though there is a risk of cold injury. Warming the kit prevents possible frost bite. The M291 kit will alleviate this problem since it is a resin-based kit. Additional information relating to decon in arctic environments is in FM 3-5.

M256/M256Al Chemical Agent Detector Kit. Arctic weather affects the kit. When temperature is -15° F (-21° C) or below, the kit can give inaccurate indications. Solutions in the capsules freeze, and the solutions will not work even if reheated. Also, it is difficult or even impossible for the heat tabs to heat the enzyme window to a reaction temperature.

Take care to keep the kit at a temperature above freezing. However, do not place it directly on a source of heat, such as a vehicle heater. If possible, warm it with body heat by placing it inside the parka.

A system of identifying a sample of suspected agent is to collect the suspected agent and place it on M8 or M9 paper. Once collected, the M8 or M9 paper is warmed and covered in a box or can while the M256/M256A1 is inside the box or can. This will heat both the suspected agent sufficiently to enable detection by the M256/M256A1 kit. Soldiers can place samples into empty ammunition cans and apply external heat to cause agent off-gassing. The external heat source may be a small fire, heat tab, burning C-4, or trip flare.

M8 and M9 Detector Paper. Both M8 and M9 detector paper are not specifically limited in the cold but can detect only liquid that would probably be frozen. If the specific substance is thickened or frozen, a sample is collected with a stick or scraper and wiped onto a sheet of wither M8 or M9 paper. The sample is placed on a heated surface, such as an operating vehicle or a power generator, to stimulate thawing of the suspected agent so that identification is expedited. Because of the possibility of off-gassing, this procedure should not be performed inside a heated vehicle or tent.

Collective Protection

For collective protection, chemical hazards become a true challenge in the cold. Successful cold weather operations are dependent upon heated shelters. Without these, combat effectiveness is decreased. Most collective-protection systems have proven to be reliable and durable in the cold. Fluctuations in pressure may occur when the system is exposed to high winds. In cold environments, indirect vapor absorption presents the greatest problem in entry and exit. For this reason it is important to have detection capability in the shelter itself, which is currently prescribed in normal entry/exit procedures. If agent is detected, soldiers in the shelter will immediately mask. The soldiers inside the shelter will be monitored to identify who has brought in the contamination. Once identification has been made, the soldier exits and the shelter is then immediately purged. If follow-on detection proves negative, soldiers may resume entry/exit procedures.

Desert Operations

Desert operations present many varying problems. Desert daytime temperatures can vary from 90° F to 125° F (32° C to 52° C). An unstable temperature gradient results, and this is not particularly favorable to NBC attacks. However, with nightfall, the desert cools rapidly, and a stable temperature gradient results. A possibility of night or early morning attacks must be considered in all planning of desert operations

Nuclear

Nuclear defense planning is generally much the same in a desert as in other areas. There are a few exceptions, however. Lack of vegetation and permanent fixtures, such as forests and buildings, makes it necessary to plan for and construct fortifications. Construction may be difficult because of inconsistencies of the sand; but sand, in combination with sandbags, will give additional protection from radiation exposure.

Blowing winds and sands can produce widespread areas of radiological contamination. The varying terrain may make radiological survey monitoring very difficult.

Biological

Most aerosolized live biological agents are ineffective weapons in desert areas. An exception is spore-forming biological agents. This is a result of low humidity and the ultraviolet radiation of direct sunlight. Troops crossing or occupying desert terrain face little danger from long-term live biological contamination except for spore-forming agents. But, because of favorable night conditions, a covert aerosolized attack could occur. Effectiveness of the live biological agent, however, would quickly diminish with daytime heat. Toxins are resistant to this harsh environment. These can be employed in the same way as chemical agents.

Chemical

Most chemical attacks will be spot or on target attacks. This is because of rapid agent evaporation. For example, with a neutral temperature gradient, 90° F (32° C) temperature, and a light wind, mustard evaporates rapidly. The concentration will be less than 50 percent in one hour.

Desert soil may be very porous. For example, an attack with an unthickened liquid agent may occur in support of a predawn attack. Soil soaks up agent. When the sun rises, it begins to heat the surface. The agent evaporates and rapidly creates a downwind hazard, and the downwind hazard area increases because of a lack of vegetation and permanent building to alter the wind flow. Soldiers must take care to place alarm systems for the widest possible coverage.

A nonpersistent agent attack is unlikely during daylight hours. Weather conditions would rapidly blow away any agent. Night brings about a reverse of weather conditions and creates ideal conditions for an attack. At night, agents linger and settle into low areas, such as foxholes.

In planning for defense, plan any strenuous activity for night hours. This will reduce the heat stress caused by wearing MOPP gear. Take care to ensure that sleeping soldiers are masked if appropriate. Also ensure that they are checked periodically to make sure that mask seals are not broken. This is because an attack is more likely at night than in the day. A way to accomplish this is to use the buddy system or to have the guard check soldiers during rounds. The unit SOP must address this subject.

Jungle Operations

Tropical climates require the highest degree of individual discipline and conditioning to maintain effective NBC defense readiness. Dominating climatic features of jungle areas are high, constant temperature; heavy rainfall; and very high humidity. In thick jungle, there is usually little or no wind, and the canopy blocks much of the sunlight from the ground.

Commanders must expect and plan for a rapid decrease in unit efficiency. They must also expect heat casualties. In addition, they must ensure that special precautions are taken to maintain unit NBC defensive equipment in usable condition. The rapid mildew, dry rot, and rust inherent in jungle areas impose this requirement.

Nuclear

Dense vegetation has little influence on initial effects of nuclear detonations except that the heavy canopy provides some protection against thermal radiation. The blast wave creates extensive tree blowdown and missile effects. Some falling particles are retained by the jungle canopy, and reduced radiation hazards may result. Subsequent rains, however, will wash these particles to the ground. Particles will concentrate in water collection areas and produce radiation hot spots.

Biological

Jungles provide excellent conditions for threat use of live biological agents and toxins. Warm temperatures, high humidity, and protection from sunlight all aid survivability of disease-causing microorganisms. Low wind speeds and jungle growth limit downwind hazards. Strict adherence to field sanitation procedures, especially vector and rodent control, is essential in jungles. These procedures will help control the naturally occurring diseases that abound. Soldiers should mask and role down sleeves to cover exposed skin from possible contact with live biological agents and toxins. Toxins are well suited to this environment, and soldiers should defend against toxins just as they defend against chemical agents.

Chemical

Chemical agents used in jungle areas can cause extreme problems for friendly forces. Persistent agents delivered by artillery shells and aircraft bombs penetrate the canopy before dissemination. These agents can remain effective on jungle floors for long periods.

High temperatures can increase vapor hazards from liquid agents. Nonpersistent agent vapors hang in the air for extended periods because of low wind speeds. However, these wind speeds minimize downwind vapor hazards. Chemical agents employed in jungle areas make MOPP gear necessary for ground operations. However, high temperature and humidity combined with the heat-loading characteristics of MOPP gear make MOPP gear uncomfortable to operate in.

Mountain Operations

Terrain and weather in mountainous areas dictate a requirement for a high degree of NBC defense preparedness. Rugged terrain limits the employment of large forces. Adjacent units may not be able to provide mutual support. Also, there is reduced logistical support and difficult rapid maneuver. In these circumstances, small US units can impede, harass, or canalize numerically superior threat forces. The intention is to dissipate threat strength and compel threat forces to fight a decisive battle under unfavorable circumstances. Mountain warfare requires friendly units to be almost completely self-sufficient in NBC protection.

Nuclear

Nuclear targeting in mountainous areas is easier than in flat terrain. The reasons are the lack of roads and trails and the slow speed at which troops must move. Digging foxholes and building other protective shelters are difficult in rocky or frozen ground. Improvised shelters built of snow, ice, or rocks may be the only possible protection. Radiological contamination deposit may be very erratic, because of rapidly changing wind patterns. Hot spots may occur far from the point of detonation, and low intensity areas may occur very near it. Limited mobility makes radiological surveys on the ground difficult, and the difficulty of maintaining a constant flight altitude makes air surveys highly inaccurate.

Natural shelters provide some protection from nuclear effects and radiological contamination. These natural shelters include caves, ravines, and cliffs. Clear mountain air extends the range of casualty-producing thermal effects. Added clothing required by cool mountain temperatures, however, reduces casualties from these effects. Rockslides or snowslides are potential problems. Units operating under nuclear warfare conditions should carefully select positions where they will not be hit or trapped by slides.

Biological

Defense against live biological agents does not differ in principle in mountains from that in flat terrain except in extreme cold. For a detailed explanation, see cold weather operations.

Chemical

Aerial delivery will most likely be the means of chemical munitions employment in mountain warfare. This results from difficult logistic problems and increased munitions requirements for cold weather employment. Troops should be constantly alert for air strikes, and they should take protective actions immediately. Defense against chemical attacks in mountains is similar to that in flat terrain where cold temperatures prevail. Refer to cold weather operations.

Urban Terrain Operations

To plan NBC defense, commanders must be fully familiar with how urban terrain will affect their mission.

Nuclear

Without some preparation, average buildings give inadequate shelter from a nuclear blast. If used correctly, ground floors and basements of steel or reinforced concrete offer excellent protection from most effects except overpressure. Soldiers should avoid windows because of possible injuries from flying debris and glass. Soldiers also may receive severe burns through openings facing ground zero. Sewers, storm drains, and subway tunnels are readily available in most urban areas. These provide better protection than ground-level buildings. Soldiers should not use structures of wood or other flammable materials, because these could burst into flames. See Chapter 4 for preparation procedures.

Buildings do provide a measure of protection against radiological contamination. Troops who must move in or through suspected contaminated urban areas should take this into consideration. They should travel through buildings, sewers, and tunnels. However, they should consider the dangers of collapse because of blast. Soldiers also should consider hazards of debris and firestorms resulting from ruptured and ignited gas or gasoline lines.

Biological

Buildings and other urban structures can provide some immediate protection from direct spray. However, the stable environment of these structures may increase persistency of live biological agents. Toxins are very effective in an urban environment, and soldiers should take the same precautions prescribed for chemical agents.

Covert operations are particularly well suited for urban employment. Existing water and food supplies are prime targets. Soldiers' personal hygiene becomes very important. Commanders must establish and consistently enforce sanitary and personal hygiene measures, including immunizations. They must also ensure that troops drink safe water and never assume that hydrant water is safe.

Chemical

Urban structures can protect against spray attacks, but this exchange for overhead cover creates other problems. Chemical agents tend to find and stay in low areas, such as those found in urban locations. Examples are basements, sewers, and subway tunnels. Soldiers should avoid these low areas. Stay times of agents, such as GB, greatly increase when settled in these areas.

Once an attack occurs, detection of chemical contamination becomes very important. Soldiers must thoroughly check areas before attempting to occupy or traverse them. They also may have to relocate some defensive positions.

Airborne and Air-Assault Operations

Airborne and air-assault divisions launch operations into specific, limited, objective areas. This provides threat forces with an opportunity to use NBC weapons effectively as a deterrent. Commanders should avoid massing troops and aircraft in and around relatively small landing zones (LZs) and drop zones (DZs). Such massing invites disaster. If the area of operation has only a few suitable LZs or DZs, the enemy may choose to contaminate them with persistent chemical agents. Any landing operation attempted in these zones would then require troops to dress in fill MOPP gear. It could also require extensive decon of aircraft (see Chapter 8 of FM 3-5). Troops operating from bases near LZs or DZs could be subjected to further chemical attacks with both persistent and nonpersistent agents. This would require extended wear of MOPP gear.

Suppression of threat fire is critical to a successful operation. Small elements should use several LZs or DZs simultaneously. This technique helps them avoid presenting lucrative targets for nuclear weapons. After landing, these elements should use separate routes to approach the objective, and they should mass only at the last possible moment before assault. Also, commanders must give planning consideration to either of two options. They can extract the force within a short time or provide a quick linkup with a ground mobile task force. These plans allow for relief from wearing MOPP gear.

Appendix B

Guidelines for the NBC Portion
of a Collective-Protection System SOP

This is intended as a guide for units in the field. Each unit should modify and expand this guidance to develop its own SOP. Each SOP should consider peculiarities of unit organization, mission, equipment, and environmental situation. An SOP should delineate operational details of a shelter or van equipped for collective protection. For example, details must include NBC-related duties of a guard (where applicable) and entry and exit procedures.

The SOP should consider the following:

- Type and location of the shelter or van.
- Frequency of and requirements for entries and exits.
- General climate of the area of operations--temperate, arctic, tropic, or desert.
- Local environmental conditions.
- Number of nonshelter personnel assigned to the same site as the shelter or van.

Use the following general guidance in preparing an SOP for operation of NBC protective shelters or vans. Modify it for prevailing conditions.

Clean Area Around the Protective Entrance

Provide procedures to decontaminate the area surrounding the shelter or van if liquid agent is present. There are several methods. Turn or remove a top layer of soil, remove snow, or add a clean layer of soil or sand. A clean surface can be obtained by laying down a piece of plastic, cardboard, canvas, plywood, or other material. Use of any one of these can prevent tracking in contaminated mud, soil, or liquid. Using either soap or detergent with water, wash the entrance steps and entrance door handle. Then decontaminate the steps and door handle, and rinse with water. Whenever possible, provide overhead cover, such as a canvas fly or similar equipment, for the area in front of the entrance. This protects removed clothing and equipment.

Personnel Entry Procedures

Cover entry procedures to ensure the least risk of contamination to soldiers and equipment inside and the least interference with tactical operations. Each entry involves a trade off. Consider this question for each person: Does the time that may have to be spent in masks and the corresponding degradation of combat mission performance justify entry of this person?

General Guidance

Provide general guidance for integration of NBC operations with combat mission operations. Guidance could include the following:

During active chemical operations, the shelter guard checks all soldiers for contamination, using a chemical agent detector or detector paper. Unless the absence of contamination can be verified, assume soldiers are contaminated, and they must perform the specific entry procedures.

Detector paper detects agents only in liquid form, most likely thickened liquid agents. Unthickened agents absorb into overgarment materials and cannot be detected by detector paper. However, agent vapor may desorb from clothing inside shelters or vans and present vapor hazards. The CAM can detect desorbing vapors.

One of the guard's main NBC duties is assisting entering soldiers. He must help them decontaminate and remove contaminated overgarments. He, therefore, must check himself periodically for contamination, especially his gloves.

Preliminary Steps

Indicate steps required to decide if a person should be allowed entry. You could use the following in your SOP:

Use a chemical agent detector or detector paper, and check for the presence of liquid chemical agent on soldiers. Check each soldier's weapon, overgarment, gloves, mask and hood assembly, helmet, and overboots. A buddy or guard assists the soldier, when necessary.

After the detector check, store contaminated items outside. Use a protective cover, such as plastic or canvas, near the entrance, and ensure items are not in the path of the entrance door.

Carefully evaluate the need for grossly contaminated soldiers to enter. Consider possible interior contamination and resulting degradation. Determine if these will be offset by combat mission performance of entering soldiers.

Entry Into Shelter or Van

Describe procedures for entering. Give sufficient detail to avoid confusion. Standardize these procedures, or at least make them compatible with and similar to those for larger shelters. Your SOP could include the procedures such as those that follow:

If liquid contamination is detected on soldiers, follow these procedures:

WARNING

When entries are performed in a contaminated environment, monitor every 15 minutes. If

---

detector changes color, or the CAM indicates more then one bar, all soldiers should mask until the source of contamination is located and removed and/or further tests indicate contamination is no longer present.

Note location of any liquid agent on the entering soldier. Use decontaminants only on areas known to be contaminated. Soldier removes LCE and unfastens Velcro tabs, tie cords, and trouser-leg zippers.

Decontaminate hood. Effective decon may require two soldiers. The soldier to be decontaminated first (soldier 1) turns and faces the shelter guard or buddy (soldier 2). Soldier 2 loosens drawstrings over the voicemitter. Soldier 1 turns, and soldier 2 wipes top, back, and sides of the hood with single passes of decon wipes. Soldier 2 then decontaminates his own gloves. He tightly rolls the hood up and off soldier 1's overgarment jacket, tucking straps into the roll. This prepares the hood for removal. After soldier 1's hood is decontaminated, he performs the same procedures for soldier 2.

Soldier 1 turns and faces soldier 2. Soldier 2 unsnaps the jacket, top to bottom, and then unzips it. Soldier 1 turns his back to soldier 2, and soldier 2 carefully removes the jacket.

Soldier 2 unfastens snap and tie cordon the waistband and opens trouser front zipper on soldier 1. He slowly rolls trousers down to the hips with one roll. (Soldier 1 can do these latter two steps if necessary). Leaning forward, soldier 1 places both hands against the van or shelter while soldier 2 pulls trouser legs off one at a time. Trouser legs turn inside out as they come off. Overboots remain on. This prevents transfer of contaminated items. Soldier 1 then helps remove soldier 2's trousers. Soldier 1 loosens own overboots.

Carrying an M258A1 or M291 decon kit and his M1/M1A1 waterproof bag, soldier 1 checks to be sure the air lock is unoccupied. He opens the entrance door and prepares to remove overboots. Soldier 1 stands before the entrance, removes the second overboot, and steps into the entrance with his exposed boot. He carefully places the overboots away from the entry path, closes the door, and starts the purge cycle.

During entrance purge, the soldier decontaminates gloves, mask, and hood including outer portion of the rolled hood, and then loosens both gloves. After completion of air purge, the soldier removes his mask and hood.

Removal and Storage of Mask and Hood Assembly

Ensure soldiers know detailed procedures for removing the mask and hood assembly. You could use the following in your SOP:

Still wearing the loosened gloves, soldier 1 bends at the waist with legs apart. He grasps the back of the rolled hood and lifts it forward over his head. He grasps the mask at the outlet-valve covers and pulls it down. He bows his head to slip his face out of the mask. Still holding the mask so filters face the floor, he lifts mask and hood off his head.

176

The soldier places the mask and hood assembly into his M1/M1A1 bag and seals the bag tightly. He loosens and drops his gloves to the floor. Then he enters the shelter, carrying his M1/M1A1 bag.

Shelter or Van Emergency Operations

Familiarize soldiers with the procedures to follow should an equipment failure occur and the alarm sounds. You could use the following procedures:

If an alert is given and the shelter or van is prepared for NBC operations, the alarm system alerts occupants to any of several types of equipment failure. Soldiers should handle equipment-related emergencies according to each system's organizational maintenance manual. If one of the following conditions occurs, shelter or van occupants should take the actions given.

Sudden Loss of Positive Pressure in the Shelter. Lights and horns on the CCM signal an alarm. Occupants put on masks. An assigned occupant confirms this signal by checking CCM power, lights, and horn. If alarms are confirmed and compartment positive pressure is lost, occupants must remain masked while the assigned operator pursues the problem. He uses the organizational maintenance manual to locate the problem, and, if possible, repair it. The operator may not find the problem readily, or perhaps he cannot repair it. In either case, occupants must dress at the appropriate MOPP level.

Malfunctioning of Gas-Particulate Filter Unit. If the change-filter light comes on, occupants put on masks. An assigned occupant determines if the filter is operating. He follows procedures in the organizational maintenance manual. If filters need to be replaced, occupants must work in the appropriate MOPP gear until filters are replaced, air is purged, and detectors indicate masks can be removed.

> **WARNING**
>
> Never change filters during a chemical attack.

Contamination of Interior by Entry of Contaminated Item or Personnel. Refer to monitoring procedures. If the interior becomes contaminated, occupants must work in appropriate MOPP gear until the airflow purges agent from the air, and a detector indicates agent is no longer present. Wipe off any unabsorbed liquid agent from equipment. Use a wet rag if moisture will not harm equipment. Warm the interior by turning air conditioner off. This may enhance evaporation and desorption of agent from materials. Selective use of forced air from a heat source can also aid in contamination removal. Decon begun shortly after agent is deposited is most effective.

Interior Procedures for Occupants

Monitoring Procedures

Describe step-by-step monitoring procedures. You could include the following in your SOP:

Each shelter or van must have a chemical agent detector kit placed at the downstream end of the airflow. This is usually near the door.

WARNING

Ensure the undressing area is well ventilated, and remove contaminated overgarments from the hot line area to avoid buildup of vapor

---

If the detector indicates presence of a chemical agent, occupants must mask immediately. Check shelter pressure, door, and power. If these are operating properly, change filters. Replace filters according to SOP and the appropriate operational maintenance manual.

Exit Procedures

Describe special exit procedures for shelter occupants. Emphasize the importance of contamination avoidance. Your SOP could include the following:

If an attack is imminent, occurring, or has occurred, occupants leaving the shelter should put on MOPP gear. The local situation and the shelter SOP will give guidance.

Occupants may need to leave the shelter temporarily or for brief periods during an attack. They should carefully avoid contamination of their MOPP gear. This minimizes contamination and reduces reentry time and risk.

In a shelter or van with more than one occupant, one may be assigned outside duties. That person should be rotated if possible. This helps to minimize low-level exposure and its cumulative effects.

Operating Procedures for Shelter Guards or Nonshelter Personnel

Describe operating procedures for shelter guards and nonshelter personnel, including visitors. Shelters or vans may be colocated with another unit. If so, assign nonshelter personnel as shelter guards, when possible. Nonshelter personnel are those not essential to the operation of shelter or van mission equipment. Guards attend to outside tasks. This reduces the number of entries and exits. You could use the following procedures in your SOP:

Exiting

When leaving the shelter, a soldier enters the air lock. Contamination may be present or suspected outside, or higher authority may prescribe continuous wearing of masks. If so, the soldier masks. If required, he dons MOPP gear, using prescribed procedures.

Monitoring

Once a chemical alert has been issued, but before an attack, the shelter guard monitors for agent presence, using a chemical agent detector and/or detector paper. After a chemical attack ceases, the guard periodically monitors outside air. Using a detector or detector paper, he determines if aerosol or liquid agent is still present. The guard also monitors the air periodically for agent vapor, using a detector kit.

Assisting Shelter or Van Operations

Shelter guards and nonshelter personnel assist in shelter or van operations. They perform such tasks as refueling generators, realigning antennas, and assisting in entry and exit of shelter personnel and visitors.

Disposal of Contaminated Equipment and Clothing

Give directions for disposal of contaminated equipment and clothing. Cover both emergency and prolonged NBC operations. You could use the following paragraph in your SOP:

Store contaminated equipment and clothing out of the way of entering soldiers. This helps avoid confusion and contamination spread. Choose a location under the shelter or van if possible. Later, when possible, take contaminated items to equipment decon stations for cleaning and possible reissue.

Supplies of Expendable Items

Cover the commander's guidance for storage of supplies of certain expendable items in protective shelters or vans. These are for use by soldiers entering and leaving the shelter or van. Include the following:

- Decon materials, such as soap or detergent, bleach, M258A1 and M291 skin decon kits, and water.
- Decon equipment including buckets, rags for wiping, and brushes for scrubbing.
- M2561M256A1 and M256A2 detector kits.
- Disposable field-expedient items.
- MOPP gear.
- BDUs in various sizes.
- Batteries for the CAM and M8A1.
- Plastic bags, trash cans, and other containers to be used for protecting uncontaminated items.

Glossary

A

AC--hydrogen cyanide, a blood agent.

ACR--armored cavalry regiment.

aerosol--
a suspension or dispensing of small particles (solids or liquids) in a gaseous medium. Examples are mist, fogs, and smokes.

AirLand Battle--
an approach to military operations that realizes the full potential of US forces by extending the depth of the battlefield and integrating conventional, nuclear, chemical, and electronic means to describe the battlefield where the enemy is attacked to the fall depth of its formation. AirLand Battle seeks, through early initiative of offensive action by air and land forces, to bring about the conclusion of battle on our terms.

ANBACIS--Automated Nuclear, Biological, and Chemical Information System.

AO--area of operations.

APC--armored personnel carrier.

ARTEP--Army training and evaluation program.

AUIB--aircrew uniform integrated battlefield.

AWS--Air Force Weather Service.

B

basic skills decontamination--
immediate neutralization or removal of contamination from exposed portions of the skin. Each soldier must be able to perform this decontamination without supervision.

BDO--battledress overgarment.

BDU--battledress uniform.

beta particle--

form of radiation emitted from the nucleus of an atom with a mass and charge equal in magnitude to that of an electron. Beta particles have a range of approximately 10 to 15 meters in still air. The primary hazard from this radiation is through prolonged contact with the skin, resulting in beta burns.

biological agent--
a microorganism that causes wither disease in man, plants, or animals, or deterioration of material.

biological defense--
methods, plans, and procedures involved in establishing and executing defensive measures against attack, utilizing biological agents.

biological operations--
the intentional use of germs, toxins, or novel compounds to cause death and disease among personnel, animals, and plants, or to deteriorate material.

biological warfare--
see biological operations.

biological weapons--
an item of material that projects, disperses, or disseminates a biological agent, including arthropod vectors.

blast effect--
destruction or damage caused by the shock wave and high velocity transient winds caused by an explosion, particularly a nuclear explosion.

blister agent--
a chemical agent that injures the eyes and lungs and burns or blisters the skin.

blood agent--
a chemical compound, including the cyanide group, that affects bodily function by preventing the normal transfer of oxygen from the blood to the body tissue. Also called cyanogen agent.

BOS--battlefield operating systems.

C

C--celsius.

CAM--chemical agent monitor.

CANA--convulsant antidote for nerve agents.

CARC--chemical agent resistant coating.

CB--chemical and biological.

CCA--contamination control area.

CCM--compartment control module.

CDM--chemical downwind message.

celsius--centigrade.

centigray--
a unit of absorbed dose of radiation. The term replaces rad.

CG--phosgene, choking agent.

chemical agent--
a chemical substance intended for use in military operations to kill, seriously injure, or incapacitate through its physiological effects. Excludes riot control agents, herbicides, smoke, and flame.

cGy--centigray.

chemical defense--
methods, plans, and procedures involved in establishing and executing defensive measures against chemical agents.

chemical operations--
employment of chemical agents to kill, injure, or incapacitate for a significant period of time man or animals, and deny or hinder the use of areas, facilities, or material, or defense against such employment. chemical warfare--all aspects of military operations involving the employment of lethal and incapacitating munitions/agents and the warning and protective measures associated with such offensive operations. Riot control agents and herbicides are not considered chemical warfare agents but are included under the broader term chemical munitions/agents collectively. (See FM 3-9 for a listing of chemical agents.)

chemical warfare agent--see chemical agent.

CK--cyanogen chloride, a blood agent.

COA--course of action.

collective protection--
the use of shelters to provide a contamination-free environment for selected portions of the force. collective-protection shelter--a shelter, with filtered air, that provides a contamination-free working environment for selected personnel and allows relief from continuous wear of MOPP gear.

contaminate--
to introduce an impurity; for instance, a foreign microorganism developing accidentally in a pure culture. Clothing containing microorganisms is said to be contaminated.

contamination--

the deposit and/or absorption of radioactive material or biological or chemical agents on and by structures, areas, personnel, or objects; food and/or water made unfit for human or animal consumption by the presence of environmental chemicals, radioactive elements, bacteria, or organisms; the byproduct of the growth of bacteria or organisms in the decomposing material (including the food substance itself), or waste, in food or water.

contamination avoidance--
    individual and/or unit measures taken to avoid or minimize NBC attacks and reduce the effects of NBC hazards. Passive contamination avoidance measures are concealment, dispersion, deception, and use of cover to reduce the probability of the enemy using NBC weapons if they are used. Active contamination-avoidance measures are contamination control; detection, identification, and marking of contaminated areas; issuance of contamination warnings; and relocation or rerouting to an uncontaminated area.

contamination control--
    procedures to avoid, reduce, remove, or render harmless, temporarily or permanently, NBC contamination for the purpose of maintaining or enhancing the efficient conduct of military operations.

CP--command post.

CPE--collective-protection equipment.

CPFC--chemical protective footwear cover.

CPOG--chemical protective overgarment.

CVC--combat vehicle crew.

CW--chemical warfare.

D

decon--decontamination.

decontaminate--
    to break down, neutralize, or remove a chemical, biological, or radioactive material posing a threat to equipment or personnel.

decontamination--
    the process of making any person, object, or area safe by absorbing, destroying, neutralizing, making harmless, or removing chemical or biological material, or removing radioactive material clinging to or around it.

deliberate decontamination--
    operation/techniques intended to reduce contamination to a level at which personnel can perform their mission without wearing MOPP gear.

detailed equipment decon--

process of removing or neutralizing contamination on interior and exterior surfaces of unit equipment to negligible risk levels to allow MOPP level reduction for extended periods.

detailed troop decon--

process of decontaminating individual fighting equipment to negligible risk levels; removing contaminated MOPP gear, including protective masks; decontaminating protective masks; and monitoring personnel equipment for decon effectiveness. This is done to reduce MOPP levels for extended periods.

detection--

measures to detect by use of chemical detectors or radiological monitoring/survey teams the location of NBC hazards placed by the enemy. It includes identifying and marking contaminated area.

detector paper--

either of two chemical agent detector papers that detect liquid chemical agents under any weather conditions: ABC-M8 detector paper or M9 detector paper.

disease--

deviation from the normal state or function of a cell, an organ, or an individual.

DS2--decontamination solution No. 2. It is available in 1-1/3-quart cans and in 5-gallon pails for filling portable decontaminating apparatuses.

DZ--drop zone.

E

electromagnetic pulse--

the high-energy, short-duration pulse (similar in some respects to a bolt of lightning) generated by nuclear detonation. It can induce a current in any electrical conductor and can temporarily disrupt or overload and damage components of improperly protected or unprotected electronic equipment.

EMP--electromagnetic pulse

EOD--explosive ordnance disposal.

F

fallout--

precipitation to earth of radioactive particulate matter from a nuclear cloud; also applied to the particulate matter itself.

fixed shelter--

collective protection, usually in a rear area in a permanent location, such as a building basement, bunker, or expandable rigid-wall, tactical shelter. Uses are field hospitals, operating rooms, maintenance shops, data processing centers, field kitchens, fire control centers, and supply storage areas.

fixed site--

the location of a military operation that requires developed real estate to accomplish its wartime mission. Examples of fixed sites are ports, airfields, hospitals, and railheads.

fixed site--
the location of a military operation that requires developed real estate to accomplish its wartime mission. Examples of fixed sites are ports, airfields, hospitals, and railheads.

FLOT--forward line of own troops.

FSO--fire support officer.

G

G2--assistant chief of staff, G2 (intelligence).

G3--assistant chief of staff, G3 (operations and plans).

gamma radiation--
electromagnetic emissions of short wavelength from the nucleus of the atom. The hazard is primarily internal. Gamma rays are the soldier's primary radiation hazard on the battlefield.

GB--sarin, a nerve agent.

GDP--general deployment plan.

germs--
a disease-producing microorganism; microbe; a pathogenic bacterium. The term includes bacteria, rickettsiae, viruses, and fungi.

GPFU--gas-particulate filter unit.

GVO--green vinyl overboot.

H

ha--hectare.

high-mobility shelter--
collective protection that can be removed with relative ease.

hr--hour

HSFC--hermetically sealed filter container.

hybrid collective protection--
> a combination of overpressure and ventilated-facepiece system.

I

ICE--individual chemical equipment.

identification--
> process of positively identifying field concentrations of blood, blister, and nerve agents, using an M256, M256A1, or M256A2 detector kit. Almost all biological agents require a laboratory facility for identification. Nuclear radiation is measured by the unit's radiac instruments.

IFV--infantry fighting vehicle.

IHADSS--integrated helmet and display sighting system.

immunize--
> to render resistant to a specific disease.

incapacitate--
> disable.

incapacitating dose--
> the concentration/dose that renders an individual unfit for duty or combat.

individual nuclear, biological, and chemical protection--
> that protection provided to the individual soldier in a nuclear, biological, or chemical environment by protective clothing and/or personal equipment.

intelligence preparation of the battlefield--
> a systematic approach to analyzing the enemy, weather, and terrain in a specific geographic area. It integrates enemy doctrine with the weather and terrain as they relate to the mission and the specific battlefield environment. This is done to determine and evaluate enemy capabilities, vulnerabilities, and probable courses of action.

IPB--intelligence preparation of the battlefield.

IPE--individual protective equipment.

K

kg--kilogram.

kmph--kilometer per hour.

L

LCE--load-carrying equipment.

lethal--
  deadly, fatal.
lethal dose--
  amount of toxic substance that has an absolutely fatal effect.

LIC--low-intensity conflict.

limited mobile shelter--collective protection that is not easily moved.

LP--listening post.

LZ--landing zone.

M

m--meter.

mask-only--
  protective posture that provides some relief from MOPP gear for personnel who must work in a contaminated environment. Personnel must be within protective shelters, some kinds of vans, tanks, or buildings where danger of transfer hazards is minimal. A soldier in mask-only posture can tolerate exposure to vapor hazards but not transfer hazards. Mask-only permits longer work periods, but personnel must assume full MOPP level before exiting their sheltered area.

MCC--microclimate coding.

METL--mission-essential task list.

METT-T--mission, enemy, terrain, troops, and time available.

mission--specific stated tasks and the purpose of an operation; implies other tasks that may become necessary by battlefield changes.

MOPP--mission-oriented protective posture. A flexible system that provides maximum NBC protection for the individual with the lowest risk possible and still maintains mission accomplishment.

MOPP gear--combination of all individual protective equipment.

MOPP closed--fill MOPP overgarment, overboots or GVOs, gloves, mask with hood, antidote, and decon kits.

MOPP open--opening the overgarment jacket (at MOPP 3/4) and rolling the protective mask hood. mph--miles per hour. m/s--meter per second

MULO--multipurpose lightweight overboot.

N

NAAK--nerve agent antidote kit.

NAI--named area of interest.

NAPP--nerve agent pretreatment pyridostigmine.

NATO--North Atlantic Treaty Organization.

NBC--nuclear, biological, and chemical.

NBCC--nuclear, biological and chemical center.

NBC-PC--NBC protective cover.

NBCWRS--NBC warning and reporting system.

NCO--noncommissioned officer.

nerve agent--
> a lethal chemical that causes paralysis by interfering with the transmission of nerve impulse.

nonpersistent agent--
> a chemical agent that, when released, dissipates and/or loses its ability to cause casualties after a passage of 10 to 15 minutes.

nuclear blast effect--
> see blast effect.
> **nuclear warfare**--
> the employment of nuclear weapons.

O

OP--observation post.

OPLAN--operations plan.

OPORD--operation order.

P

PASGT--personnel armor-system ground troop.

PE--protective entrance.

percutaneous--
through the skin.
permafrost--
permanently frozen subsoil usually 3 to 6 inches below the surface.
permeable--
having pores or small openings that allow liquids or gases to penetrate.
persistency--
a measure of the ability of NBC weapons to continue in their casualty-producing effects after they have been released and downwind for indefinite distances.
personal wipedown--
performed by each soldier on mask, hood, gloves, and essential gear. For chemical and biological contamination, soldiers use the skin decon kit to decontaminate. Soldiers should not attempt to remove chemical contamination from their BDOs; special protective properties of BDOs minimize the effects of chemical hazards. Soldiers should brush radiological or biological contamination from BDOs.

POL--petroleum, oils, and lubricants.

PT--physical training.

purge--
act or process of removing unwanted substances, such as contaminated air.

Q

qt--quart.

R

radiac--
derived from the words "radioactivity, detection, indication, and computation." Radiac is used as an all-inclusive term to designate various types of radiological measuring instruments or equipment. Radiac is usually used as an adjective.
radiac dosimeter--
an instrument used to measure the ionizing radiation absorbed by that instrument.
radiacmeter--
portable, battery-operated radiation detector and indicator used to detect and measure beta and gamma radiations.
radiation dose--
total amount of ionizing radiation absorbed by material or tissues, commonly expressed in centigray. The term is often used as the exposure dose expressed in roentgens, which is a measure of the total amount of ionization that the quantity of radiation could produce in air. This should be distinguished from the absorbed radiation per gram of specified body tissue. Further, the biological dose, in reins, is a measure of the biological effectiveness of radiation exposure.

RCA--riot control agent.

rd--round.

RES--radiation exposure status.

residual contamination--
that amount that remains after steps have been taken to remove it. These steps may consist of nothing more than allowing the contamination to decay normally.

riot control agent--
chemical compounds that produce only temporary irritating or incapacitating effects when in field concentrations.

RTO--radio telephone operator.

S

S2--intelligence officer (US Army).

S3--operations and training officer (US Army).

S4--supply officer (US Army).

SCALP--suit, contamination avoidance and liquid protection.

SCPE--simplified collective-protection equipment.

sec--second.

SOP--standing operating procedure.

spore--
an asexual, usually single-celled, reproductive body of plants such as fungi, mosses, or ferns; a microorganism, as a bacterium, in a resting or dormant state.

SWO--staff weather officer.

T

TAI--target area of interest.

TAP--toxicological agent protective.

thermal effect--
heat and light produced by a nuclear explosion; energy emitted from the fireball as thermal radiation. The total amount of thermal energy a unit receives at a

specified distance from a nuclear explosion. It consists essentially of ultraviolet, visible, and infrared radiation.

threshold dose--
the smallest amount of a toxic substance that can produce the first recognizable injuries (for example, irritation of skin or eyes, nose; or miosis).

TOE--table of organization and equipment.

total system--
a collective-protection overpressure system plus environmental control.

TOW--tube-launched, optically tracked, wire-guided.

toxins--
a class of biological poison resulting from the byproduct of living organisms. A toxin may be obtained naturally, that is, from secretions of various organisms or synthesized.

transfer hazards--
liquid or solid contamination.

TREE--transient radiation effects on electronics.

tundra--
marshy, vast, level, treeless plains of the arctic.

V

VB--vapor barrier.

vector--
a carrier; especially the animal or intermediate host that carries a pathogen from one host to another, as the malaria-carrying mosquito.

ventilated facepiece--
a series of individual respiration systems or masks serviced by a common filter system.

VGH--relating to V-and G-type nerve agents and H-type blister agents.

W

WBGT--wet bulb globe temperature.

References

All references with information on the subjects in this publication may not be listed here. New material is constantly being published, and present references may become obsolete. Consult the applicable directory of publications and instructional material catalogues to keep updated.

Required Publications

Required publications are sources that the user must read to understand or to comply with this publication.

Field Manuals (FMs)

FM 3-3, NBC Contamination Avoidance

FM 3-4-1, Fixed Site Protection

FM 3-5, NBC Decontamination

FM 3-6, Field Behavior of NBC Agents

FM 3-100, NBC Operations

FM 34-1, Intelligence and Electronic Warfare Operations

FM 34-3, Intelligence Analysis

FM 34-81/AFM 105-4, Weather Support for Army Tactical Operations

Soldier Training Publications (STPs)

STP 21-1-SMCT, Soldier's Manual of Common Tasks, Skill Level 1

STP 21-24-SMCT, Soldier's Manual of Common Tasks, Skill Levels 2-4

STP 21-II-MQS, Military Qualification Standards II, Manual of Common Tasks.

Technical Manuals (TMs)

TM 3-4240-207-12, Operator's and Organizational Maintenance Manual: Filter Unit, Gas-Particulate... ABC-M6

TM 3-4240-241-12, Operator's and Organizational Maintenance Manual for Filter Unit, Gas-Particulate... ABC-M6Al

TM 3-4240-264-12, Operator's and Organizational Maintenance Manual: Shelter System, Collective Protection, Chemical-Biological: Inflatable, Trailer-Transported, M51

TM 3-4240-279-10, Operator's Manual: Mask, Chemical-Biological: Field ABC-M17, M17A1, and M17A2

TM 3-4240-279-20&P, Unit Maintenance Manual for Mask, Chemical-Biological; Field, ABC-M17, M17A1, and M17A2

TM 3-4240-280-10, Operator's Manual for Mask, Chemical-Biological: Aircraft, ABC-M24 and Accessories and Mask, Chemical-Biological, Tank, M25A1 and Accessories

TM 3-4240-288-12&P, Operator's and Unit Maintenance Manual including Repair Parts and Special Tools List for Collective Protective Equipment NBC, Simplified, M20

TM 3-4240-300-10-1, Operator's Manual for Chemical-Biological Mask: Field M40

TM 3-4240-300-10-2, Operator's Manual for Chemical-Biological Mask: Combat Vehicle, M42

TM 3-4240-300-20&P, Unit Maintenance Manual (Including Repair Parts and Special Tools List) For Chemical-Biological, Mask: Field M40

TM 3-4240-312-12&P, Operator's and Unit Maintenance Manual for Mask, Chemical-Biological, Aircraft, M43, Type I

Related Publications

Related publications are sources of additional information. Users do not have to read them to understand this publication.

Army Regulation (AR)

AR 40-63, Opthalmic Services

Field Manuals (FMs)

FM 8-9, NATO Handbook on the Medical Aspects of NBC Defense Operations

FM 8-285, Treatment of Chemical Agent Casualties and Conventional Military Chemical Injuries.

FM 21-10, Field Hygiene and Sanitation

FM 21-10-1, Unit Field Sanitation Team

FM 21-11, First Aid for Soldiers

FM 90-3, Desert Operations (How to Fight)

FM 90-5, Jungle Operations (How to Fight)

FM 90-6, Mountain Operations (How to Fight)

FM 90-10, Military Operations on Urbanized Terrain (MOUT) (How to Fight)

Technical Manuals (TMs)

TM 3-4230-204-12&P, Operator's and Unit Maintenance Manual... for Decontaminating Apparatus, Portable... ABC-M11

TM 3-4230-214-12&P, Operator's and Organizational Maintenance Manual... for Decontaminating Apparatus, Portable, 14 Liter M13

TM 3-4230-216-10, Operator's Manual for Decontaminating Kit, Skin: M258A1 and Training Aid, Skin Decontaminating: M58A1

TM 3-4230-224-10, Operators Manual, Decontamination Kit, Individual Equipment: M280

TM 3-4230-229-10, Operator's Manual for Decontaminating Kit, Skin: M291

TM 3-4240-229-12, Operator's and Organizational Maintenance Manual for Collective Protection Equipment... Hawk, M10

TM 3-4240-284-20&P, Organizational Maintenance Manual... Collection Protection Equipment, Fire Direction System, Artillary (TACFIRE) AN/GSG-10(V)

TM 3-4240-285-30&P, Direct Support Maintenance Manual... for Collective Protection Equipment, Guided Missile System, Patriot..

TM 3-4240-286-20&P, Organizational Maintenance Manual... for Collective Protection Equipment, Air Defense Command and Control System, AN/TSQ-73...

TM 3-6665-307-10, Operator's Manual for Detector Kit, Chemical Agent M256 and M256A1

TM 3-6665-311-10, Operator's Manual for Paper, Chemical Agent Detector: M9

TM 3-6665-319-10, Operator's Manual for Water Testing Kit, Chemical Agents: M272

TM 3-6665-327-13&P, Operator's, Unit, and Intermediate Direct Support Maintenance Manual... Chemical Agent Monitor System (CAM)

TM 10-277, Chemical, Toxicological and Missile Fuel Handlers Protective Clothing

TM 11-6665-213-12, Operator Manual and Organizational Maintenance Manual... Radiacmeter, IM-174/PD

TM 11-6665-214-10, Operator's Manual: Radiacmeters, IM-9E/PD, and IM-147/PD.

TM 11-6665-230-12, Operator's and Organizational Maintenance Manual for Radiac Set, AN/PDR-27R

TM 11-6665-236-12, Operator's and Organizational Maintenance Manual for Radiac Set, AN/PDR-75

TM 11-6665-251-10, Operator's Manual for Radiac Set AN/VDR-2